Starting a Theatre Company

Exploring everything from company incorporation and marketing, to legal, finance, and festivals, *Starting a Theatre Company* is the complete guide to running a low-to-no budget or student theatre company.

Written by an experienced theatre practitioner and featuring on-the-ground advice, this book covers all aspects of starting a theatre company with limited resources, including how to become a company, finding talent, defining a style, roles and responsibilities, building an audience, marketing, the logistics of a production, legalities, funding, and productions at festivals and beyond. The book also includes a chapter on being a sustainable company, and how to create a mindset that will lead to positive artistic creation. Each chapter contains a list of further resources, key terms, and helpful tasks designed to support the reader through all of the steps necessary to thrive as a new organisation. Resource pages contain links to a wide range of industry created templates, guidance, and interviews, making it even easier for you to get up and running as simply as possible.

Starting a Theatre Company targets Theatre and Performance students interested in building their own theatre companies. This book will also be invaluable to independent producers and theatre makers.

Karl Falconer is a director and educator and Managing Director of PurpleDoor. His work has been staged and screened across the UK and Ireland, and has been supported by Arts Council England and the Paul Hamlyn Foundation. His work has been nominated for a National Lottery Award and he currently serves on the Arts Squad for Northern Broadsides.

Starting a Theatre Company
How to Become a Theatre Maker and Create Your Own Work

Karl Falconer

Designed cover image: ©PurpleDoor

First published 2023
by Routledge
605 Third Avenue, New York, NY 10158

and by Routledge
4 Park Square, Milton Park, Abingdon, Oxon OX14 4RN

Routledge is an imprint of the Taylor & Francis Group, an informa business

© 2023 Karl Falconer

The right of Karl Falconer to be identified as author of this work has been asserted in accordance with sections 77 and 78 of the Copyright, Designs and Patents Act 1988.

All rights reserved. No part of this book may be reprinted or reproduced or utilised in any form or by any electronic, mechanical, or other means, now known or hereafter invented, including photocopying and recording, or in any information storage or retrieval system, without permission in writing from the publishers.

Trademark notice: Product or corporate names may be trademarks or registered trademarks, and are used only for identification and explanation without intent to infringe.

by Taylor & Francis Books

Access the Support Material: www.routledge.com/9781032251318

Library of Congress Cataloging-in-Publication Data
A catalog record for this title has been requested

ISBN: 978-1-032-25133-2 (hbk)
ISBN: 978-1-032-25131-8 (pbk)
ISBN: 978-1-003-28172-6 (ebk)

DOI: 10.4324/9781003281726

Typeset in Baskerville
by Taylor & Francis Books

To Jim and Josie, for encouraging me

Contents

List of illustrations   viii
Acknowledgements   ix
Foreword   xi

1. Introduction — 1
2. Defining Your Style and Company Voice — 16
3. Becoming a Company — 32
4. Roles and Responsibilities — 50
5. Building an Audience — 65
6. Marketing and Branding — 87
7. Logistics of Production — 111
8. Legal and Safety — 133
9. Finance — 147
10. Raising Funds — 172
11. Festivals — 191
12. Putting on Work — 208
13. Business Sustainability — 232
14. Failure, Endings, and Exit — 246
15. Final Words — 254

Index   256

Illustrations

Figures

5.1	Mapping marketing with audience demographics	72
5.2	The audience funnel	73
9.1	Financial management system overview	148
9.2	Balance Sheet example	155
9.3	Profit and Loss Account example	157
9.4	Risk register example	162

Tables

6.1	Four week marketing plan	94
6.2	Three week marketing plan	94
8.1	Overview of responsibilities	134
	Document Control Sheet	137
9.1	Cash debit example	151
9.2	Cash credit example	151
9.3	Debit and credit example	152
9.4	Simple budget expenditure example	160
9.5	Simple budget income example	163
9.6	Project income	164
9.7	Project expenditure	165
9.8	Budget costing headers	165
9.9	Spreadsheet items listed individually	166
9.10	Spreadsheet items accumulated	167
9.11	Spreadsheet layout example	167
9.12	Spreadsheet cell identification	167
9.13	Spreadsheet costings for adding	168
10.1	Grant application tracker	182
10.2	Grant aims and outcomes tracker	186
10.3	Milestone tracker	186
10.4	Win theme tracker	187
13.1	Identifying goals	235

Acknowledgements

Every actor and creative, every drop-out and last-minute replacement, every technician, theatre manager, colleague, tutor, and audience member, has unwittingly contributed to the development of this book. Special thanks firstly to Chris Spring, Michelle Morris, and Andrea Wainman for encouraging a really annoying student to find the rules and break them. Eternal thanks to Calum Green, Thomas Williams, and Siobhan Crinson. Your patience, passion, and support were more important than you will ever realise, and your talent and creativity is the foundation behind everything we have achieved collectively. Special thanks to Con O'Neill, for taking a chance on me early on in my career when, in his words, I looked like Jesus, to give me guidance and advice from the very best, including to change my hair style. A huge thank you to Sian Prime, Debbie Forster, Vasken Jermakian, Rachel Cooper, and Mel Larsen for your friendship, mentorship, and guidance through the hurdles, and for answering a million stupid questions to make me a better leader. Special thanks to Janet Butler, Leon Scott, Nadia Papachronopoulou, Victoria Armstrong, and Andrew Pritchard for wanting to be a part of making PurpleDoor's journey happen and for your guidance when we have stumbled. Thanks to Matt Anderson, Paul Muhammad, Lucy Palmer, Andy Smith, Jazz Andrews, and Jason Dale for your friendship, encouragement, and for being the most outstanding team: how I wish our time together had been longer. Thanks to all the incredible people who have been a part of shaping our ideas and providing fantastic feedback, encouragement, and support, to Vicki, Lou, AnneMarie, Paul, Veda, Adrian, Ruth, Andy, Hannah, Rachel, Claudia, and Kylie. Enormous thanks to Linsey Marrow for support in the early days, which made all the difference. Special thanks to Lynne Wolff and Mavis Taberner for your incredible generosity and warmth: you made a special mark on my life in our short time together. An enormous thanks to all those actors at PurpleCoat who contributed time and again to helping make a crazy, silly dream come true. Thank you to Jack, Olivia, Rhiannon, Anna, Caitlin, Antony, Lee, Alicia, Justine, Ellie, Callum, Emma, Evie, Nicola, Jamie, Beth, Sam, Clayton, Ellie, Cerian, James, Jess, Al, Jack, Rhea, Katie, Jackie, Aimee, Lisa, Jay, Russel, Cathy, Tom, Phil, Paul, Simon, Gary, Stewart, Nigel, Dan, Douglas, Albert, Lauren, Agata, Chris, Simone, Dorcas, Lois, Harleyia, Jack, James, Louise, Ian, and all of our incredible Young Actors Company. Special thanks to the incredible Abigail Rokison-Woodall, Tracy Irish, Helen Nicholson, and Oli Mould who gave me the confidence, without realising it, to think that writing a book was something I could do. Your guidance and support has been without compare. Thank you to the fantastic team at Routledge who have shown patience in putting up with my endless questions, particularly Stacey Walker and Lucia Accorsi, without whom I wouldn't have been able to get this far. A huge thank you to my family for always supporting me, laughing at me when I'm being dramatic, and being there for me when I've needed it most. Mum, Dad, Cameron, Oscar, Harvey, and Nicola, who will be furious that this book isn't dedicated to her. And finally, an enormous thank you to Tash for putting up with my tantrums, for supporting me while I took time off to write, and for always encouraging me to be my best self. Every day your love, encouragement, and support has been the thing that has kept me going. Thank you.

Foreword

PurpleDoor is a Liverpool based theatre company and venue, supported by the Paul Hamlyn Foundation and The School for Social Entrepreneurs.

Information can be found at www.thedoorisopen.co.uk or via social media by searching for Liverpool PurpleDoor.

The author regularly supports new theatre makers, offering advice, mentorship, and guidance, and can be contacted at info@thedoorisopen.co.uk.

1 Introduction

Creating theatre is one of the most stimulating and challenging things you can do. You have the joy of creating worlds, of sharing those creative experiences with a whole raft of fellow creators and audiences, and you are guaranteed a life as diverse and changeable as a 'traditional' job is predictable. You have the privilege of deciding which stories to tell and figuring out how they should be told, who by and to whom. You will meet partners, friends, enemies, co-creators, co-conspirators, divas, clowns, psychopaths, and virtually everybody in between. You have the opportunity to visit new places and possibly to become very well known, to hold a mirror up to nature and bring joy, education, empathy, and compassion to people's lives.

You will also likely run out of money, barely sleep, constantly feel underpaid and underappreciated, probably hold down a job alongside a side hustle, and be the person everyone else blames when it all goes wrong. It is thankless, it is hard work, and you'll be daydreaming about the simplicity of life for those lucky enough to work a regular job.

Who is a theatre maker?

Producer, theatre maker, amateur hobbyist, company, student. There are many different guises under which you may have arrived at this book, and if you've made it this far, the chances are that you're probably the right person for it. Titles such as theatre maker and producer can sound so grand and well established, but here I use them for clarity and simplicity only, and you should not be put off by them.

You might be a theatre student, an actor, writer, or keen hobbyist wanting to know more about how work is created. You might work alone or as part of a larger group. You might be a member of a local amateur dramatic society or somebody returning to the arts later in life. You might have been inspired to explore your own creativity for the first time, or you may be looking for ways to monetise your hobby. If you have an interest in creating something from scratch, this book is for you.

DOI: 10.4324/9781003281726-1

Why this book exists

This book exists to be the book I wish I had when I was starting out. Theatre making is hard, and the impenetrable lack of information and reliance on previous experience, good connections, and the bank of mum and dad is unnecessarily prohibitive and at odds with the apparent liberalism of the arts as a whole. The systemic inequalities embedded in our industry are forcing more and more people into creating their own work, but here there also exists an information, access, and privilege divide, where those with the most cultural capital are better supported to succeed.

The wake of the Covid-19 pandemic highlighted stark differences in the way theatre venues treated their makers and creators, who are paid poorly and treated unfairly at the best of times. More devastatingly, the pandemic showed us just how vital the role of culture and storytelling is to the richness of our lives, whilst highlighting how little importance the plight of theatres held for many of the audiences we are there to serve.

In running my own company, I found myself regularly running into hurdles when I didn't know how to do something, usually business related. Although the internet has answers to most of this, the wealth of information was overwhelming, confusing, and often contradictory.

Business related information was full of jargon, with different rules and implications if it was written in the US to the UK, and it often left me with more questions than I started with. I regularly found myself feeling inadequate and scared that I had got things wrong. Financial information seemed to rely on a pre-existing knowledge of basic information and theatre information was often secretive and vague. In some cases, it was many, many years before I got over that fear and imposter syndrome.

In the UK, a reported one in five businesses fail each year. In the US, almost one in three have failed by year two. After a decade, 70% have closed. There are obvious caveats to this – local and yearly factors and what we consider to be a failure – but this is still a large volume to consider. Often as creatives we don't like to see ourselves as part of the business world, but perhaps a failure to recognise and appreciate this side of our work is a big factor in the knife edge our industry spends much of its time carefully balancing.

I hope that in writing this book I can help you to develop your confidence and tangibly improve your skillset, both as a theatre maker but also as an entrepreneur. For whether you're running a modest theatre-in-education company in your school drama studio, or preparing to take over the industry with your epic theatrical masterpieces, appreciating that there is a whole world to consider in the second half of that word show*business*, I hope will make your work stronger and ensure that you are still doing what you love in years to come.

Existing companies

You may be coming to this book as a student or a new starter, but you may equally have experience running a company currently or in the past. Many amateur dramatic societies have extensive historical legacies and I hope you will find the methods and advice in this book useful to help you streamline and enhance your current work. Those working in the theatre industry have often had to learn their skills on the job, particularly when it comes to business and financial matters, so taking time to strategise is almost always a positive and productive use of time. Whatever stage your journey is at, I hope that you will find genuinely useful tips and techniques to apply to your operations to help make them more successful, more authentic, and more productive, whether this be to start out as strong as possible, or to find new and improved ways of running your existing company.

Why now?

The Covid-19 pandemic has changed the way we engage with our communities, with work, and with culture as a whole. High streets are desperate for the need for radical change, which all but the most forward-thinking councils have plans to embrace. As the streaming wars range in our homes, the question about the role and relevance of going to the theatre – with all of its costs, rules, and assumptions – shows no sign of being resolved any time soon. At the same time, we face the prospect of a further squeeze on living standards in the short to medium term.

In our own industry, the pandemic has helped to highlight stark inequalities of access and opportunity. Although these systemic injustices have been around for a long time, the pandemic helped shine a light on these issues – which range from geographical inequality to pricing barriers for training – and many in the industry are considering alternatives, including potentially leaving the creative arts altogether.

The rise in convenience services offered us the promise of greater leisure time and freedom from oppressive work patterns. But many of us are working harder and longer than ever before, keeping down second jobs and side hustles just to get by. In this context, many training academies have started to value the importance of creating your own work as a way of circumnavigating the lack of opportunity for so-called 'traditional' work. Drama schools and universities, driven by a changing student–consumer relationship, are finally tilting towards offering students practical skills and support to succeed, once their studies end. In short, more people than ever before are seeing the advantage in creating their own opportunities, rather than waiting around for opportunities to come to them.

Against this climate, it becomes more important than ever for there to be accessible and reliable support to help those people wanting to take control of the means of production. There may never be a perfect time to start a business, but there are definitely challenging times and plenty of excuses waiting to get in the way. I hope that this book can be the guiding light I needed, built through years of my own experience making the same mistakes I hope I can guide you to avoid.

PurpleCoat: a case study

Who am I and why am I worth listening to? I feel it is important to contextualise my own background so that you, as the reader, can appreciate my own experience and equally my failures in times when I have made bad decisions and got things wrong.

In 2008 I founded my own theatre company, PurpleCoat Productions. I was finishing my A-Levels in the UK, based near Liverpool, and didn't know what I wanted to do with my life. Or, to be more accurate, I knew exactly what I wanted to do and had no idea how to do it. Since a very young age I had been hugely inspired (read, obsessed) by *The Lord of the Rings* film trilogy, and particularly their extensive behind-the-scenes footage of the making of the films. I was in awe, not just at the technical and artistic wizardry that helped bring those films to life, but at the sense of family, the camaraderie, and the fact that the director, Peter Jackson, had started out with his friends making low-budget horror movies in his back garden. The fact that some of those same friends went on to win Oscars for their work on these ground-breaking movies was, and still is, a massive inspiration to me.

However, in 2008, growing up on a council estate, and coming from a family who understandably wanted me to pursue a 'secure' career, I faced a crisis of decision making. At that time, London was the only viable place for study and work, and this was simply out of my budget. I had no savings or family finance to fall back on and even the maximum available maintenance support from the government fell short of covering my full living costs. Instead, I opted to stay at home, study at a local university in a course I wasn't invested in, whilst I channelled the savings into fully establishing PurpleCoat.

PurpleCoat was a collective of four creators who had all met at college and who had produced a few short films together during our time studying. We shared wildly different backgrounds and experiences, but we got on well together and had a fantastic working relationship. When two of the co-founders moved to London for university, we readjusted and refocussed and instead decided to put on a play. Our first plays were basically remounts of shows we had worked on in college, and the fact that they were a Greek tragedy and a Shakespeare play meant that we didn't have to pay performance licence fees. We had £10 when we started, and we lied to a local club (yes, a club) that we could sell enough tickets to cover their hire fees. We pulled together a cast from a collection of friends of friends and somehow got these early productions on their feet. They were certainly rough around the edges, but they carried a spirit and established a strong set of working relationships, which inspired us to want to continue.

It was in those early years that the first seeds of our DNA began to grow. As we became an unofficial ensemble, with a core group of artists returning for subsequent shows, it dawned on me that my position was not unique. Many of the people I was meeting were extremely talented, hardworking, and dedicated individuals, who had to make a choice between moving to London or giving up. For the first time, I was starting to see the local and political consequences of inequality within the arts, where those with the luxury of time and money were most likely to excel, rather than those with the most talent. Our shows became about supporting and championing that talent, and we spent a great deal of time trying to get our work seen, blindly following opportunity after opportunity. Looking back, this seems naive and misguided, and indeed our artistic output was precariously undefined: we made films, we made theatre, we did classical work, we did contemporary work. At that time, PurpleCoat was more about the people behind it and the spirit of wanting it to work, than about knowing what that work was.

As a result, the core group we had built up began to change and break away, as people moved away, started or left education, and went to work on other projects. The people had been so integral to what we were that we faced an identity crisis when those people started to change.

Our tunnel-vision determination did lead to some early successes though. Early on we managed to get a few reviews that went in our favour, and we were part of the RSC Open Stages project, which was an open call, but which allowed us to perform at some regional theatres. At the same time, a range of fringe venues popping up locally enabled us to stage more productions cheaper and easier, which developed our skills and extended our repertoire. We were, essentially, a repertory company (where a semi-consistent group of performers stage published plays, often in quick succession with little rehearsal time), with little artistic specificity but a knowledge that the work we created was always thorough, intense, and deeply personal. Our work with Shakespeare, in particular, gave us the chance to develop our flavour for high-concept theatre, with productions of *Romeo and Juliet* set in Las Vegas and lesser known plays such as *Titus Andronicus* set in a cyberpunk alternative reality.

In 2014 we reached our peak output, staging productions of *Noises Off*, *Shirley Valentine*, *The Caretaker*, *My Mother Said I Never Should*, *Macbeth*, *A Midsummer Night's Dream*, a tour of *Twelfth Night*, and a short film. Reading that sentence should make your knees wobble: I have no idea how we didn't collapse. It is clear to me now that our own sense of insecurity, of having to justify our existence, led to this feverish level of productivity that was unsustainable. We did finally establish some direction by deciding to apply to Arts Council England (ACE) to establish a youth theatre, and going through this process led to our first budget and planning session in the whole time we had existed!

Meanwhile, the sense of frustration and injustice was festering in my mind. I knew we were creating good work and I knew we could do work just as well as other, much more established companies. I felt we had earned a seat at the table: we had toured the country and performed in venues with a capacity of 900 seats and fringe venues with a capacity of 40 seats. We had sell-out shows and five-star reviews, as well as our fair share of half-star reviews and times when the cast outnumbered the audience! Our work had been championed by people like Con O'Neill, Ian McKellen, and Stephen Fry: due in large part to a very tenuous connection from one of our ensemble members, who pestered Stephen Fry's Twitter account incessantly.

As we entered 2015, everything went wrong. Reading this summary, that might sound obvious, but you have to take a moment to appreciate how this felt at the time. Being productive was a good foil for feeling as if we were making progress. Being able to access increasingly large spaces was equated with greater success in our minds. Each performance carried the hope that this might be the one show where things take off, where we get noticed, where a theatre will programme us. We were desperate for somebody to pay attention to our work, to give us a fair hearing and to help us. Although things are better now, back then there was little to no support for artists locally and the number of people starting their own companies was much lower than it is today. We were outliers, and although we were strategically lacking, we did have something to offer.

This rate of work was not to last. The pressure of each show having to sell so many tickets just to cover costs was enormous, and as people returned to work with us on multiple shows, this pressure turned into fatigue and irritation. We weren't growing and we were largely dependent on grass-roots flyering to shout about our work and hope we had an audience. Each show could have been our last if we'd have failed to sell any tickets. At the same time, I was working a full-time job and we had yet to be paid for our work at PurpleCoat. Our ACE bid for our Youth Theatre had been successful, although none of this support was allocated for us to pay ourselves, and the pressures of formally registering as a company, submitting accounts, and managing a grant properly was building all the time.

At Christmas 2015 we decided to stage a double bill of Shakespeare's *Henry IV Part I* and *II*. An ambitious retelling would bring you into Shakespeare's world of intrigue, battles, and realpolitik, and aimed to throw off the assumption that his History plays were stale or boring. At the same time, our Youth Theatre were to stage a production of Ben Johnson's *Volpone*, as part of our Shakespeare's contemporaries season.

Towards the end of rehearsals for our youth production, our director and my co-founder secured a really wonderful full-time job and had to step back. I stepped in to help, meaning that I was now directing three shows at the same time, and working full time. When it came to the shows themselves, *Henry IV* failed to sell many tickets (we had more cast than audience in one show: a personal low) and to top things off, the set fell over, which in turn hit a speaker hanging from the roof, which in turn triggered a smoke machine to blast smoke incessantly. A better metaphor you could not have written.

I am now very open about the fact that I went through something of a breakdown during that time and that I hit a very low point in my life.

Whatever merits the show might have had were eclipsed in my mind by the financial fear that we were finished, and that after seven years we had nowhere else to turn. The prospect of falling back to my dead-end job with no plan or hope of escape terrified me and I hit a very, very low point. I was unable to express this in any sort of eloquent or reasonable capacity to our fantastic cast, and I had an ugly episode where I let them down tremendously and didn't respect their time or energy in getting these shows on. It took me a hugely long time to accept that the show did have its strengths and that a failure of programming (who wants to see *Henry IV* three days before Christmas?!) was not a failure of the artistic accomplishments of the company or the actors involved.

We limped on in 2016 and 2017 to fulfil our obligations to the ACE before practically calling it a day. As is so often the case, it was from the wreckage of this time that I was able to finally address the issues that had been plaguing us for so long. For the first time in so long I didn't feel the millstone around my neck to keep producing work. I was able to discover new hobbies, and to meet people who didn't just define me as 'Karl who puts on plays.' I was able to spend time with myself and to invest time in my relationships. I was able to accept that I am more than my work.

In many respects, the Covid-19 pandemic gave me an excuse to finally stop and reflect on my journey as a theatre maker. I had originally wanted to be a director, but had lacked the finances and probably the courage to move to London and try and do this the 'proper' way. People will often say that there is no clear path in this industry, but at that time it certainly felt as if creating our own work was not a path anybody seriously recognised or understood, particularly as we weren't funded or attached to a venue. Added to this is the fact that creating a company was probably something I did out of necessity, rather than choice. I lacked the mentors, the access, and the support to know how to do the best thing for me when I was leaving college, and the subsequent eight years had been a constant worry that I was doing the wrong thing. I couldn't help compare myself to my peers, and to second guess whether I should have moved to London, auditioned for drama school or tried to get a job. I knew that I enjoyed directing and I felt I had some skill at it, but what should I do next? Without that guidance I was left to make my own decisions.

In the years following the pausing of our work I decided to quit my job and study an MA in Shakespeare and Education at the Shakespeare Institute in Stratford-upon-Avon. I did this remotely (before it was fashionable!) and used the new government postgraduate loans to afford to do this. This was a short-lived but incredible time for me, returning to my love of learning, making up for the mistakes I had made during my BA, when I was so consumed with PurpleCoat that I made little effort with my studies. I came to realise that my time with the company had given me transferable skills that I could use to great effect elsewhere. I don't want to give the impression that this was a simple rags-to-riches transformation from my failures in 2015: I was so unwell that I found it almost impossible to engage with my fellow students and I spent precious little time engaging with the wider culture of that year as a result. Healing was a long process for me, one that I'm sure continues today.

I finally moved to London! I lived with my partner in an awful flat in the outskirts of the Metropolitan Line and took up teaching positions, lecturing in film production. This was my life as the pandemic began: I had graduated to the position of course leader at a fantastic college teaching students who have shaped my life in so many ways. These incredible, diverse, rowdy, unapologetic young people shaped me into the teacher and the person I am today, and I was finally able to channel my creativity, energy, and passion for supporting others into a profession that showed me tangible results.

As the pandemic began, I started to think about our work at PurpleCoat and to reflect upon our long-held belief that if we'd have had our own space we would have been so much better prepared to reach the audiences and deliver the impact that we always intended. I successfully applied to some fantastic funders for money to help develop these ideas, which have grown now into plans for PurpleDoor, the first free theatre in the UK. Exploring the role theatre should play in its local community, PurpleDoor aims to direct all of the years of experience and learning from PurpleCoat into a tangible offer to support artists and encourage local creativity. We're using our experience to question why theatres look and feel and operate the way they do, and we're excited to see where this leads us. In so many ways, the work and ethos, the struggles and rewards of our years with PurpleCoat have shaped every aspect of PurpleDoor.

Choosing to come back to theatre and doing it on my own terms has helped to develop a much healthier relationship for me. My work has gotten stronger and opportunities have arisen to create work with some wonderful people. My work now has a strength of conviction, an artistic focus and a defined understanding of what I want to say and how I want to say it, I think in large part because I am doing it for the right reasons. All of these come through life experience and learning from my mistakes, and I am much, much happier as a result.

I share this extensive account of my journey for three reasons. Firstly, it is good to understand the context and validity of the person claiming to have provided, in these pages, a know-all guide to creating your own work. So often our industries are dominated by people who will claim that their success 'just sort of happened,' often because they had the financial and support networks to fall back on. This may be you, and I have no issues with that, but I believe we are richer when people from a range of backgrounds are practically able to navigate the tough route of creating work in a way that enables them to succeed.

Secondly, I confidently predict this might be the first time you have read such an honest admission of failure and mistakes in a creative context. We are embedded with such toxic habits of success and achievement in this industry that to talk of our failures is seen as embarrassing or an admission of weakness. I am neither of these things. I don't believe I have made any failures in my journey, only misguided decisions, which I would reconsider with reflection and hindsight. I am proud of my journey – mistakes and all – and you should be too. They have, without doubt, shaped my practice and made me stronger. By sharing my story, I hope to prepare you for your own mistakes, and to let you know that they need not define you.

Finally, I hope that sharing my story in this way makes our positives and negatives much clearer than they were to me at the time. It can so often be much easier to support, critique, and analyse the work of other people than it can be to objectively assess our own situation. As a teacher I give feedback on students' work all the time. Retaining this level of distance in my own work remains a challenge. I hope that you are able to read the story above with a dispassionate 'what an idiot, I'd never have done that!' Hopefully, by knowing this, your own journey will be a breeze.

Going behind the filter

This book is about the reality of running a company. In a way, it's about going behind the Instagram filter and looking at what happens behind the scenes. To that end, I feel it important to make an aside about jobs, to break down a preconception, and to hopefully make you feel more empowered in your own position.

Unless you are in an incredibly lucky position, you are probably reading this book whilst holding down some way of paying the bills. You might be a student working part time in a bar, or you might be working full time and worrying about fitting your company into the evenings and weekends.

You won't often hear people in the performing arts talking about this, but it is completely fine and normal to have a job. These jobs are often what make the art affordable, and although people will have a whole host of reasons not to be open about this on social media, it doesn't mean it isn't happening.

For ten years running my theatre company I worked full time. The only exception to this was during my Masters degree, when I couldn't afford to create any work anyway. This was incredibly taxing, making me exhausted most of the time. I used to joke that I worked both nights and mornings, often getting up before seven to go to work and not getting home until past midnight. Early on, I couldn't drive or afford a car, so I was spending most of my life on buses eating takeaways. I don't say this for sympathy or for respect, but merely to provide one example of reality behind what you see on social media.

It isn't limited to small-scale independents either. I know one actor who has played numerous title roles at the Royal Shakespeare Company, who works as a parcel courier when between jobs. A writer colleague trained at drama school and worked professionally for several years before spending a few years working at Argos to pay his rent. These are the realities, not of tortured artists but of real people getting by. Do not feel as though you aren't fitting a prerequisite if your life circumstances aren't ideal: most people's aren't. In the best circumstances, the daily grind can give you the finance to carry on and the fuel to keep creating.

Mentors

The most important thing I have learnt throughout my time as a creative is the importance of mentors. It is so important that I am putting it right at the start of the book, outside of any of the chapters that follow, in the hope that it can be an area you can hold in your mind as you go forward.

Mentors are an invaluable tool to guide and support, as a shoulder to cry on and a confidant to open up to. There is no stock mentor type: they may specialise in a certain area or be more broadly based, they may be an industry specialist but they may equally be a tutor or colleague.

Coming into this industry with absolutely no experience and no connection to the theatrical world, it took me a long time to find mentors and to appreciate their importance. The earliest mentor for a lot of people will have been a teacher. For me it was Chris, who was invaluable during my theatre A-Level in recognising and encouraging my enthusiasm for storytelling. Chris pushed us all to be inquiring and reflective, and he opened our eyes to what was possible. In fact, Chris was such a strong support that it took time to adjust when we were thrust out into the world without that guidance.

I have found wonderful support and advice, and grown as a person as a result, from a host of people throughout my life and career. Some have been my boss, others have been teachers and practitioners with more experience than me. I haven't actively sought these mentors out but by being open to connections and being willing to hear their perspectives and to learn from them, we have formed relationships that have helped me to grow. I like to think I might also have helped them, in a small way, in return.

I have only been appointed formal, dedicated mentors for the very first time in the year of writing this book. This was through a scheme run by the Paul Hamlyn Foundation and the School for Social Entrepreneurs; companies who I would advise all readers to connect with. These mentors are experts in their field and have been appointed to support me in areas where I felt I needed guidance. This year has truly highlighted the importance of these roles, not just to my learning, but also for my resilience, confidence, and well-being. Debbie, Rachel, Mel, and Vasken have made this book stronger through their wonderful advice, and have helped me more than they know. If only I'd have had access to this earlier, perhaps I wouldn't have needed this book to exist!

So: seek out your mentors. Have those people in your life who you can learn from and who you can be honest with, truly honest with. Make it formal, or make it a coffee once every couple of months, it doesn't matter. But have those roles where you can express your fears and concerns without worry or recrimination. Tony Fadell, the genius behind the iPod and iPhone recommends therapy. I think the principle is the same. Sometimes we have to take the mask off and come up for air.

One last note. It is particularly prescient to me that none of my mentors are from within the theatre industry. I'm not sure why that has been the case historically, but when it came to working with the School for Social Entrepreneurs this year, I deliberately wanted people who came from different sectors and who had no experience of the theatre world. I think there is a legitimate argument to be made that theatre itself can be enhanced by moving outside of the bubble and bringing in different perspectives: in all areas from programming to marketing and finance. Even teaching, working every day with students who couldn't give two hoots about theatre, has shaped and informed me as a practitioner. For me, this has helped massively, as I know there is no conflict of interest from their part, but also because it has opened my eyes to my wider skillset and the wider applicability of my skills. I can make theatre, yes, but I can also do marketing, finance, and leadership. I would not have been confident enough to recognise that before working with these mentors.

How to use this book

This book is divided into fourteen chapters looking at every aspect of creating your own work. It is deliberately intended to act as a thorough and practical guide for every stage of your creative journey. Ideally you would read the book chronologically before starting to produce your own work, as developing a holistic understanding of the whole process will assist you in taking those exciting but daunting first steps. However, I expect that you are just as likely to want to flick through to sections that are most useful to you, and I would encourage you to do this where it helps. Do know that there will be greater learning and skills development from exploring all aspects of the book, however, as many of these areas speak to and feed into each other. You are equally likely to find a way to improve your work by spending time with the chapters you think you already know as you are by facing those areas where you think you are weak.

I hope that this will become a book you return to throughout your career, and I have taken efforts to ensure that many different scenarios and case studies are explored, so that you will come to trust that the book has your back. So much theatre making can be isolating and scary, and I trust that the depth and breadth of this book at the very least help you to remember that other people have trodden this path before and that in your journey, and particularly in your struggles, you are not alone.

Resources

Each chapter concludes with a detailed resource list, allowing you to dive deeper into sections that interest you. I have tried to focus this towards online resources where I can, recognising that books and other resource materials could be a cost that is prohibitive to some readers. While there are some excellent books suggested in these resource lists, equally useful research can be found for free online.

I believe strongly that quality resources can really enhance our understanding, and these resources have each been picked because I have found them to be the most useful, the most accessible and the most supportive. At the same time, I have found through bitter experience that other people's resources can sometimes intimidate and overwhelm me, so feel free to ignore these if you have alternative ways of working, where appropriate.

Chapter breakdown

Chapter 2

In Chapter 2 we explore the artistic side of creating theatre. From establishing working patterns to exploring ethics and privilege in the stories you choose to tell, Chapter 2 is about the importance of defining your own artistic style as a company: what makes your work become your work, and why does that work deserve its place? What are the responsibilities of creating art in the divided world of the 21st century and how does a new company establish practices that can benefit its art and its people, right from the first day?

Chapter 3

Chapter 3 breaks down the business of forming a company. Taking a step-by-step guide to incorporating a company, this chapter explores company structure, governance, registration, setting up a bank account, and more. Appreciating that readers may be coming to this chapter with a deal of apprehension about the 'business side of things' this chapter aims to break down the complex world of company formation in a way that is simple and easy to understand and to follow, in real time. If you already run a company, this chapter should provide a brief guide to ensure that you are doing everything properly, and to ensure all of the groundwork is in place.

Chapter 4

Chapter 4 looks at job roles and responsibilities within your new organisation. From discussing the importance of how to define individual roles in a shared ensemble, to exploring ways of finding and attracting new talent, this chapter helps prepare your journey from a group of friends to a professional outfit.

Chapter 5

The challenge of finding an audience for your work is the subject of Chapter 5, where we explore aspects of audience development to help ensure that your work gets seen. Linked very heavily with the creative choices and responsibilities you will have developed in Chapter 4, this chapter aims to find ways of linking your audience development to purpose, to ensure you are growing as an organisation and reaching those audiences who need to see your work.

Chapter 6

From audience development, we move to branding and marketing, exploring in Chapter 6 the practical strategies for taking your work into the world and getting the word out; from considering tools and techniques for developing a marketing strategy, to a comprehensive guide to videography, website speed and streaming, this chapter takes a sweeping approach across many of the elements your business needs to be seen and heard in the 21st century. Learning from the latest changes in technology and the experience of the pandemic, we will explore strategies for making your work digitally accessible and open to the opportunities of the digital age. We also discuss some much needed tips for how to make your work accessible to as wide a range of potential audiences as possible.

Chapter 7

In Chapter 7 we work through the process of producing a theatrical performance, from conception through rehearsal, right through to the final night. Breaking down the logistics of every step of the process, including working with venues and how to run a tech, this chapter introduces some of the 'need to knows' that help ensure your production runs smoothly and comes together without a hitch.

Chapter 8

Understanding the legal requirements of running a business is vital to ensure your operations are above board and in line with the law. Knowing your obligations in line with things such as health and safety and insurance is essential, but can be difficult to know where to start. Chapter 8 aims to provide you with an introduction to what is needed from you as a company manager, but also to explore those issues that are not legally required but are expected from any business wanting to take themselves seriously in a 21st-century arts landscape.

Chapter 9

Chapter 9 explores the ins and outs of company finance, including budgeting, accounting, and how to run a financial system within your company. This chapter takes an accessible approach to understanding the key fundamentals of accounting, to give readers a basic language and guide to follow. The chapter aims to empower readers by breaking down finance in easy-to-understand language, which aims to leave you feeling more confident about numbers and ready to embrace their potential to make your company a financial success.

Chapter 10

Chapter 10 considers ways in which you can fundraise for your company. Looking at the different methods of income generation, from grants and loans to crowdfunding and philanthropy, Chapter 10 provides an overview of the different ways you can get the finance you need to get your plans into action.

Chapter 11

Understanding the different avenues for getting your work into the world is crucial so that you can take full advantage of the opportunities out there. In Chapter 11 we take an overview into festivals, with a need-to-know survival guide exploring everything from potential flyering technique to poster design and accommodation choice.

Chapter 12

In Chapter 12 we will look at the main ways theatre makers can create work, with a particular focus on getting programmed and dealing with venues. We will also explore alternatives such as hiring a space, creating education, community engagement, or site-specific work and organising your own tour.

Chapter 13

After the success of your first show, it's time to start thinking strategically. Chapter 13 thinks about long-term planning, including issues around sustainability and environmental impact. With a focus on growth and future-proofing, this chapter aims to ensure that the success of your initial show can be long lived.

Chapter 14

Redefining and reclaiming failure is a big part of my philosophy and the focus of Chapter 14, which considers what happens when things don't go to plan and what to do about it. Sometimes things will go wrong and eventually you, or your co-founders, might want to leave or shut down your organisation. It also focuses on the importance of evaluation and reflection, including helping you to map out your transferable skills for longer-term success.

A note on order

For obvious reasons, choices have to be made when structuring a book of this type to ensure the information you need to access is clear and easy to follow. There are many possible critiques to be made of the way I have categorised and ordered the content in this book, and I want to make clear that this is not to imply a suggested hierarchy or 'right way of doing things.' Indeed, in the early days, it can feel as if everything needs doing at once. That aside, I have tried to follow a process of logic in ordering the material here, and you could follow this to the letter with some success.

Chapters are designed, in the whole, to stand alone and can be read in any order depending on your interests, needs, and perspectives. The fact that sustainability comes near the end of the printed volume, for example, does not and should not diminish its perceived importance any more so than any other category.

Final words

I have taken a great deal of time to ensure the tone of this book is both supportive and critical, to ensure that you have the best chance of success in your journey ahead. Some of you might be creating content with no real long-term aims, but I still hope that the direction of this book will focus your mind so that you question the purpose and validity of your work in a business-like way. I am working from an assumption that, whatever your starting point and level of expertise, your ultimate aim is to make art that people want to see. Whilst the content of this book, on its own, won't guarantee you artistic or creative success, I hope that having a reference to work against will help to focus your own output.

In writing this book, I have tried to be mindful of a tone that implies 'Do this, don't do this, do that, don't do that' but this is inevitable in a book whose primary aim is to help you avoid mistakes and achieve success. I have made the assumption that, in purchasing this book, you aspire to creating the best work that you can, and this has led to a focus on rights and wrongs, which I hope you can appreciate in context. My aim is to support you not just to create work, but to create the best work and to be business minded in starting a company that can last for years to come. This needs encouragement as well as a firm hand, and there is little room for complacency or bullshit, as you will find when you start putting your work out into the world. You will make mistakes, and you certainly shouldn't believe that this author knew all of this when he was in your shoes. But what I lacked was a firm, supportive mentor who had trod these waters before and could tell me where the quicksand was: I aim to replicate that role for you in these pages.

So, with all that out of the way, let's begin at the beginning: creating a style.

2 Defining Your Style and Company Voice

Your style is both your brand and your artistic voice. It is what people come to recognise, appreciate and want from your work and it is how people will come to define a piece of work as clearly, unarguably, yours. It is highly likely that you have come to this stage because you yourself were inspired by the work of a company or director, and you have fallen in love with the aesthetic, political, or theoretical frameworks that shape their practice. Now it's time for you to hone yours and to figure out what you want to say.

Why style is important

When we talk about style, we're not necessarily talking about the sort of aesthetic that the word implies. Your style can mean a range of things, from the types of shows you put on, to the people you work with, to the themes and messages that appear in your work. Another way to think about this is your artistic voice, but I tend to stray away from this definition as it tends to imply an insular and individualistic model of thinking. It can be helpful to think about style in terms of the values you want to communicate, and who you want to communicate them to.

The nature of style can feel difficult to define and risky to analyse, and sometimes creatives will shy away from discussing too much of their process for reasons of doubt, protectionism, or lack of insight. Why do we need to talk about style at all?

When founding our first theatre company, myself and my business partner began with the mindset discussed above. Thinking about style, or theme, or voice, felt too self-conscious and pretentious and we simply fell into a way of working that seemed to yield results. For our first production we decided to adapt a text we had already worked on in our college studies, and the result was a show that carried some weight.

Difficulties only began to emerge as our company grew. Lacking any central style or defined process, we moved from our first production – a Greek Tragedy – onto a Shakespeare play, then a short film, then a piece by a contemporary local writer, and so forth. This wasn't necessarily a problem, but in lacking a central artistic vision for our work, it became harder for us to

DOI: 10.4324/9781003281726-2

summarise what it was and why it needed to exist, both to ourselves and for other people.

Style then is important for both internal and external purposes. Internally, we need to understand the framework within which our work operates so that we can define and express ourselves against it. I think of this a bit like a gallery. The central understanding of who we are and what we stand for becomes the walls, pillars, and ceiling of our gallery. The work we produce becomes the varied, beautiful, interesting artworks we can display within our gallery, but without that central structure, our work exists without context and without purpose. What's more, it can be much, much easier than you might think to create those individual pieces of art whilst neglecting the need for that holding structure.

Externally it becomes increasingly necessary for us to communicate a sense of cohesion as soon as our work moves beyond its first show. Whether we are selling our work to audiences, summarising it for funding bodies, or evaluating its impact for a report, external bodies need a set of guidelines with which to interpret our work and to judge its impact. There is a reasonable argument here against the need to please external forces, but this shouldn't be seen as a compromise to help you get funding, but instead about enhancing the experience of those we want to engage with your work by providing a framework within which to appreciate it.

Audience and purpose

In the theatre, the audience is too often a focus of the marketing department and occasionally an afterthought for the creators. Although there is a legitimate reason to focus on audience in marketing and branding, no product or service can survive if there is not a need for it or interest in it. As you work through this chapter keep your audience in mind. They are the ultimate arbitrators of your work and will be the reason you hopefully keep producing work for decades to come. I am not suggesting that you seek to produce work with the sole aim of it being popular, but to create work in a vacuum away from audiences and without much thought for who they might be seems counterproductive. I believe we can sometimes be fearful of our audience in the arts, not really wanting to engage with them but cursing them when they don't turn up or when they don't laugh when they should. In establishing and refining your artistic purpose and process, we would do well to remember our audience alongside the sorts of stories we want to tell. It's all very well deciding that we want to create work on a particular theme or topic, but when we later discover that the audience have no interest in this, have we brought value? Equally, are we making the change we would seek to create if we are essentially preaching to the converted?

For this reason, it is important that your audience and your product – the work – are in conversation with one another. Theatres and funders are finally starting to move away from traditional top-down leadership models which sees work made for audiences in the hope they will turn up. This is both risky financially and also treats the audience as little more than by-products of the artistic process. Thinking instead about how you can be in conversation with your audience, indeed, how the audience can be part of creating, shaping, and influencing the work you create, is something you should certainly build into your thinking at this stage.

Start with the 'why'

It's the word I'm using again and again in this chapter, but that should tell you something about its importance. Entrepreneurs can often rush to the how or the what, as a natural outcome of their enthusiasm for their new idea. If you can, start with the why and everything else will follow much more organically. Too many ideas are invented in search of a problem, and if you reverse this process your work will find its feet and convince others to get involved. Why would an audience member come and see your show?

What do you want to say? Why do you want to say it?

Why are you starting a company? What are you hoping to achieve that you don't believe isn't already being said? It is important to think about these things at this stage because they help to inform everything that comes next. There may be many answers to the questions above. Below are a few of the answers I would have given when starting my theatre company:

- Because I believe Shakespeare can be rediscovered for a different audience in my local area
- Because I want to develop my skills as a director
- Because I enjoy working with my friends
- Because I want to develop opportunities for local talent, and I don't believe the current theatre provision is doing that.

While it is perfectly acceptable to create work for the sake of it, and no one is ever going to come and stop you, I would argue that it is becoming increasingly important for all of us to define our sense of purpose in a world facing any number of threats. Against the large-scale issues of climate change, pandemics, and continued inequality, it becomes more important for theatre to articulate clearly what it is for and what purpose it serves. This is not to impose an external sense of value on theatre, but instead for theatre to understand and articulate its case against a backdrop where we have already seen the arts devalued and sidestepped. I am not suggesting that your work needs to seek to change the world, but having a solid understanding of what you do want to achieve is the best antidote to the numerous forces that would seek to undermine it. You may simply want to create work to entertain people – great! You may want to solve world inequality – also great! There is no hierarchy or purpose here, but instead a plea to know the value and purpose of your work and how to communicate it. In a world where every show leaves a carbon footprint and where audience congregation can pose health risks, can we afford to create art in a vacuum that sits separate from the world outside? I have become increasingly convinced, including in the development of my own practice, that thinking about the purpose of our work is, in fact, essential.

Knowing what you want to say and why you want to say it also helps on a practical level throughout the creative process. This level of detail helps to add complexity to the framework your practice exists within, which makes it easier to consider whether decisions sit within that central view of the world.

Why you, why this, why now?

Think back to the last book you read. Whose perspective did you encounter the story from? In most cases, this will be the protagonist, and the language of the narrator helps us to experience the story as it unfolds through their eyes. Every story is told from a perspective, and it is usually the job of the writer, or the director, to help shape and formulate that perspective for us.

Taking this same idea to our own work, we must ask ourselves: what is the perspective of this piece of work? I'm not exploring this down to character level yet, but again thinking conceptually about style and perception to help us answer the question of *why*. If we are staging a piece of work, either newly created or an adaptation of something previously published, we have to answer this question in order to create work that is meaningful and distinct.

Many funding bodies have increasingly taken this question and framed it as such: *Why you? Why this piece of work? Why now?* Some creatives hate this question, but I believe it has its merit. At its heart is a desire to drill down the purpose for creating a piece of work that speaks to the world and the contemporary moment. It is not, as some have claimed, about limiting creativity, but about appreciating that impactful and memorable work can speak to the contemporary moment and to highlight and enhance our understanding of our role within it. Shakespeare's cannon is wide ranging in almost every respect, but what remains consistent across his entire career is his ability to speak to the events of and concerns of the day, whether writing comedy, history, or tragedy. Whether it be reflecting upon the death of Elizabeth I or the gunpowder plot, Shakespeare's work illuminates the minds of his audience, even whilst taking them to Ancient Egypt or Prospero's island.

Our work should aim to speak to us now because it exists now. And unlike almost any other art form, the very nature of theatre is to exist within its defined moment. If it is to live beyond its fleeting lifespan, its challenge is to enhance that moment through its ability to speak to it.

To be clear, I am not advocating a particular political view or perspective on the relevance of theatre here, but merely suggesting that artwork should have a defined purpose for existing if it is to expect an audience to share in its journey. Audiences come to our work with expectations, and we should respect their effort by presenting them with work that can define its own reason for being. Audiences are free to like or dislike our creative decisions and to respond accordingly, but to leave indifferent to our work and having forgotten it twenty minutes later is, I think, a failure of purpose. From a business perspective, we want to create an offer that our audiences want to come back to again and again. They won't do this if they don't know what we stand for and what we can offer them.

What drives you?

A lifetime of experience helps us to form our views, experience different things, and develop a sense of our place in the world, and what's more, this is a shifting journey that changes with us throughout our life. Some people are particularly in tune with these aspects of their identity and perhaps shape much of their life in response to it. For others, it can be a bit more of a journey of discovery. Again, to be clear, I'm not implying here that your work should necessarily be noble or life changing, but, to simplify an example, even comedians need to think about their views and perspectives to shape the tone, style, and focus of their jokes.

Earlier on in your journey you may find it more difficult to know what drives you. This can be a similar situation as experienced by young actors who may not have the wealth of 'life experience' that can shape authentic performance. There is no shortcut to life experience! But although life experience can inaccurately be assumed as a short-hand for something dramatic, we all have a wealth of experience of *our* lives, with their various pleasures and turmoil. To be clear, I am certainly not seeking to condescend or discourage those of you who are younger. I experienced much of this myself, starting my company at eighteen, it was a constant frustration dealing with other people who would make judgements about our work based on the age of the people running it. Now that I'm older, I know a lot more and have a lot more life experience, but I'm not necessarily sure that this has improved my work in any tangible way. If anything, understanding more has made me more self-conscious and critical. I now spend my days willing myself back to a state of wilful ignorance! Some of the most inspired and creative work is created through daring risk taking and through learning on-the-fly, just as incredibly powerful work can be formed through authentic life experience.

Ask yourself the following questions as a starting point:

- What brings you joy?
- What makes you angry?
- What do you want to see more of?
- Is your world represented on stage enough? If not, why not?
- Who is making the work you aspire to?
- What are the shows, films, and TV shows that inspire you? What are the common crossovers/themes between them?

- If you could make any change – in life, in politics, in theatre – what would it be and why?
- What is your dream?

Whatever your situation and context, take ownership of it. You can never say that you know everything in this game, and the old adage is true: you don't know what you don't know. The only real thing that changes is that, with experience, you become cripplingly aware of how much you're unsure about!

Authentic storytelling

There are a range of considerations to explore if we are approaching the question of 'Why you?' for a funding application, but here I want to reflect on its more philosophical implications regarding authorial ownership and intent.

One of the greatest joys and benefits in the creation of art is the development of empathy. As actors and creatives, we seek empathy with the stories and characters we engage with in order to truthfully represent their experiences and perspectives, even when they differ hugely from our own. Occasionally this requires us to move beyond the realms of what we know, to explore stories and worlds that do not exist in our reality.

It goes without saying, then, that a large part of our *raison d'être* in the arts is to use our imaginations to help bring different stories to life. More broadly, however, society is beginning to reflect in ways it has not done before, upon the authenticity and legitimacy of who is telling those stories.

We have come some way on this journey, but there is certainly a long way to go. We may yet wonder at the widespread casting of Caucasian actors in the popular pantomime, *Aladdin*, or the titular Joseph of technicolour dream coat fame, or at the casting of able-bodied actors in the role of Richard III. These cases, and more, reflect the complexity of a situation that is both unconscious and deliberate. We have a responsibility as creatives to interrogate the limits of our own imagination when representing, inhabiting, and commenting upon the experiences of stories that differ from our own. If the best we can hope to present, in those circumstances, are stereotypes, perhaps we were better not to present them at all. We are not neutral bodies in space, and your position in running a theatre company in itself denotes a degree of privilege that should be reflected upon and considered carefully.

> **Task:** Taking inspiration from the section above, consider creating a list or Venn diagram of stories you feel you have the right to tell, and those stories and areas that you will not approach. This requires conceptual as well as practical thinking. Will you be proactive about staging plays by both men and women, for instance? Will you stage work by authors whose views on particular topics vary from your own? Identify your red lines as a group.

Locality

Location is an important factor for many businesses. A shop on a busy street is much more likely to attract footfall than a shop that is difficult to find. Unless you are running a theatre, location is unlikely to appear as highly on your list than if you were running a venue-based business.

However, for a theatre company, location matters in a different way. Your locality brings with it a whole host of associations and implications, some more helpful than others. Where you are based determines the audiences and creatives you have access to, and how easy it is for people to commute to you. A company based in the middle of the countryside may find their pool of available creatives smaller than a company based in the middle of a huge city. The affluence and diversity of your local community will form a large part of your potential audience, and you may find it easier to reach a wider demographic in places where the local community itself is more varied. Indeed, the local community itself may determine the sort of work that is valued, which will in turn shape the function of your art. This may not be something you have considered before, particularly if you are starting your company in a place you have spent a lot of your life – it's likely that you have long stopped noticing the intricacies of your own community.

Locality and a sense of place may feed into the aesthetic and focus of the work you choose to tell. All of these artistic decisions make important statements about your work. Where you choose to perform your work is also an important consideration with regards to locality. Do you perform locally or do you take your work to others? Is your work presented in theatres or the community hall? Do you perform in the mornings or the evenings?

There is no right or wrong approach to locality, only what works for you in the aesthetic and political context of your work. Your location may be entirely incidental, but it is something to consider when assessing the purpose, impact, and need for your work.

New vs old

Your company is likely to fall into one of two broad categories. You will either create entirely new creative pieces of work – through a variety of wild and wonderful methods – or you will stage or adapt work that has already been written by playwrights throughout history.

There is no inherent benefit to either of these approaches, but they do imply different things externally and you should think twice before trying to tackle both under one umbrella. Similarly, if you work across different mediums – film production, for example – it can be distracting to your audience if your company appears to produce both theatre and film. This is not to discourage a multi-disciplinary approach by any means, but it needs to be clear to yourself and to your audience what your work is and is not. Successful companies tend to articulate a specific artistic vision: theatrical feminist adaptations of Bronte novels, for example, and stick to doing that really well.

Being broad in your output can lead to mission creep, where your long-term plans change as a result of shifting and vague aims and objectives. This can be one of the main symptoms of the disease I have diagnosed as 'the secret director.' Are you forming a company because you want to form a company or because this is a way of developing your directing experience? Having a go at a musical, followed by a classical drama, followed by a devised piece, can be beneficial for those purposes. Again, there isn't anything inherently wrong with this, but think back to the companies who inspire you and you are likely to find a more focussed approach.

New plays are incredibly exciting and immediately relevant to the 'Why you? Why this? Why now?' question, by the very fact that it has been created by you in this space. What could be more exciting than that? There tends to be a lot of subsidies for new plays, and they can build a reputation very quickly. On the negative side, it can be much harder to sell tickets to 'My New Play' than it can to a production of *Macbeth*, because there is more unknown risk for an audience. Starting with nothing puts much more pressure on the process to be robust, and it is often a longer process of refinement and development before your 'final' piece is ready to be seen by a paying audience.

On the other hand, pre-published plays can create an exciting opportunity for experimentation and are a chance to bring to life everything from undiscovered gems to timeless classics. They can be costly if *performance licences* are involved (see Chapter 8 for more on this), although older pieces are free and can be altered to your heart's content, perhaps to create something entirely new. On the negative side, you will automatically be compared to others who have worn those shoes before you, particularly when staging well-known work, and it is rare to find a theatre company who deal specifically in the staging of pre-written work. Frustratingly, due to changing tastes over time, older plays that have gone out of copyright tend to have larger casts (more actors, more expensive), whereas many newer plays (performance rights, fewer actors = less word of mouth?) tend to work with smaller casts. This is a generalisation, of course, but again something worth thinking about before embarking down a particular road.

Task: To make this decision easier, it can be helpful to plan ahead. Regardless of whether or not you have a production in mind, draw up a 'wish list' of five–ten other performances you could theoretically explore in the future.

For those of you working on new pieces, this wish list can explore topics or themes you would potentially be interested in developing.

For those considering pre-published plays, this could be a list of works that fit your requirements in terms of cast size, author etc.

If, after completing this task, you found it difficult to compile a larger list, this may be an indication of future difficulties, perhaps because your requirements are too stringent or because of logistical reasons. Use this analysis to reflect and position yourself in the best way going forward.

How style shows itself

Style is ephemeral to begin with but should be specific in the context of your own organisation. With this knowledge in place, your style communicates itself through every facet of performance, from play choice and casting, to marketing decisions and access in performance. If your style isn't consciously shaped and moulded into everything you do, you will find it will leave its mark regardless, and for better or worse, others will use this to judge you by and to make their own assessment of your values and ethics.

Think about the last time you saw a poster or flyer for a show. If it was effective, it should have told you something about the show, allowing you through that one interaction to make a rough judgement call about whether or not it'd be something you'd enjoy watching. A director who sets out an expectation to have all lines learnt before the first meeting sets a different tone and style to a director who sets up a group chat and hosts their first session in a pub. A show that ends with a Q+A invites a certain interpretation, as does a company who audiences come to know always start their shows exactly on time. There are an exhausting number of ways in which style presents itself, and none are inherently better or more professional than others, but each must be taken in the context of the broader tone your organisation seeks to operate by.

As the leader of this organisation, it is important that you remain consciously aware of this balance and how decisions reflect your values. This is not about PR and making sure that things *appear* a certain way to the public, but instead about ensuring that processes evolving from your activities accurately reflect the mindset and ethos of the people running them. If actors can be heard laughing when they leave stage, for example, or if your show ends with a badly coordinated curtain call, it may give an audience an air of unprofessionalism. Similarly, if your marketing materials contain typos or are badly designed, audiences will form conclusions about the mindset of the people running the company. You should aim for professionalism at every stage of the process, not just because it gives off a better impression of your company – which it does – but because you should aspire to create the best work that you can in the context you are working in. Without this, your company might not be around for long enough to give it a second chance!

Developing your process

Every artist has their own method of working and their reasons for doing so. These may be artistically driven, logistics based or, more than likely, a mixture of both.

It is not in the scope of this book to discuss the plethora of rehearsal practices available to you (although there are several recommendations in the resource section), but instead to consider the ways in which your creative practice as a whole should be shaped and considered to reflect who you want to be as a company and what you want to say.

Everything discussed so far in this chapter should be equally applied to your working process as it is to the final piece of work. In fact, the two should be seen as connected and essential to one another, for one cannot exist without its twin. Your process artistically and ethically should reflect the values of your organisation, and you should be cautious about ensuring those you work with – from actors and creatives to external agencies and venues – reflect and enhance that vision and don't contradict it.

Mimicking style

When we begin our creative journey, we often have strong influences who may have inspired our choice to create work in the first place. Those influences can be from within the same sector, or they may be diverse and varied. A lot of the time, our desire to create work stems from a desire to create work *like theirs*. Something about their process or the finished product appeals to us and makes a mark in such a way that we feel compelled to share in it.

It is fairly easy, therefore, to create work that is heavily routed in respect of our inspirations, essentially to create work that mimics the style of others. There is a fine line between inspiration, mimicry, and copying. For your company to be successful, it needs to create its own style that is as distinct, inspiring, and exciting as those who you were initially inspired by.

> **Task:** Considering the artists or companies who have inspired you, do some research into *their* influences. Who inspired, shaped, and influenced their work?

The task above is useful for a number of reasons. Firstly, it may well introduce you to further work that inspires your own practice. Secondly, it can be a useful reminder of the fact that art is a process, and inspiration leads to innovation in the right circumstances to create something new. All art is a conversation, and in being inspired by somebody else's work, you are in conversation not just with the artist themselves, but with their inspirations and, by extension, a whole history of artistic creation. In time, perhaps your own work will form part of that timeline which others will look to for their inspirations.

Experimentation and failure: developing style

How then do we develop style in practical terms? The answer to this is frustratingly simple: practise. We uncover a way of working and the stories and ideas that speak to us through exposure to different creative experiences, creating a small legacy of breakthroughs and setbacks. Without running the risk of sounding like a broken record, experimentation should pre-date your decision to form a theatre company so that the work you are putting out into the world is ready to carry your name. Of course, the ability to experiment implies its own privilege, and some of you reading this will not have the time or resources to play and may see this as a luxury. Some of you will have already benefited from that process, perhaps through the years of your university study, and may be well on that path towards establishing what makes your work distinct. Experimentation shouldn't be seen as a static process that can only happen at the start of your journey, however, and instilling an ethos of experimentation can help your work from becoming stale as you develop.

When I founded my company I was debating whether or not to go to university. My drama tutor, Chris, gave me some excellent advice which I, of course, ignored. 'University,' Chris told me, 'is three years to fuck things up.' I didn't appreciate or understand this at the time, but I certainly do now. When your work is out in the world, it is out in the world, for all to see and judge. Our work needs time to develop and to grow, and our voices need experimentation and support to find our unique expression. Putting work straight into the world, as I did, was a fantastic practical learning experience, but it removed from us the chance to get it wrong. You can search our reviews, good and bad, from our first ever production to our latest work. Is this a good thing? Perhaps it depends on how you look at it. It is certainly something to consider, so that you can foster a positive relationship with experimentation and development, and so that you can see the power and potential in getting things wrong. Our rush and need to create work and put it out to the world made each show an existential threat as we hoped and prayed for good reviews and for enough money to cover our costs.

Managing people: managing yourself

One thing you will be doing more than any other during the life of your theatre company is working with others. These will range from regular collaborators to venue staff you meet only once or twice. One of the biggest ways in which your values and ethics will present themselves is through how you work with other people, so it's important to build this into your interactions with others.

Regardless of the nature of your relationship with other people, as a representative of your company, your words and actions reflect the company as a whole. For better or worse, you are the face of your company, and that means taking the success when it comes and being the person others turn to when things go wrong.

As the face of a company – the main point of contact – your experience is different from everybody else. Period. You are operating on two levels always, at one time enjoying and being in the experience and at the same time, maintaining a birds-eye view. You may wish to celebrate when the curtain goes down, but you'll be the first person the venue will come to if there's a set to be removed. You might want to spend an hour before the show getting into character, but it's likely the venue will want to speak to you five minutes before the house opens to ask about the interval arrangements. Being the leader of a company, particularly at the stage where you're likely to be wearing multiple hats, is a constant balancing act. Particularly when we're tired or emotional, how we continue to follow the example of our values speaks volumes about the integrity of our company. It can also be our greatest challenge.

Managing yourself can be the hardest part of the whole process. We might not have thought about this before – after all, we are the one responsible, so the last thing we can do is stop and think about ourselves! So I thought when running my own company. The sense of personal restlessness I felt to be constantly creating, and the crippling pressure I experienced to make the company deliver for those working with us was all-consuming. At one point I was managing three shows simultaneously, whilst keeping down a full-time job, which was necessary to cover my rent. It's little surprise, in hindsight, that this led to burnout. And although the road to this destination was well intentioned, the results were less sympathetic.

We can easily move into a territory where we convince ourselves that our sacrifice is somehow noble and worth it for the good of the company. Indeed, in our wider economy we are often encouraged to give ourselves substantially to our work and it can easily become all consuming. In the arts, where working practices and work–life balance are traditionally problematic, it can be all too easy to become defined by our work and to wear this as a badge of honour.

Being passionate and driven to create art is, of course, no bad thing. What we must recognise is the inevitable road this drives us on towards burnout. I have come to realise that avoiding burnout requires incredible, and persistent, self-discipline, and that as a rule of thumb, by the time we realise we might be headed down that road, it can usually be too late.

If the pandemic has taught us anything, it should be that there are huge personal benefits from redefining our relationship with our work and to striking a better balance with our health, with the economy, and with the environment. We must become better skilled at recognising burnout in ourselves and others and in creating working practices that are supportive and not exploitative. Of course, there will be times of squeeze and increased demand, but when this becomes our usual working pattern, we must reflect honestly on the sustainability of such a model. Furthermore, we should all make more effort to recognise this in others and to support them, especially if the work somebody else needs to do for us is untenable.

My business mentor gave me a brilliant story to summarise this problem. She told me about how, when she was younger, she would revel in the struggle of beating the system, being a poor student, and not filling her car tank until the last possible second. Her warning light would be flashing at her and on more than one occasion she would practically role the car into the forecourt, getting every last penny from her fuel. One day when her dad asked her what she was doing, she proudly told him how running the car to empty was helping her to save a bit of money. Her dad wasn't impressed. Didn't she know that running the car dry can create all sorts of problems in the exhaust and pipes, running down the life of the car and slowly killing it each time she ran it to empty? I'm sure you can see where this is going. The process is exactly the same for us, and although it can be easy and sometimes even desirable to run ourselves aground, the longer-term damage can be hidden and devastating, and we should avoid it at all costs.

Working from home

As the world continues to develop in the aftermath of the pandemic, home working has become more of a reality for many of us. In reality, I'd been home working with my theatre company for nearly ten years, working away into the small hours after returning home from my day job.

Today, however, we are more aware than ever of the reality of this process for many people, and where we may have a shared experience of this from the first wave of Covid-19, our new world of varied working patterns has seen some of us return to our offices whilst others are set to remain working from home indefinitely. How we manage the pitfalls of home working, and recognise the reality of them for others, is an important factor in supporting our overall balance in life. Although some of these considerations are not exclusive to home working, they are issues we should be attuned and responsive to in establishing working expectations for our companies.

Considerations to include are:

- Social isolation
- 'Zoom' fatigue
- 'Blue light' from electronic devices
- The need for natural light, exercise, and fresh air
- Group chats and working-hours.

There are many benefits to the 'new normal' for supporting theatre companies, particularly in the ease of hosting a remote meeting or rehearsal, and we have exciting opportunities to develop our practice by taking advantage of these. Where every rehearsal contributes towards our carbon footprint, or where distance can be expensive for your creatives in travel costs, remote meetings and rehearsals can be an exciting development to the typical formula. But, equally, we should also be mindful of the issues this can bring. I have found that a simple notification blocker has significantly helped me with this, and I always outline at the start of any new project that I will only pick up emails or messages within usual working hours. The temptation to be responding to messages or group chats during my own time is too strong without this rule, and I try as much as I can to reinforce it throughout, in respect of the fact that other people may not appreciate those notifications at that time. As with everything else in this chapter, our conduct in such matters again outlines our values and helps others to follow them.

Vision, mission, and values

How do we begin to think about and communicate this framework? One of the simplest and most effective tools for accomplishing this difficult task is the Vision, Mission, and Values statements. Straight out of the handbook for most business start-ups, the Vision, Mission, and Values statements shouldn't be viewed with corporate wariness but seen as a valuable starting point towards articulating and summarising all of the things we have discussed so far in this chapter.

Let's break this down to understand the differences and begin to consider how you might apply this to your own company.

Vision: Articulating your vision is about the future. What is your goal? What do you want the world to be as a result of your company? Be bold, inspiring, and ambitious and tell us what you want to achieve, clearly and directly. Consider the Alzheimer's Association: *A world without Alzheimer's*, or Microsoft: *A computer on every desk or in every home.*

Mission: Think of a mission statement as a roadmap for your company. Whereas the Vision Statement thinks about what you want to achieve in the future, your Mission Statement thinks about *how* you will do it. Think about what you want to achieve, who you will support and why. What is the current purpose of your company? Consider the Mission Statement of a company such as TED: *Spread ideas* or Tesla: *To accelerate the world's transition to sustainable energy.*

Values: The values of any brand or organisation can be thought of in terms of the standards you hold yourself against. You might write this as a broad paragraph or perhaps as a list of specifics. How will your company conduct itself and what values will it uphold? How will you hold yourself to account?

Task: Having worked through the above, create your own Vision, Mission, and Values statements. If you are a group, you may think about brainstorming these together or perhaps you could develop drafts independently before comparing notes, to see each person's perspective.

Think about the following questions as a starting point for articulating your vision and mission.

- Who are you?
- What kind of work do you want to make and who for?
- How would you like your customers to describe you?
- What kind of company would you like to be in five years' time?
- What kind of art would you like to be creating in five years' time?

Tip: It can be easy to spend a lot of time debating the detail of specific words in your statements. Although wording is important, to a degree, you will reach a point where further editing is almost unnecessary, so keep one eye on the big picture here.

> Repeat the above process for your Values statement. Start with key phrases – you should aim for somewhere between five and ten – and keep this statement simple to understand and remember. Don't pack it with jargon, but do give yourself permission to dream and be idealistic.
>
> Remember that these should be treated as live documents, and you can and should update them as and when appropriate, so that they continue to reflect the purpose and nature of your organisation as it moves and develops.

Creating Vision, Mission, and Values statements and making them visible can be a purposeful start to a company. They help to outline your aims, your concerns, and your perspectives and ensure that everyone who works with you understands and respects this same perspective. In many ways, everything else flows from this task: from the work you choose to stage, to the way you work with others, it is an investment of time that will pay dividends for a long time to come.

Vision, mission, and values in practice

So far throughout this chapter we've talked a lot about the standards and framework you hold yourself to in the creation of your work. In breaking it down in this way it can seem as though there is an obvious, and binary, division between a right and wrong way to do things. But while there is a clear distinction of values at a societal level, where there often is, and should be, a defined and shared understanding of right and wrong, thinking about this in your own organisation should be refined and specific to your own circumstances. I would take it as granted that your work and practice will follow the broad values of your wider culture, but the values of *your* company and the voice *you* give to those values are about *your* privilege and perspective as an artist with an entirely unique perspective in the world.

This is about refining yourself as a practitioner, about recognising your burning need to create something in the world and helping you to bring it to life. In this, your vision, mission, and values should be entirely unique to the circumstances of *your* company because nobody else can say what *you* want to say, the way *you* want to say it. Recognising this, refining this, and articulating this, are the steps towards becoming a true artist.

Chapter Resources

Vision, mission, and values

Duncan, Rodger Dean, 'Leading with vision: A blueprint for engaging your workforce,' Forbes.com, www.forbes.com/sites/rodgerdeanduncan/2017/06/13/leading-with-vision-a-blueprint-for-engaging-your-workforce/

'How to develop vision, mission and values,' DIY Committee Guide, www.diycomm itteeguide.org/resource/vision-mission-and-values
'How to use leadership vision to lead your business,' Indeed, www.indeed.com/career-advice/career-development/leadership-vision
'Mission and Purpose,' Social Enterprise Toolkit, https://socialenterprisetoolkit.ie/chapter-2-mission-purpose/

Ensemble work and rehearsal practice

Alfreds, Mike, *Then What Happens? Storytelling and adapting for the theatre* (Nick Hern Books, London, 2013)
Berry, Cicely, *From Word to Play: A handbook for directors* (Oberon Books, London, 2008)
Bloom, Michael, *Thinking like a Director: A practical handbook* (Faber & Faber, New York, 2001)
Caird, John, *Theatre Craft: A director's practical companion from A to Z* (Faber & Faber, London, 2010)
Callery, Dymphna, *Through the Body: A practical guide to physical theatre* (Nick Hern Books, London, 2001)
Donnellan, Declan, *The Actor and the Target*, 2nd edition (Nick Hern Books, London, 2005)
Etchells, Tim, *Certain Fragments: Contemporary performance and forced entertainment* (Routledge, London, 2001)
Harvard Business Review: On Leadership (Harvard Business School Publishing Corporation, 2011)
Harvard Business Reviews: On Managing Yourself (Harvard Business School Publishing Corporation, 2010)
Hauser, Frank and Russell Reich, *Notes on Directing: 130 lessons in leadership from the director's chair* (Bloomsbury Methuen Drama, London, 2003)
Hope, Russ, *Getting Directions: A fly-on-the-wall guide for emerging theatre directors* (Nick Hern Books, London, 2012)
Manfull, Helen, *Taking Stage: Women directors on directing* (Methuen Publishing, London, 1999)
Mitchell, Katie, *The Director's Craft: A handbook for the theatre* (Routledge, Oxon, 2009)
Rodenburg, Patsy, 'Why I Do Theatre,' YouTube (9th October 2008) www.youtube.com/watch?v=L9jjhGq8pMM&t=1s
Savran, David, *Breaking the Rules: The Wooster Group* (Theatre Communications Group, New York, 1986)
Trefor-Jones, Glyn, *Drama Menu: Theatre games in three courses* (Nick Hern Books, London, 2015)
Unwin, Stephen, *So You Want to Be a Theatre Director?* (Nick Hern Books, London, 2012)
Wright, John, *Why Is That So Funny? A practical exploration of physical comedy* (Nick Hern Books, London, 2006)

3 Becoming a Company

Starting any new project can feel overwhelming. Everything seems equally urgent, you don't feel as though you have the skills to do anything properly, and you don't know yet what you don't know. For many, the first logical step is to explore company formation, which can itself feel like a minefield. The good news is, forming a company is logical if you follow the steps as outlined here and give this process the time it needs.

You may not yet be at the stage of wanting to form a company but reading this chapter can help you to create a mental mind map of the journey ahead. I would encourage all readers to work through this chapter and highlight the bits of information that might be useful later – even if this is the sort of stuff that terrifies you, knowledge is power and taking ownership of this stage of the process will make your art more sustainable and more enjoyable. Trust me, I was not a 'business person' either. If I can do it, so can you.

Let's dive straight in.

Becoming a company

The decision to form any legally recognised company – whether a theatre group, a bar or a toy shop – is a landmark moment filled with huge excitement and risk. There are a myriad of benefits and positives that come from registering your company as a legal entity, and you may be considering this move through necessity as much as through choice. While it is easier than you might think to get started, it is something you should give plenty of thought to, to make sure it's the right thing for you and your team.

Picking your moment

Forming as a legal entity involves a lot of ongoing work and responsibilities. Your relationship to your co-founders and your work will change profoundly, so you need to be confident in your decision to take the work in this direction. The process of becoming a company in a legal sense is called *incorporation*, but it is important to remember that you don't need to incorporate the moment you start working together. For many, the decision to do this comes because of

DOI: 10.4324/9781003281726-3

conversations with a funder such as Arts Council England. We were using the name of our theatre group, PurpleCoat, for over five years before we decided to incorporate, and we did so because we felt that we were at a stage to best take advantage of the opportunities it offered, whilst being confident in our ability to navigate the paperwork and extra challenges it brought.

> **TASK:** Use the questions below to help assess your current situation. These questions are deliberately broad and leading: if you still feel ready despite some of the implications, go for it.
>
> 1. Have you put on a piece of work as a group yet?
> 2. Did it go as well as expected?
> 3. Have you finished your education?
> 4. Have you worked with your colleagues for an extended period, in good *and* challenging circumstances?
> 5. Have any of your team had experience with business or finance?
> 6. Do you have the time and energy to commit to the company?
> 7. Do you have an idea for a new piece of work?
>
> If you answered Yes to the majority of these questions, the timing may well be right for you to think about moving to the next stage of incorporation. However, this is not prescriptive and should be judged by instinct and common sense, two key skills you will need again and again for your future venture.

Take the time to think carefully about your future. If you find yourself rushing: ask yourself why. Are you avoiding looking at the details and hoping it'll figure itself out? Are you letting the excitement carry you away from logic? There will be no singularly right moment when it is *the* perfect time to incorporate – any new company is founded with a great deal of *risk*. The skill, and the key to a successful venture, is being able to take the right steps at the right time, having fully researched and concluded that the potential benefit outweighs the potential risk. Notice in the questions above, nothing suggests a particular type of person being the best fit to start a business. Ultimately, it doesn't matter if you have a degree or not, whether you've studied at drama school or live in a certain part of the country. If you are savvy, you can use your individual circumstances to your advantage and distinguish yourself from the crowd.

How do you like pizza?

It's not for nothing that the industry you're planning to enter is known as show-*business*. There's two words there, and to be a successful theatre company you will need to know how to put on a show, for sure, but it's the business side that can so often be overlooked. Through my many years of figuring out the obstacles and making many of the mistakes I want you to avoid, I've always found it useful to think of my organisation not as a theatre company at all. The entertainment business is uniquely different from many other sectors in several ways – it's one of the reasons this book exists: so much of the business advice that's out there doesn't relate to a theatre company, at all. But when it's hard to see the wood for the trees, looking at your business through a purely *business-focussed* lens can really help clarify your intentions and goals.

So, let us do that now. Imagine there are five of us who all really, really like pizza. We like them so much we start to create our own. Realising how good they taste, we decide we'll start a company. We're based in London, so let's open there. We'll register as a company and throw together our collective savings.

There should already be some alarm bells ringing. Clearly the selling of pizza is a big business – worth £2b per year in the UK alone – and as a city with a population of nearly 9 million, not to mention a significant number of tourists, London might be the ideal spot. But let's hold our horses for a second. London is a huge city – should we open in Putney or Paddington? Would we be better off as a sit-down restaurant or a takeaway? If we're a takeaway, we need to get onto the major delivery platforms, but is that better value for money than hiring our own delivery driver? Market research is essential – there's a whole section dedicated to it in Chapter 5 – but the important thing to bear in mind for now is how much you know and how much you might still have to find out. London is a big city. That means rent and competition will be higher – maybe it'd be a better investment and less risky to start in Milton Keynes? Or Cardiff?

The next alarm bell that should start to ring is the number of founders. Five people seems excessive in a small pizzeria – is everyone contributing something unique? Often, proposed new theatre companies are bloated – picking the right people is something we'll look at in more detail in Chapter 4.

Just because our plucky young chefs made some nice dishes in their kitchen, none of them have experience of doing this professionally. Does this mean that they wouldn't be successful at opening a new business? Of course, not – but they do need to assess this. Would you give them £100,000 on that basis? What if there were only two of them and one had once been a high-ranking sous-chef for Gordon Ramsey?

Conducting a full-scale analysis of your potential business may seem premature at this stage, but it is going to be a step you'll be thankful for taking when your business succeeds.

SWOT

A quick way to make a detailed assessment of your business is through a *SWOT* analysis. Your Strengths and Weaknesses are specific to you as an organisation, and are generally things you find relatively easy to control. Opportunities and Threats, however, are those things outside of your control which you can either take advantage of, or need to protect yourself against.

> **TASK:** Grab a piece of paper and think about how each of these applies to your potential new business. Start by splitting your paper into four segments.
>
> - Strengths – *where are your strongest assets, what do you excel at?*
> - Weaknesses – *what could you be better at?*
> - Opportunities – *what opportunities can you spot in, say, the next twelve months?*
> - Threats – *what could be a threat to your new organisation?*
>
> Having completed this exercise, you should already be feeling a lot more in touch with your current position. Broadly speaking, if your Strengths and Opportunities outweighed your Weaknesses and Threats, this might be a good indication that taking the next step is the right thing to do. Alternatively, now that you have had the opportunity to think about your Weaknesses and Threats, you're immediately in a better position to be able to do something about them. This is an activity with endless application – you can do it together as a company, you should even do it as individuals. The important thing to remember is that it shouldn't be static. In a year's time, you will probably compile a completely different set of results, as you combat some of your Weaknesses, and as new Opportunities and Threats present themselves.

Still a hobby?

Is your organisation a hobby or a company? It's important to ensure you're on the right side of the law when you start to sell tickets and make money, as you could suddenly be in a very different legal position from when you were making shows in your educational institution as students. In the UK, *HMRC* refers to 'badges of trade' to establish if you are running a business. These include:

- Are you intending to make a profit?
- Do you buy or make goods with the intention of selling them on?
- Did you borrow any money to get things going?
- Does the frequency and number of transactions suggest that you are running a business?

For a lot of people, this breakdown can be a realisation that things are a bit more established than first thought. Tempting as it may be to think that you're still pursuing a hobby and that HMRC will never find out, the punishment for not notifying them can be severe.

The pros and cons

So, what are the benefits of forming a company and how is that different from what you've already been doing? In brief, forming as a legal entity allows:

- Reduced personal *liability*
- Significantly increased fundraising options
- Potential credibility, through commitment to responsible management.

Simply put, being registered as a company is a mark of professionalism and a statement of intention for your planned permanence. It shows that you're serious, that you're committed to good management and leadership, and it will influence the way other people perceive you. This will be especially important when dealing with funders, banks, and venues, and will open doors that may otherwise remain shut.

When registering your company, you will be expected to identify at least one person with significant control (PSC). This is another benefit of incorporation. A PSC has ownership or control over your company because they have at least 25% of the voting rights at board level. More on the board below and how this works in practice, but for now, it's important to remember that ownership formalises both your relationship and your responsibility.

How companies work

Much of the language around company formation may be new to you, so before we look at company types, it is important to lay out some basics.

When we're talking about directors in a company context, it's important to reiterate that this is not in the sense of a theatre director, but a company director. A company director is a person or persons legally responsible for the company and for ensuring financial and tax information is sent to the appropriate bodies correctly and on time. If you decide to form a company, you will become a company director.

Company directors are the people who do the leg work of running the business, but who holds them to account? The board are a group of people with responsibility for overseeing the organisation's governance: making sure that the long-term future of the business looks healthy and ensuring that those running the company are doing a good job. The board may be referred to by several names, including trustees, the management committee, governors, or directors. This can become a bit confusing, but their function is always the same. In a company primarily designed to make profit, the board are the ultimate beneficiaries, and individuals may sit on the board because they have invested a large stake into the organisation.

This is only useful to know to understand how arts organisations tend to be different. A company that is driven by social aims rather than purely financial – such as a charity – will have slightly different rules for how profit and governance works. Organisations such as charities are allowed to make a profit, but that profit will be invested back into the company, rather than used to give a bonus to the directors. This is what is meant by the phrase not-for-profit. In order to specify the benefit provided by a charity, the company will have a list of charitable aims, so that its impact against those aims can be measured and tracked.

Charities and organisations with a social purpose – also known as social enterprises – will still have a board, but their relationship to the company is slightly different. Where the principle of the role remains the same, trustees on a charitable board aren't paid: they are giving their time and expertise because they believe in the mission of the organisation.

Most companies operate what are known as shares. When a company is limited by shares, it is owned by shareholders, who exercise certain rights over the company. Shares represent a chunk of a business, so if you imagine that total shares of a company come to 100%, if you owned twenty shares you would own 20% of that business. An individual share can be any value. As the fortunes of the company hopefully increase and the organisation is worth more money, the value of the company shares would also increase, making your ownership of those shares a sound one. Shares are important to understand in principle, but the majority of arts organisations don't have them. A company limited by guarantee, on the other hand, has no shareholders, instead it has guarantors. Guarantors each agree to pay a fee towards company debt if the organisation is closed, usually only to the tune of £1.

Company names

One of the most exciting things you will need to decide for your company is its name. You will need to do your research, because your company name cannot be too similar to an existing one – so the *Royalish Shakespeare Company* probably isn't going to work – and you are barred from using certain sensitive expressions and words. In the UK, *Companies House* has a simple name search, where you can check that your proposed company name is available. Don't just search Twitter and use that as a basis for whether your company name is unique or not!

New theatre companies tend to opt for weird and wonderful names, on the one hand, or shockingly obvious names on the other. Be wary of both traps. Although you are creative by nature, you will want your name to tell people what it is, particularly in our age of information overload and the rush to capture people's attention online. Move away from in-jokes or names that only make sense to a few people and think ahead to those audiences who will book to come and see your show. Likewise, think carefully before complementing your name with terms such as Productions or Ensemble. It's been done so many times before, and often by much bigger players, that it may sound pretentious and unoriginal. Finding a name is a complex balance between memorability, originality, and clarity. Why not test a few out in some market research?

One final note on names is to consider your online presence. We delve into this more in Chapter 6, but your social media handles and website URL will need to be memorable and linked to your company name, and it can be tricky to work around if they have already been taken. You ideally want consistency across these platforms, and names already being taken tells you that the name has already been used by another company, so bear all of this in mind when making your selection.

Company types

Although there are many different types of company, here I am going to introduce you to the main types used within an arts context.

Limited Liability Partnership: A flexible company structure for formalising partnerships and offering some of the benefits of company formation. In an LLP, the partnership is a distinct legal entity from the founders, meaning that it has independent legal status and offers limited liability to the members.

Company Limited by Guarantee: This company structure doesn't involve *shareholders*, and the main benefit of this for a theatre company is that you can be *non-profit distributing* (meaning any profit you do make gets reinvested into the company) and have *charitable aims*. This option is extremely common; it opens opportunities with public funders and can be an indicator of a *social enterprise*.

Community Interest Company (CIC): This company structure combines enterprise with social welfare. If you aim to be non-profit distributing but don't want *charitable status*, this may be the structure for you, and although you can still have charitable aims, you are not allowed to gain charitable status by registering as a CIC. CICs can be attractive to funders who see this structure as an indicator of stronger social ambitions than that of a traditional limited company. As a relatively new type of company, many trusts will still only fund charities, which can be a disadvantage. In the simplest terms, a CIC exists to serve a specific community.

Sole traders and self-employment

Although not a company structure in its own right, it is important to mention sole traders and self-employment, as it often relates significantly to freelancers within the creative sectors. An individual is self-employed if they run their own business for themselves, are responsible for its success, or when you work for several customers at the same time without a standard contract of employment guaranteeing regular working hours or pay. The specific distinction of being self-employed is complex and varies depending on your territory, but actors and theatre freelancers tend to fall into this category due to the nature of the project-specific, inconsistent working relationships they undertake with venues and producers.

A sole trader is essentially a self-employed person who is the sole owner of their business, so if there's more than one of you this won't be the method for you. Sole-traders aren't incorporated and it is not a business structure in the manner of the examples listed above. Setting up as a sole trader is the most popular legal structure in the UK, accounting for 60% of small businesses, likely because it's the simplest structure to set up. Despite this, there are some clear differences which you should be aware of before pursuing this route.

Whereas a limited company remains a separate legal entity in the eyes of HMRC (meaning the company and the people who run it are separate legal entities), sole traders are completely and wholly responsible for their business. If, for example, you ran a bookshop and for some reason I wanted to take you to court, if you were a limited company, it would be the *company* I'd sue. If you were a sole-trader, I'd be suing *you*. Whereas limited companies are treated as a separate legal entity, sole traders are classed as one and the same in the eyes of the government. This means that if your company goes bankrupt, or if someone sues you, it is you who picks up the flack. It is also marginally more tax efficient to be registered as a limited company.

When you start a contracted job with an employer, you always need to fill in information regarding your tax status. This is so that the government knows how much you have earned that year and how much tax you should be paying as a result. When starting a job with a contract of employment, your employer deals with this for you, but what happens when your employment status changes regularly, when you don't have a guarantee of how much you'll earn (if anything) each month, and when your work is inconsistent and time-limited? This is the case for many freelance creatives and the solution is to register as self-employed. This process achieves the same effect of declaring your income so that you can be taxed appropriately, but the process is different to reflect the different terms of your working life.

You should register as self-employed if you anticipate earning money from your new organisation in an ad hoc, inconsistent way, or from running things like classes and workshops. You may have successfully applied for funding and plan to pay yourself, for example. If you already have a job elsewhere, you also need to register as self-employed so that your extra earnings are declared above what you have already declared in the salary from your first employment. If you are lucky enough to have enough money to pay yourself a regular, fixed salary, it is likely to be more appropriate to operate a payroll and pay yourself through PAYE, which is explored in the next chapter.

Being a sole-trader and registering to be self-employed is a big step, which requires you to be directly involved with your finances and to manage them accordingly. I have linked to a step-by-step guide for how to do this in the UK in the resource section, and other readers are advised to research information specific to your territory, to find the most up-to-date information. It is likely that many of your colleagues and tutors will have experience of self-employment, so they are also worth referring to if you need support setting this up.

How to set up your new company

When you are ready to set up your organisation as an incorporated structure, you need to follow a set of key steps, which vary slightly depending on the company type. This does not apply to sole-traders but organisations which are distinct legal entities, including LLP, CIC, and charities. There are entities that can provide you with assistance in registering a company and offer tailored advice on your plans for company structures. Some will even register the company for you. Think carefully about the added benefit of these before shelling out; however, as you might be able to save money just by doing your research. Registering a limited company online yourself currently costs £12.

- Company Limited by Guarantee: must register with Companies House.
- Community Interest Company (CIC): must register with Companies House and pass a 'Community Interest Test' as part of the process.
- Community Interest Organisation (CIO): registered at the Charity Commission and not companies house. Must be able to demonstrate a public benefit from your work.

Copyright and trademarks

Copyright comes in many guises, but in this context, we are thinking about the safety net of ensuring that nobody else can steal your name and logo. Happily, Companies House prevents a new company from being named too similarly to an existing business, and at the small to medium scale, this should be satisfactory. Registering a *trademark* is a timely process, but it does give you the legality to take legal action against anyone who copies your brand too closely, and once completed, your registered trademark lasts for ten years. Search 'Register a trademark' at gov.uk for a full list of rules about trademarking and to complete the process. Although this can be a fruitful step once you reach a certain size as a company, this is not something you should worry about too much when starting out.

IN01, Memorandum and Articles of Association

These fancy sounding documents are much easier to complete than they sound. They are the three main ingredients you will need to register a limited company. You will be taken through these automatically as part of the online registration of your business.

- *IN01*: This is the form you will first need to complete to register a limited company. It contains the essential information about the name of your

company, the names of the directors and their respective addresses, and the type of business you are going to undertake. Here you will also declare the *Registered Office Address*.
- *Memorandum of Association*: This document is a legal statement, signed by all the initial shareholders or guarantors, agreeing to form a company. It lists the names and addresses of each of the directors in your organisation. *Note*: if you are registering as a CIC, there is a slightly different format for your M+A, as these need to be approved by demonstrating how your organisation will help an at-need community. Search 'Community Interest Companies: Model Constitutions' and follow the steps.
- *Articles of Association*: This is slightly more in depth and explains how the company will be run, including administrative arrangements and the powers and responsibilities of company directors. You either have the choice to use standard articles (known as 'model articles') or you can write and upload your own. Given that this document outlines how your organisation will be run, it is advisable not to use model articles, but to write your own. This is where the expertise of an organisation such as the Independent Theatre Council can be of benefit, as they have resources for the sort of things theatre companies such as yourself should seek to include.

Registered office address

This is the official address for HMRC and Companies House to deliver statutory mail and legal notices. If there are several of you and you don't have an office or don't live together, this is an important piece of information to decide. This is where you will be legally registered, and if you are a public company, as most of you will be, this address will be searchable and visible online and on all your communication. Important posts will be sent to this address so you need to ensure you have access to it, and it's where people will come to if things go wrong, so if you're living at your parents' place, it's a conversation to have before you take on that responsibility. If you are living in a rented property, your tenancy agreement will likely state that you must not run a business from the property, so this is also something to investigate. Your business address does not need to be in the same part of the country as your business activities, and there are many companies online who advertise budget friendly city office addresses. If you have used a lawyer in helping to set up your business, you usually have the option of using their office as your registered address.

The Government Gateway

When you first incorporate a company, you'll be bombarded with a lot of paperwork, including from HMRC and Companies House, which includes confidential and important information about your company, such as your

Unique Tax Number (UTR). The Government Gateway, which is HMRC's online system for you to submit important documentation such as tax statements and your *Confirmation Statement* (more below), is extremely secure and confidential, with your log on information being posted to you in separate letters. If you lose this log on information, it'll be sent again securely via mail, which HMRC says can take up to two weeks. There's no quick 'Forgot your password?' solution here. Obviously, this is to protect your company information, but you do need to make sure you're safe and secure with storing those key documents (and, in fact, all your paperwork) to avoid headaches in the future.

Confirmation Statement

The *Confirmation Statement*, formerly the Annual Return, is a form you submit each year to Companies House, which confirms the key information about your organisation. Most of the time, if nothing in your company has changed (no changes of address, no new directors etc.), this is a fast and simple process to complete. It's usually due around the anniversary of the date of incorporation, and joyfully, it's something you must pay to complete, even if nothing has changed. Doing it online is vastly more cost effective at £13, whereas completing a paper form currently costs £40. You'll get an email reminder but there's a hefty fine if you don't send your Confirmation Statement off, so make sure you prioritise it.

Annual accounts

As a company director of a limited company, you have a responsibility to submit *annual accounts* and an *annual return*. Your trustees have overall responsibility for ensuring good financial governance. Finance is often the area many creatives shy away from, believing they 'don't do maths,' or that it is endlessly complicated. The truth is that it doesn't need to be, and by knowing what you're signing up to in advance and by getting it right from the start, you can save yourself huge headaches later. There is an extensive breakdown of your financial requirements in Chapter 9.

It is beyond the scope of this book to provide a detailed investigation of how to account for your business (see the end of the chapter for recommendations) but what follows is an overview of each part of the process.

Annual accounts, sometimes referred to as Financial Accounts or Company Accounts, show what the business has been spending its money on, how much *turnover* and profit it has made and how well it has been doing during the last *financial year*. The information in your annual accounts will be used to prepare a Company Tax Return for HMRC. Your accounts are how people will assess the health of your business, and for public companies this information will be available for all to see via the Companies House website. It's a significant undertaking and one that must be accurate – for this reason alone it is worth enlisting the skills of an accountant, because mistakes can be costly.

A *financial year* (you might have heard the term fiscal year in the US, which is the same thing) is a twelve-month period, over which accounts are prepared. One financial year starts the day after the previous one finishes. For new companies, your financial year starts on the day of incorporation. The Accounting Reference Date (or ARD) for your company is the day you must submit your annual accounts by and comes on the last day of the month when your company was first registered. Let's make this easier by considering an example:

A business that was incorporated on the 8th July 2023 will have an accounting reference date of the 31st July (the end of the month). This means that the following year the ARD will be on the 31st July 2024.

Directors' report: This section varies in length depending on the scale of a company's activities. Here the director lays out the main business of the company during the last financial year, where they usually draw attention to the main achievements and hurdles the company has experienced, as well as laying out some ambitions for the following financial year. If you're interested in seeing this in practise, you can easily pick a theatre (or any public company), search for them on Companies House and read their own latest accounts, including their directors' statement. For a small enterprise as you will likely be, this tends to be nothing more than ticking a few pre-formed sentences when you submit your annual accounts.

Balance sheet: A balance sheet outlines the value of everything owned by your company at that specific moment in time.

Profit and loss: The profit and loss account details where spending has happened over the last financial year and in which areas. As a result, this document calculates the profit or loss a company has made in its last financial period. Together with the balance sheet, these documents provide a detailed report of the financial health of the company and can be used to chart a company's growth.

Auditors: Accounts are highly sensitive documents which must be accurate to ensure companies pay their equal share of tax to the state. Enter the *auditor*. Run a Google Image search for 'auditor' and you are met with a raft of stock images of people in suits with magnifying glasses scrutinising piles of paper. The reality is that auditors are authorised to go through your accounts and to check and verify their accuracy. The good news is that if everything is above board you have nothing to worry about. The even better news is, if you're a small company you don't have to have your accounts audited, at all.

Small and micro-companies: Some good news. Companies that are deemed to be small or micro entities are allowed exemption from several aspects of annual accounts, meaning they can submit what are known as *abridged accounts*. A micro company is listed as one with an annual turnover of £632,000 or less and fewer than ten employees. A small company is listed as one with a turnover of less than £10.2m. As a small or micro company, you can apply for audit exemption, and the directors' report is optional.

Listing your company information

Being an incorporated company means that you must display certain information on all your communications. By law, you must include your company name on all communication, both electronic and paper based (check out Chapter 6 for information on setting up email signatures). This includes websites, emails, letters, bills, order forms, and receipts. Additionally, official business communication must also display the company number (you will receive this when you incorporate), whether the company is registered in England and Wales, Scotland, or Northern Ireland, the company's registered address, and the fact that your company is limited, if you've been granted exemption from showing this in your name. As an example:

FivePizza Guyz. Registered in England and Wales.
No: 09111111 Limited by Guarantee
Registered Office Address: 1 Pizza Place, Covent Garden, London, L1

The board

As alluded to earlier, the board of trustees (or governors, or directors) are the highest authority within a company, and as such are responsible for its *governance*. A public limited company must have at least two directors, and there is no definite upper limit, although more than seven might be considered unwieldy. A strong board is essential to a company's success, and the right board can be instrumental to ensuring you are able to weather future challenges.

The board is the ultimate authority in a company, with power even to fire the CEO. Their responsibility is to ensure the company is well managed and meeting its financial and legal obligations, as well as acting as a critical friend to the CEO to help ensure the company meets its long-term ambitions. Board meetings take place at a rate that is deemed appropriate: companies growing fast may want to meet once a month. It is helpful, though not essential, to appoint a chairperson, who sets the agenda, runs the meeting, and ensures everyone can have their say. Similarly, although this is no longer a legal requirement, it can be helpful to appoint a *company secretary* (this can be the same person as one of the company directors) who is chiefly responsible for the administrative duties of the company.

The decision to appoint a board is a big one and there is no defined threshold to mark the perfect moment to do so. Some funders may require an organisation to have a board, but you shouldn't just appoint one to get a successful funding bid, as the board are an integral and permanent part of your company DNA. Depending on your company type, it is likely that your board will be unpaid volunteers, but this is not to diminish the importance they have to your company.

The board of trustees are responsible for promoting the company's success, for ensuring good governance and due diligence, for managing their conflicts of interest, and for ensurig record keeping of the board's decisions is kept. A board member is not a mentor and they're not just coming along for the ride. There are legal and moral expectations of a board member and the decision to join a board is a big one. You are, in effect, signing yourself up to the fate of the business, with rights to affect decisions and to look out for its best interests.

A board has responsibilities, and they also bring a wealth of advantage that you cannot hope to have on your own. Key to this is experience, and this should be your starting point when thinking about appointing a board. Typically, board members will be well connected, with experience in areas such as HR, legal, finance, and management, although this does predispose the majority of boards to being older, white, and male, which may be something you'd want to address. The important thing is that your board should bring something new to the table and they should be more experienced than you – members with previous board experience, ideally with another theatre company or venue, are also invaluable. You want your board to help you open doors you cannot open alone.

The level of experience required from a board can therefore make them difficult to appoint. A good potential board member will be in demand, and where a person can technically sit on more than one board, it will be difficult to get their attention while you are a small player. But this shouldn't put you off. Remember that your board can grow and change over time, as more trustees join, others leave, and your needs change. Most of the key art recruitment websites in your territory will allow you to post adverts for trustees, although it can be more challenging when trying to find those with experience outside of the sector, in areas of law and business management, for example. In this case, search for sector-specific trustee support; especially if you're a charity or CIC, there are lots of sites to help connect you to willing members.

It is worth clarifying here that, as one of the company directors, you are automatically part of the board. In a company limited by guarantee, you need at least two directors to form a company, so the pair of you form the board, and you each have 50% of the voting rights when key decisions are made. Although you might be undertaking a role within the company itself – the Artistic Director, for instance – as a company director you are part of the board. This can become tricky in the setup of certain business types. Trustees in a charity can't be paid; however, those performing roles in the business can be. It's important, therefore, to research the roles, requirements, and implications of the board within your company type and based on your territory, before committing to a decision.

Having a board means that important decisions need to be approved and voted on. This is one of the simplest and most democratic means in which a board helps hold the company to account, where proposals need to be approved by a majority in order to pass. Rules about how your board will operate should be in your Articles of Association, but typically this will require a simple majority of the board to be present to vote on key issues. If the vote passes with a majority, the motion is approved. There are a number of steps if there is a deadlock in your voting, but perhaps the easiest is to appoint a chairman to have the casting vote in the event of stalemate.

Board observers can sometimes be appointed, usually as a way of giving the person appointed confidence about the progression of the company. This will possibly be unlikely in your early stages, but may be something stipulated as part of a funding requirement further down the line. Observers don't have direct power over a company and they don't exercise the same rights as a trustee.

Meeting minutes

Companies are required, by law, to take *minutes* of all meetings by its trustees. This is to ensure transparency and accountability, and the minutes recorded must accurately reflect the resolutions and decisions made in the meeting. Copies of board minutes must be retained for at least ten years from the date of the meeting. There are serious repercussions for failing to comply with what is a relatively straightforward task, so set up a process that works for you and stick to it.

Bank accounts

Setting up a *business bank account* is a relatively straightforward process which can increasingly be completed online. Some banks may still want to see you in person, and this isn't unusual. Signatories (those who must sign for funds to be released from an account) will need to provide several pieces of ID (relating to personal ID and proof of address), so make sure everyone has these available before beginning the process or this will cause delays and complications. Bills to prove your address will need to be relatively recent (usually dated within the last six months) and you will usually have to prove three years of address history. You will also need to show your company registration forms and proof of your registered address, so this is the first test to make sure you've safely stored all those documents from earlier!

Banks will usually want to know some other information during registration, including the main activities of the business, where your money will come from, your expected turnover, and whether you have any suppliers based outside of the UK. You can find out what information you will need in order to apply on banks' websites before starting the process (just search the name of a bank followed by 'business banking', for example, 'Lloyds business banking'), which will usually take about seven days.

Business bank accounts allow you to securely store your company's cash and electronic sales, which removes any ambiguity about how the finances in your business are handled. Your business bank account should be used only for business spending and should not be mixed or confused with personal transactions, as you must account for each of these in your annual accounts.

When choosing which bank to go to, here are a few key pointers to bear in mind:

- Do you have to pay? Many banks will entice you with attractive starting offers, but several business accounts require you to pay a monthly fee (usually after six or twelve months).
- Who has access to what? As a business bank account can be accessed by more than one person, how to handle spending is something that must be considered so that a business knows who is accessing and using their money. This adds a layer of protection but can also be cumbersome: sometimes purchases over a certain amount must be signed for by multiple *signatories* – people who can sign for payments – or need a main signatory to be appointed.
- How do you get out? If it all goes wrong or if one of you decides to leave, how easy is it to remove that person from the bank account? Most business bank accounts, just like limited companies, require a minimum of two directors and if your second in command resigns, what will that mean for your account?
- Is smartphone access available? We are becoming increasingly accustomed to easy payment access via debit cards, contactless payments, and banking apps. Check which features your bank offers and compare them: not all banking apps are as user friendly as others. Banks increasingly offer a range of flashy services – think about which you might need (as they often come with additional costs) and assess which is the best for you. Don't be afraid to shop around at this stage, even if your organisation is small.

Increasingly technology is stepping in to support the small-business founder, and there are now a number of app-based banks that are worth giving serious thought to. Each of them has pros and cons, and you should never join any bank without first conducting a bit of independent research to check that, ultimately, your money will be safe with them. Some offer attractive fee options, where you pay as little as 20p on each transaction that comes in and out of the account, rather than a monthly sum. You may only be dealing with small amounts of money at the moment, and you can change your bank in the future, but there's no harm in planning ahead.

People often avoid switching bank accounts for fear of huge amounts of administration. There can often be significant benefits and cost savings to be found from switching all suppliers, but the good news for small businesses (those with under fifty employees and a turnover of less than £6.5m) is that you can now use the Current Account Switch Service, which is a free tool offered by the government to help you switch banks with minimum hassle in as little as seven days. It's a lot less admin intensive than it was previously and allows you to fully integrate with your new account for minimum fuss. Remember to connect your new account to your bookkeeping software and again, it's worth repeating, you cannot mix your business and personal transactions and banking.

There is a lot to pack into a relatively short amount of time here, but the truth is, much of this is a one-time headache which you won't give much thought to after the event. Debating the pros and cons of business bank accounts or worrying about removing the name 'Ltd' from your name are big moments, but once they're done, your path is clear to get on with the real business of making theatre. Well done on reaching this stage, now the fun can really begin.

Chapter Resources

Theatre business support

'5 things you must do when you become self employed,' Byte Start, https://www.bytestart.co.uk/5-things-self-employed

'Am I employed, self-employed, both or neither?' Low Incomes Tax Reform Group (7th September 2022), www.litrg.org.uk/tax-guides/self-employment/am-i-employed-self-employed-both-or-neither

Caines, Matthew, '15 tips on setting up a theatre company,' *Guardian* (28th August 2013), www.theguardian.com/culture-professionals-network/culture-professionals-blog/2013/aug/28/expert-tips-setting-up-theatre-company

Company Bug, www.companybug.com/

'How to start a theatre company,' getintotheatre.org, https://getintotheatre.org/blog/how-to-start-a-theatre-company

Independent Theatre Council, www.itc-arts.org/

Stage One, https://stageone.uk.com/

UK Government Website, www.gov.uk/

UK Theatre, https://uktheatre.org/

'What are board observers and should you have them?' Bonaccord, www.bonaccord.law/blog/what-are-board-observers-and-should-you-have-them.html

Company names

Glover, Bryn, 'Choosing the right business structure,' Startups (19th May 2021), https://startups.co.uk/setting-up/choosing-the-right-business-structure/

Harroch, Richard, '12 tips for naming your startup business,' Forbes (23rd October 2016), www.forbes.com/sites/allbusiness/2016/10/23/12-tips-for-naming-your-startup-business/?sh=2c90b940904e

Smithson, Brent, 'Choosing the right business structure,' Companies House (18th July 2018), https://companieshouse.blog.gov.uk/2018/07/18/choosing-the-right-business-structure/

Accounting and finance support

QuickBooks, https://quickbooks.intuit.com/uk/

Rice, Anthony, *Accounts Demystified: The astonishingly simple guide to accounting*, 7th edition (Pearson, Harlow, 2015)

Sage, www.sage.com/en-gb/
Xero, www.xero.com/uk/

General business tools

Google Drive, www.google.co.uk/intl/en-GB/drive/
iCloud, www.icloud.com/
OneDrive, www.microsoft.com/en-ww/microsoft-365/onedrive/online-cloud-storage
Open Office, www.openoffice.org/

4 Roles and Responsibilities

Some of the most important decisions you will make about your business will be selecting the people in it. You may think this is a decision that has already been settled – if you're thinking of forming a theatre company it is highly likely that you have already identified a few key collaborators with whom you enjoy creating work. But remember the five guys starting their pizza restaurant from Chapter 3? Across this chapter we will look at how you build a strong team, how to analyse the skills of yourself and others and how to find collaborators in the future. As a growing theatre company, you will constantly be on the lookout for new collaborators – whether they be producers or technicians or actors. Knowing how to find people and building lasting relationships with them when you do is essential for the long-term success of your company, especially if you plan to work as an *ensemble*. Lastly, but by no means least, we will explore the complicated and sometimes controversial issue of pay, so that you're always on the right side of the law when working with others.

What is an ensemble?

Many young companies may take the form of an ensemble – a repeated group of actors working together in a set style. Some of the most exciting and distinct companies operate in what can be described as an ensemble model. An ensemble doesn't have to be rigid, though. If you're working in this way, take time to think about what you want your constant element to be. Is it all about the performers: perhaps you want the audience to repeatedly come back to see the same faces? Is it about the style? When one thinks of a company such as Gecko or Frantic Assembly, elements of an aesthetic style immediately spring to mind. For these companies, their use of movement, theme, and style is the consistent element, which means that, ultimately, you know you are watching one of their shows.

Your current roles

Depending on the nature of your company, this might have already established itself in your early explorations together as a creative unit. Your friend

DOI: 10.4324/9781003281726-4

might be, 'the one who writes plays,' and you're the person who acts in them. Alternatively, as the style of your ensemble dictates, you might all share the responsibility of devising a piece of theatre, with each of you mucking in and pulling together to get the job done. Perhaps it's impossible to say who truly does what.

Thinking about job roles requires you to remember that your organisation is a business as well as a theatre maker. It is perfectly legitimate for your theatre maker's ethos to be collaborative and without hierarchy – we certainly need more companies willing to be bold with their power structures if we are going to create work that is truly inclusive and collaborative. However – and I'll be reiterating this a lot in this chapter – planning for the future now is essential to avoid problems later. Don't let the unspoken rules of your organisation remain unspoken: open, clear, and constructive communication will be hugely important for your practice going forward. Have the conversation – give each other the right to be heard and the right to refuse.

Assessing your skills

Let's return to our five budding chefs and their new pizzeria in Chapter 3. From the outside looking in, it seemed like a ridiculous business idea to have five founders. How would that work? If they could achieve the same thing with three, or two, or even one, surely it would be more cost effective to reduce their numbers? On the other hand, let us imagine that one has the real flair for cooking, whereas their brother is training to be an accountant. The other has worked all their life in Italian restaurants and the fourth is half-Italian. The fifth just likes pizza and is ok, but not great, at making pizza, but they're good fun to be around and they lighten the atmosphere.

Alright, so we're being harsh here, especially to poor old founder number five. But the rule of averages always seems to dictate that, in any group, there's someone doing more work than the rest. That's fine, you might like that. But it's worth thinking about as you plan. When I started my company, we did so because four of us had enjoyed working together, with no real structure other than the fact that I was the director. As things became more serious, it was obvious that there wasn't an equilibrium between all the members (beware the person who just 'helps out'!) and the tough decision was made to go ahead with just two of us. If you're serious about your company, you must be serious about its personnel – you literally can't afford not to. Four people would mean four sets of wages whenever we applied for funding or had costs to cover, and if we weren't getting four times the amount of quality as a result, it was a decision that was inevitable.

Now, this all sounds pretty gruesome and serious. On the one hand, it is, and you will need to know when to put on your CEO hat if your business is to succeed, long term. On the other hand, this doesn't have to be a black and white situation. Encourage a discussion between your founding members and ascertain everyone's thoughts and feelings. Listen out for language which may suggest a half-committed attitude, or someone who is going to play the field and jump on your bandwagon if they sense opportunity. If you feel that different people are at different stages, have different relationships to the company, or different visions for its future, it's time to plan your next steps.

> **TASK:** Ask everyone to write down the following and use this to stimulate a discussion point.
>
> - What are your hopes for the company in the next year?
> - What does success look like?
> - What other commitments may clash with the company?
>
> These are reasonable questions to ask your co-founders, and indeed, yourself. Most job contracts have a clause that states that you must work exclusively for them, so it's a helpful approach to take with your fellow co-founders. Clearly this doesn't mean everybody should give over their lives to your company, far from it, but it's a useful way to flesh out a conversation that may need to be had.
>
> If, after doing this, the findings suggest that people are on different journeys, there is a simple solution. Make it ok for everybody to have a different relationship to the company. I wish somebody had told me this when I was starting out. I was so invested, emotionally and physically, in the idea of our new company and what we could do with it that I took it as a personal injustice if somebody couldn't dedicate the same amount of time and attention to it that I could. This doesn't mean that people shouldn't pull their weight, they should, but my advice to you, especially if you are a large group, is to consider the possibility that two or three of you register as directors, and anybody else becomes a temporal member: somebody who comes and goes and works with you in a different way.

Whichever way you get there, the essential thing to understand is that your company directors are ready for the challenge. As we saw in Chapter 3, there is a lot of responsibility riding on these early decisions.

Working as a team

Whichever way you form, it is important that each of you knows each other's skills and is aware of your skills gaps. If you're clever, you will seek out and work with people who complement your personal skills shortages. This is how many successful writer/director or director/producer partnerships work. One of you might be great at organising and scheduling and be fantastic with money but not strong creatively. On the other hand, one of you might be an incredible director, great at working with actors, and in possession of a unique creative vision, but you're not so great at organisation. Together you could be a strong team, if you learn to complement each other's method of working, and – here's the crucial point – you'll be far better together than either of you could be alone. This is at the heart of all effective collaboration. Find people who bring out the best in you, who complement your skills, who challenge you creatively and who encourage you to be your best. A brilliant colleague of mine always tells their students the sobering message: if you're the smartest person in your friendship group, get better friends. It's rather a brutal way of looking at it, but the idea has merit – seek out people who lift you up, and who inspire you to push for more.

> **TASK:** Repeat the SWOT analysis from Chapter 3 for yourself. Once you have completed this, and without sharing what you've already written, repeat the exercise again but complete the analysis for your co-directors. The key here is that you shouldn't share what you have written about yourself originally, and you'll be really surprised by what others say about you from this exercise. They will often see qualities that you don't, and it can be a constructive and safe space in which to highlight any bad habits.
>
> You can expand this further with a full-scale skills audit. This maps out and visualises the areas of strength and relative weakness within your team. There are skills audit templates available online, and I have linked to one in the resource section. At their heart, the skills audit lists a range of common skills, knowledge, and experience needed for your organisation, and thinks about the challenges, opportunities, and gaps within your current collective. Work through the skills audit in the resource section. Once complete, identify between three and five main areas of focus. Draw up a plan for addressing each of these. Will you undertake training? Do you need to find further expertise? You might need to speak to a mentor if you are unsure how best to fill those gaps.

In reality, you will never cover all the skills you'll need, so take time to identify the skills that you are lacking as a collective. This is a good exercise to visualise how much each person is potentially bringing to the table: poor old pizza founder number five might need to do some re-thinking. However, it shouldn't be a negative activity: as a result, they might realise that they're actually much stronger at social media than their co-founders and this is an asset they are going to need in order to spread the word.

How are you getting on? This might be a good time to step back and reflect upon your practice as a collective. You're working through some pretty tough territory. Relax – there's no need to rush these stages. Do them in an environment that is conducive to focus and safety – opening up about each other's flaws with a 'creative' glass of wine is not going to end well. Are you supporting one another? Is one person dominating the conversation and not letting anyone else speak? Pick up on these early signs – they're strong indicators and you should do something about them.

Relationships

It is very likely that you will be thinking about forming your new theatre company with friends. This can be great – there is nothing quite like creating something you are proud of with people you enjoy being around. Let's take a brief look at how best to support this.

Communication is clear and you should be aware that, in choosing to work together, no matter how informally, you are developing your friendship in a new way. Where are you at in your relationship with the people you work with? You may end up working with your collaborators intimately for years – my co-founder and I literally moved in together at one stage because we were spending so much of our time calling one another between rehearsals – and this can be both exciting and suffocating. You're going to need to trust that your relationship will cope with these new pressures; as anyone who has ever been in a tech rehearsal will know, working in the creative industries can be as frustrating and stressful as it is thrilling.

Maintaining healthy relationships is intimately bound to your own wellbeing and is something you should not overlook or simply expect to survive without care and attention. You are going to form relationships with many people during the life of your company – imagine how many people the boss of the National Theatre meets over the course of a year – and each of those relationships needs fostering. Of course, there will be people you spend every day with, there'll be people you shake hands with once and never see again, and there'll be people you have to direct in an intimately emotional scene for a play, and each will require a different set of skills whilst maintaining the same sense of integrity.

Communication and boundaries are important to establish from the outset. This helps everybody to understand your working rules and sets clear parameters for your working relationship. Group chats can be a useful and quick way to reach everybody but are also ripe for sabotage. A new rule I've been working on recently is that I won't answer company-related business outside of nine–five hours. I've decided that this is an important step for my own wellbeing and energy, and setting these boundaries helps to create a professional practice within the organisation. To facilitate this, I have notifications muted after this time, with messages responded to the next day. Of course, this always needs to be done in negotiation with the other people in the group: those with children, caring responsibilities, and certain disabilities may need to work differently from this. The best way of establishing these expectations is to be open and to agree it as a group. Putting on a show is an emotionally bonding experience for all involved, but, as anyone who has ever watched *Noises Off* will know, the drama backstage can often be just as explosive as what's happening on it.

Regrettably, in such highly emotive circumstances, relationships will occasionally break down. This could be because of something highly dramatic, or it might simply be that one of your colleagues has had a change in circumstances and they now want to move on from the company. It can be difficult to prefigure so early on in your foundation but take time to have the conversation. Statistically, your new company, like most small businesses, may close after a few years of trading. If this is the case, and hopefully it won't be, you should commit focus now to ensuring you can walk away with the friendships that made it still intact. We will look in more detail at the nuts and bolts of winding up in Chapter 14.

Volunteers, workers, and employees

When working with other people you must make sure that you are clear about how exactly they are involved. Particularly in the early days, people might be helping you out for free, or you might have decided to cover travel costs or split profits in exchange for their help.

Whatever your preference, you need to be aware of the specifics of employment law in your territory, as volunteers, workers, and employees have distinctly different rights and expectations. Employees are defined as having a contract of employment and an expectation of regular pay and hours. This is important because if you are working with people – a group of actors, for example – with the expectation that they turn up at certain times and provide a specific service, you might have strayed into the role of employer without even realising it.

This is important to be aware of so that you don't fall foul of employment law when the people working with you become your employees accidentally. There have been successful cases brought against small-scale producers who either didn't realise, or actively avoided, this distinction. If there is an expectation of work, you are likely to have employees, which brings with it rights around contracts, working conditions, and, of course, pay.

Similar, but separate to this is the role of worker. Somebody is a worker if there is more of a casual relationship between them and the employer, often without the guarantee of regular hours and less of an obligation to make themselves available for work.

An individual is a volunteer when there is no expectation of payment and no obligation for them to work. Volunteers can be paid expenses – such as for food, drink, travel etc. – but not a wage. If there are other rewards, payment, or promise of future work, it is likely that the individual has moved to become a worker or an employee.

If you are unsure about the nature of your work and how it falls in regard to the people working with you, you should search for the legal distinctions between employees, workers, and volunteers in your territory and contact your local actors union for advice. They will be able to point you in the right direction and should be happy to help you out.

Finding talent

At some stage you'll find yourself looking for new collaborators. Maybe you need a producer, or you need new actors for your next show. When you're starting out, this can seem very daunting, and in most cases, the best place to start is with the people you already know. If you've been to drama school or studied at university, you might be at a bit of an advantage here, but if you haven't and you only know a few people, work with what you've got and use this to reach more people. Don't overstretch your resources: is it worth staging *Henry IV Part II* (which has sixty characters) if you only know three actors?

Finding actors

If you're looking to work with new talent on your next production, you will need to audition. There is more information about the casting process in Chapter 7, but here we will look at some of the common places to find performers.

The first thing to consider is what type of performer you are looking for. If you're working with a low or no budget and you've never put on a show before, with the best will in the world you're very unlikely to secure Orlando Bloom. Instead, you will have much more luck seeking out non-professional actors, or those who are still students, or recent graduates. Websites such as Starnow generally cater (though not exclusively) to actors who may not have the same wealth of experience, agents, or formal training behind them, and can be a good starting point for finding collaborators. Facebook groups for independent actors cover most regions of the UK, as well as groups for student actors. Find your local am-dram groups – the term feels outdated and condescending today, but most major cities will have a plethora of non-professional acting groups regularly staging work. Your new organisation may intend to be one such group. Members of such community acting groups or youth theatres are always amazingly well connected to other actors, so get involved, join, and go and see a performance. Your network will grow quicker than you might think.

What should you be looking for in collaborators? I find it helps to turn this question around on you. What do *you* look for when you meet new people? What qualities appeal to you and make you want to work with a person? What qualities do the opposite? Especially when you're starting out, you are going to want people who are sympathetic to your situation, who add value and who don't make your already challenging circumstances worse. Often, in the early days, you may need everyone to 'muck in' and do a bit of everything, and the last thing you need is somebody causing a stink or not being part of the team. Think about the personal qualities as well as the professional qualities when choosing people to work alongside.

Remember, when you're networking, auditioning, interviewing, or simply greeting audiences, the way you present yourself speaks volumes about your organisation's ethos and attitude. For better or worse, you are now a representative of your brand, and however you articulate that to the outside world will have a huge impact on the way that people interact with you. We're not thinking about this in a branding sense here, but in the sense of how you appear to embody your values as a creative practitioner. Would you prefer to meet your new director if they were wearing a suit, or dungarees? There's no right answer, of course, but think about what it says. Whichever way you outwardly choose to show this, remember to be courteous, curious, and respectful to everyone you meet in the course of your business activities.

Professional actors

The time will come when you want to work with professional actors. The difference between a professional actor and non-professional is that the professional actor has been paid to work professionally in the past and is likely to be a member of an actor's union. Don't dismiss someone just because they haven't been to drama school; it's not the route for everyone and many actors are developing their careers in very different ways. Castingcallpro is a great intermediary website, where users have to pay a fee (usually a good indicator that the people on it are serious). In the UK, professional actors will most likely be a member of Spotlight and will have a Spotlight profile where you can see their credentials, past work, headshots, and showreel, if they have one. You can become a member of Spotlight yourself as a casting professional, which will allow you to search and post casting calls, but this does come at quite a fee. However, if you are given a link, you can view a specific actor's profile for free. You can be amazingly specific with your search criteria but remember that some of the best casting is surprising and against form, so bear this in mind before specifying that someone should be exactly 5 ft 4 with green hair and a South Shields accent.

Most professional actors will have an acting agent. An agent's job is to find an actor work and in exchange to charge a small fee – usually a percentage of the actor's payment for a job. Dealing with agents can seem scary, but when you're offering interesting work, you're going to be popular with them! You should contact agents with a casting breakdown for your piece – this lists the specifics of each of the roles along with any key info such as gender, hair colour etc. They will then match a few of their clients who may be suitable so that you can run auditions. It's a great idea to build up relationships with casting directors as they are always looking out for exciting work for their clients. Understandably, they're busy people and they represent professionals, and they will be rigorously committed to ensuring good working conditions for their talent. But reach out to them – especially smaller casting agencies – as they may be willing to help you, even for an unpaid project, if they think you could show potential for the future.

Payment structures for freelancers

The decision and ability to pay people is a key milestone in your company's life, and you should be mindful of the ongoing debate within the fringe sector about how various payment options are discussed and viewed.

The debate about free pay is one fraught with strong opinions. On the one hand, newly founded organisations such as yourself may see it as an impossibility to have enough money to pay for your talent. If you had to do that, you'd never get a show on the stage in the first place! The fringe is a great training ground, not just for actors but for directors too. The bigger your show, the more talent you'd have to pay, and there's nothing to automatically suggest that a play with fifteen actors would generate three times the box office of a cast of five.

On the other hand, if somebody is working for you, and HMRC views this act as work, then they are doing a job, and if they're doing a job, they have a legal entitlement to be paid at least minimum wage. Actors and creatives have already sunk vast sums of money into their training to enter a precarious industry. It's tough to earn a living. If I'm giving you work, you should be paying me fairly.

Ah! You may reply, but if you're not working at the moment anyway, what's the problem with doing this job for free? It's going to be a fantastic show, we've got some acting agents and theatre producers coming to see it and you're getting to play a fantastic role, perhaps a much bigger role than you'd be getting seen for at this point in your career. It would be a great exposure for you.

Yes, you might reply, but I can't pay my electricity bill with exposure.

And so, the debate goes on. In recent years, one or two eminent critics have stuck their flag in the ground and announced that they will only review shows in which everyone is being paid. Equity have recently produced their response to the ongoing dilemma with their Professionally Made, Professionally Paid scheme, which commits producers to recognising and remunerating fairly the creatives who work to produce these shows. The aim of this is to stop exploitation – although the stereotype of the suited producer walking off into the sunset with a cigar and a stack of money may seem slightly far reaching for you at the moment. The reality, which is often missed out of the debate regarding payment, is that even within the fringe theatre scene there are differing levels of production. A two-night hire in a fifty-seat venue in Aberdeen, which you have paid for yourself, could be seen as totally different from a four-week programmed run at a major London fringe venue. Ultimately, if you can pay, you should do. Whatever your financial situation, it is essential that you are transparent about it at the earliest stage, so that collaborators don't feel cheated – being deliberately vague about your situation is disingenuous. Better to work with people who know your situation and are happy with it than to try and convince people to work for less when they thought otherwise. How would that make you feel?

When it comes to paying freelancers (or employees for that matter), you need to establish a system at the outset and do your research before taking anybody on. You cannot simply send money to somebody's bank account or make this up as you go along, for obvious reasons. If you are expecting to pay regular, consistent salaries to employees you will need to operate a payroll. It is unlikely that you will be at this stage for some time, however, and when you do reach this milestone, it is recommended that you should absolutely consult the services of both an accountant and an experienced HR person. PAYE is the UK system for collecting tax and National Insurance from salary payments, and is reasonably simple to run in principle, but given the importance of getting this right, this is something you should seek guidance and mentorship with to ensure best practice.

When paying freelancers for ad hoc and time-limited work, the invoice system is more regularly used. You may have experience of this yourself from your own work as a freelancer. The freelancer will send you an invoice for the work they have completed, and the sum agreed, and then you will pay those invoices within an agreed time frame. For this to work effectively it is essential to confirm the payment terms, including the sum and time frame of payments at the outset. Make sure you keep the invoices stored safely as evidence of the payment, and ensure you earn your chops as a reliable employer by paying your freelancers on time. Late payment is a massive issue in our industry and can have real implications for those freelancers who need payment, so do aspire to pay promptly.

How do I make it work?

In an excellent blog, a performer who had enjoyed nine fringe shows in one year estimated that the cost to him of maintaining this hobby varied between £180 and £400 per month, once his travel and food costs had been taken into account. Tellingly, he titled this blog entry, 'An Expensive Habit,' and having an idea of the cost to your actors is useful, especially when you can't afford to pay. It is important to talk about pay, even at the very beginning. Although we all do theatre for the love of it, putting on shows does cost money and you should aim to at least try and break even, especially when you don't have funding. There's no quicker way to cause disputes than when people are out of pocket, so let's look at some of the ways to make it work.

There are several different structures of pay for the fringe company to consider. Each of these allows you to be open, honest, and ethical within challenging circumstances.

The profit share model

Profit share is an extremely common fringe production model where any profits made at the end of a run are split between the company. It's simple and easy to manage, but unfortunately it can often be an empty gesture as, more often than not, there may not actually be any profit to split. Does everyone get paid equally? Does Hamlet get the same share of profit as Flag Bearer three? Profit sharing creates its own problems, and unfortunately everyone has had experiences where their final envelope is empty whilst the producer is sitting drinking cocktails. Beware the pitfalls.

The open book model

The *open book method* has been used in the business world for some time. The premise is simple: the finances of the company are made available to all members, so that everyone can see exactly how much money is available, where it's being spent, and how much profit has been made. This means that all company members are able to see how the budget is being split across the various departments, how many ticket sales have been made and how far away the production is from turning a profit. The argument for the open book model is that by being transparent, everyone is invested in the finances, and everyone has a stake in its success. As a result, the people you are working with know that their work is not being exploited.

When you can afford to pay fairly

When you reach the fortunate stage of being able to pay, your first port of call should be your actor's union. Dealing with a big body such as Equity can seem intimidating but remember that everyone wants the same aim: to support talent so that they can continue to work and create a thriving industry. If you're offering paid work in an industry of high unemployment, you're doing a great thing and your actor's union will want to help you. Unions will be able to support you in drawing up a contract that is fair and legal, and to update you on the current recommendations for paying cast and crew. If you're receiving public funds, from an Arts Council, for example, it is increasingly likely that you will be required to pay the minimum wage of your territory, or the minimum agreed by an actors union such as Equity. More and more venues, particularly in key markets such as London, will also require you to provide evidence that your performers are being paid the Equity minimum, so it is essential to check these things before making plans for performance. Beware that the rate of minimum wage changes regularly, is different for different age groups, and should be seen as an absolute minimum where possible.

Where to find people

Don't underestimate the power of social media and word of mouth when searching for a freelance creative. It can often be the quickest and most direct route to finding somebody, especially useful when time is tight, and many people have direct links from their profiles to websites or portfolios.

One key resource worth knowing about is the Directors' Program, operated by the Young Vic Theatre in London. It's free to join for emerging directors and designers and is worth checking out for several reasons. Primarily, it provides a platform in which to connect with other independent creatives across the country. I have made multiple lasting connections through callouts via the network, which can also be a great way to spread the word to fellow creatives when your show is about to open.

Of course, drama schools are brimming with new talent about to make their first steps into the industry. Attend showcases and public performances where possible, but look beyond simply scouting the actors, as this can be a great way to find technical talent as well. Contacting course leaders can be helpful, as they may be willing to advertise your position to prospective students but be respectful of their busy schedules and don't expect a result. All courses operate differently, some encourage students to build up external experience whilst others prefer students to stay internal during the period of their training, and different courses will have differing busy and quiet periods.

Beyond social media and drama schools, websites such as www.mandy.com are a great place to find crew members and collaborators. Some sites charge a membership fee, or a cost for posting an advertisement, and you should weigh up whether the cost of posting the fee will be of benefit to you in helping to reach potential employees who you would not have known otherwise. Seek out the prominent arts and theatre websites in your territory, as well as those operating locally. You might also find traction with Facebook groups.

The best way to decide what information to include on your job advertisement or call-out is to engage with these networks and to see what other people are doing. Speaking in the broadest sense, people are time poor and want to quickly establish whether a job is (a) something interesting to them and (b) something they can technically afford to do, whether that's about pay or time or location. Make people's lives easier to engage with your work and you'll have a much better response rate.

Paying creatives

Paying your freelancers is exactly the same principle as paying actors but note that different roles carry different suggested rates of pay. Obviously, when paying people, you need to pay at least minimum wage, but you should consult with the Independent Theatre Council (ITC) for the most up-to-date guidelines for industry payment. Different roles may be part of different unions – for creatives or actors – and some individuals may not be part of a union at all, which further complicates the process. Some roles, such as a director or designer, are often paid a lump sum for working on a show, rather than an hourly or weekly rate. Again, check the latest guidance – for the UK, the ITC breaks this down clearly on their website and their resources regarding pay are very clear and accessible. You do need to become a member to view this information, but this is recommended.

Many people struggle with knowing how much to charge or ask for their services. There are different schools of thought on this, but a helpful strategy is often to turn it around the other way and to talk about the budget. If you approach me to run a workshop, for example, and you say that your budget is £50, I'll be able to make a relatively informed decision as to whether or not that opportunity fits with my usual expectations and can cover my costs. This is a useful way of avoiding the embarrassment of wildly underestimating how much you should pay for someone's services, when you're unsure of where the ballpark is. The good news is, there are lots of templates and extra resources to help make sure you are following best practice when it comes to payment. Many of these resources have been linked at the end of the chapter.

Company culture and expanding

There will come a stage when your company expands. Depending on how your organisation works and what sort of art you want to create, new people will come and go as your organisation develops. I remember this being a particularly emotional issue for me in the early days of my organisation – this particular group of about twelve recurring actors had worked together so well that we wanted to keep everyone together again and again. Of course, this wasn't possible, and arguably wasn't a proactive way to go about trying to re-create rather than looking ahead; you should embrace the development of your organisation, which will happen with or without you. One of our actors at the time told me, 'the company's spirit will stay the same, it's just the DNA that will change.' The message stuck with me, and I realised that as our company became established and developed an audience, my job was to develop and continue that sense of spirit and ethos.

When bringing in new people, be sure to take time to get a feeling for whether they'd fit into the spirit of the way you work. This is for everybody's benefit – and is why we're always reminded to use job interviews to feel out whether you would enjoy working for that employer. Most of the time we forget about that because we just want the job, but of course it's important. A disruptive member could be a big headache for the rest of your ensemble.

At the same time, nobody wants to join a group and instantly feel like the odd one out. Be mindful of how you induct new people into your work, and make sure everybody is on the same page. This will always require a bit of tact. I remember one occasion when bringing in a new cast member, somebody greeted her by saying, 'well you're taller than the girl you were replacing, will that work for Scene Four?' Funnily enough, I was back on the hunt again the day after.

People 'dropping out' is a curious phenomenon that you will have to become expertly used to, especially if you're not in a position to pay people. Sometimes this might be for perfectly understandable reasons – actors will offer to work for free but with the proviso that if a paid job comes up, they'd be obliged to take it. That's a risk you must weigh up. But performers dropping out for a million other reasons is one of the occupational hazards of running a new company: if you're not paying people, remember that the actors hold a lot of sway over the production if they want to wield it, so it's vital to maintain a positive working environment. Over ten years I have known actors drop out the day *before* a show, the day *of* a show and, in one particularly fun memory, as the audience were walking into the auditorium. Of course, in those situations it's tempting to search for blame and list a million reasons why that person is a jerk. It's not worth it – the situation has happened, and you must assess how it can be salvaged. When any relationship breaks down, I always ask myself honestly what part I could have played to avoid such an event. Even when I've not been directly involved, I'll usually find some gut memory – maybe at a first audition, maybe in the way the person was always slow to respond to emails – that makes me realise I should have acted on my instinct earlier. Perhaps I didn't induct that person to the group well enough – and the later you're bringing in a replacement the better you need to do this – and as a result perhaps they've been feeling isolated. When push comes to shove, the actor in this type of setting can decide that 'it's only a play,' and cut their losses. If you've got £10k sunk into the show and three show programmers sat outside tonight, can you afford to lose them?

What should you have done in that situation? If your instinct was strong, perhaps you shouldn't have cast them in the first place. Always avoid casting the person who seems like a bit of a nightmare to work with, but you loved their audition. That's a disaster waiting to happen. Remember the importance of those shared values on which your ensemble runs – remember your founding rules. However, if the situation was less dramatic than that – say, for example, your actor was repeatedly turning up late or you'd noticed they carried a distinct dislike for someone else in the company – it is your job and your responsibility to be the mediator. Find a quiet and discrete moment to raise the concern with the actor and to let them know why that behaviour isn't helpful. Give them a chance to air their grievances – perhaps this way you'll find out that they're always late because they're a carer for their elderly mother. The more you take responsibility towards building and maintaining the relationships within your company, the stronger your organisation will become.

Chapter Resources

Payment support

Baggaley, Laura, 'Does it matter if we don't get paid for theatre work?' *Guardian* (22nd March 2007) www.theguardian.com/stage/theatreblog/2007/mar/22/doesitmatterifwedontgetpaidfortheatrework

Cook, Laurence, 'U.K. Actors: should you work for free?' *Backstage.com* (9th September 2019) www.backstage.com/uk/magazine/article/uk-actors-work-free-1741/

Freelancers Make Theatre Work, https://freelancersmaketheatrework.com/

Myles, Rob, 'An Expensive Habit: The true cost of working in fringe theatre,' Rob-Myles.co.uk, https://robmyles.co.uk/an-expensive-habit-the-true-cost-of-working-in-fringe-theatre/
'PAYE and payroll for employers,' Gov.uk, www.gov.uk/paye-for-employers
'Professionally Made, Professionally Paid,' Equity, www.equity.org.uk/getting-involved/campaigns/professionally-made-professionally-paid/
'Rates of Pay,' Independent Theatre Council, www.itc-arts.org/rates-of-pay/

Skills audit

'How to complete a skills audit,' Reach Volunteering, https://reachvolunteering.org.uk/trustee-recruitment-cycle/reflect/how-complete-skills-audit

Education and training resources

Broadway HD, www.broadwayhd.com/
Digital Theatre, www.digitaltheatre.com/
DramaOnline, www.dramaonlinelibrary.com/
FutureLearn, www.futurelearn.com/
Haydon, Christopher, *The Art of the Artistic Director* (Methuen Drama, London, 2019)
Hytner, Nicholas, *Balancing Acts: Behind the scenes at the National Theatre* (Vintage, London, 2017)
Marquee, www.marquee.tv/
National Theatre at Home, www.nationaltheatre.org.uk/ntathome
National Theatre Live, www.ntlive.com/
#OVConnect
SCONUL, https://sconul.ac.uk/
The Stage, http://thestage.co.uk/
The Young Vic Director's Program, https://creatorsprogram.youngvic.org/

Finding talent and unions

'A guide to hiring freelancers,' FreelanceUK, www.freelanceuk.com/become/guide-hiring-freelancers.shtml
ArtsJobs, www.artsjobs.org.uk/
BECTU, https://bectu.org.uk/
Equity, www.equity.org.uk/
Mandy, www.mandy.com/
Spotlight, www.spotlight.com/
StarNow, www.starnow.com/

5 Building an Audience

Without an audience, your hard work will be for nothing. Art is nothing without somebody to experience it, and when you are starting out the mystery, cost, and discipline involved in finding an audience can seem crippling. What's more, as you don't need an audience until the end of the process, it can be all too easy to push this under the carpet until right before performance day. In a festival, you might literally be finding your audience hours before they get in front of the show.

Building an audience is a key to growth. Developing work that you know people want to see is essential to ensuring that your company continues to achieve its aims. Audience development can seem scary, and out of all the topics covered in this book, can put you most outside your comfort zone, but with a clear strategy it can be tackled and even made enjoyable.

Assessing need

'If you build it, they will come' goes the adage. Unfortunately, this is not always the case in the real world. In a saturated economy with many demands on our audience's attention, we cannot simply rely on the audience finding us. Sadly, we can no longer assume quality as a predictor of audience interest and in the theatre, we often can't spare the time for word to build gradually by playing the long game.

The problem of finding an audience will be familiar to anyone who has created a piece of work. Desperately messaging your friends and family to buy tickets, or standing on a cold street handing out flyers to disinterested strangers; the pressures of audience numbers are particularly difficult for theatre makers to face. A small audience not only brings financial worries but can affect cast morale. Depending on the size of venue, a smaller gathering can seriously impact the performance – particularly when working on a comedy – and low audiences can seem to imply an inherent lack of quality of the finished product. All of these challenges are difficult for creators to balance, and it can often be a significantly draining surge of effort right at the end of a creative process to try and pull this together. Even when your company has been paid by a venue to perform, the fear of an empty audience can linger and affect reviews and goodwill.

DOI: 10.4324/9781003281726-5

Establishing need

Our first step to addressing audience building is to establish need. Let's follow an example, let's imagine for a moment that we are going to develop a new type of hat. This super modern smart-hat will provide a head massage when you are stressed and can stream music over Bluetooth. It's going to change the world as we know it.

In our first example, we rush out to find a designer and create some outlines for our new hat. We decide to develop a few different styles and we also decide to introduce a child sized version. With our designs complete, we contact a manufacturer, put in an order, and a few weeks later our pride and joy is delivered to our house ready to be sold.

We set up an online shop on a couple of sites, develop a website and an Instagram page, and pay for some adverts. And then we wait. And wait. And wait. A month later, we've sold half a dozen hats and the boxes are taking up a lot of room in our kitchen. We haven't recouped our costs and the postage price to send the hats costs more than we expected.

> **Task:** Think about the scenario above. What do you think has gone wrong? Do you recognise this in your own scenarios? How would you reorganise the turn of events to produce a more positive outcome?

There are two issues here that are linked together and that lead to the failure of this business venture. If we design a product and then hope to find an audience, we open ourselves up to the risk that it isn't wanted. By rushing ahead with the design and manufacturing of the hat without finding an audience and communicating with them, we have taken what we perceive to be a good idea and assumed that other people will be willing to spend their hard-earned cash on it. To be clear, I am not implying that the idea is a bad one – a massaging Bluetooth playing hat might well be brilliant – but if we'd have spoken to our audience we might have found out that a similar product already exists, or that our target audience only value high quality wool, or that the design is too childish, or any other number of things.

So we need to know an audience exists and we need to know whether they would buy our product. Let's tackle these two challenges below.

Who are our audience?

It is often the case that new theatre companies start with a show and then hope an audience will come and watch. Perhaps their work was popular when they were at drama school, when friends and family would happily come along for a cheap ticket, but this is not necessarily representative of having created work that the wider public want to see, and that has a future beyond your first year of graduating.

The arts have fallen into a habit of working in top-down hierarchies. If we build it, they will come! Well, not quite. Rather than seeing our audience as a by-product of our work or as a necessary evil to be bought, we should be thinking about this exchange as a two-way street. So often, the language of outreach, engagement, and 'reaching out' keeps us remote and places our audiences as passive participants. Instead, we should be viewing our audience as our community, understanding why we want to work *with* them, and using that process to reflect back what they want to see. Yes, there are plenty of examples of top-down 'here is something shiny and you are going to like it' entertainment, but is that ultimately satisfying, and do you have the resources to compete, even if it was? We will make much more profound work, and crucially, our audiences will have a stake in it and will value the impact theatre can have on their lives, if we enable methods of genuine community listening and co-creation. Experience your company from your audience's perspective.

Although in your earliest days you will be grateful for any audience you can get, as you start to position yourself and develop a greater understanding of what you want to say and why your work needs to exist, your audience should be an integral part of that journey with you. Is work ever great if nobody wanted to see it? We could conceivably argue that this represents a failure of marketing, or that the audience weren't reliable, or that they were simply too 'hard to reach.' But in practice, work that has significance and importance gains that significance and importance from the very fact that its community wants to experience it. Otherwise, we fall into the trap of sitting in our ivory towers dreaming up ideas that we think some nebulous group of 'the audience' will want to see. Or worse, creating work purely for ourselves.

Wants and needs

Finding a gap in the market and discovering a potential audience isn't enough to guarantee that your product will sell. Read that sentence again. Just because you have identified a gap in the market and you think people have shown interest, this is no guarantee of bums-on-seats when it comes to performance day. Why? Because people are busy, there are other shows to see, they already went to the theatre last week, they forgot, they were running late on the day, it was raining, etc. etc. etc.

We need to shift our focus away from what people *want*. This is an unreliable metric. People might follow you on social media and like all of your posts. They might have come to see your last show or they might have promised you that they'll be at your next performance. None of this means anything until they are sat on that seat in front of you or, from an economic perspective, until they have bought that ticket.

Instead of thinking about what people want, we need to focus on what they *need*. It is part of our biological makeup to desire things throughout our lives.

We are all on an unending, unquenchable mission to want, want, want. As soon as we get what we want, we want something else, whether that be human affection or the latest smartphone. Wants are fickle and when we're being asked by a friend or a very nice producer if we'd be interested in a really exciting new production opening next week, our instinct is to say the right thing. Perhaps we just want to end the conversation, or perhaps we genuinely do convince ourselves that we will go.

But as time passes and our wants fade, we become less and less likely to attend. The price is too expensive or the theatre is too far away. We don't know when it'll finish, and we've realised it's going to be raining. We don't recognise the name of the company and can't establish their track record.

Appealing to our audience's wants is futile. Instead, let's turn our attention to what they need. This is where things become a bit trickier. When we need something, we cannot function without it. Think about the incredible rise in streaming services. If Netflix or Disney + sold themselves as something we wanted, they wouldn't be nearly as successful as they are now. But as soon as they invested in exclusive shows, or spin-offs from popular franchises, audiences need to buy in if they are to keep up with the latest developments of their various cinematic universes. In the early 2000s, the idea of paying for music was becoming laughable as the internet saw music piracy reach new heights. Spotify and other streaming services seemed like an outlier, but tapping into an audience's need for more choice and, crucially, for simplicity, the service engineered a new form of behavioural norm.

Theatre has a difficult job here, more so than most other art forms. As audiences expect more and more convenience, theatre remains largely anchored to a set of dated principles. Audiences must travel to a venue and pay an entry fee, shows must be enjoyed in silence with designated toilet breaks and codes of behavioural norms. At the same time, theatre cannot realistically be said to be meeting a physiological need for its users, in the same way as a car solves our need to get to work, or food solves our need to eat.

Audience's might not *need* to come to the theatre per se, but they do need a framework of reference in which to decide whether visiting will help them with one of the levels of needs visualised by Maslow's hierarchy. Unless we're offering free food and shelter, there is little point trying to sell a theatre ticket to somebody who has no food. Likewise, if we are trying to reach communities for whom attendance at the theatre is not typical, we might need to acknowledge that deeper levels of need (such as financial, community, etc.) may need to be addressed before we will succeed in selling them the benefits of our outreach.

We can probably assume that most audiences would like more time and money. With that in mind, the decision to attend your show involves both a financial and a time risk. To appreciate this, let's think about all of the things an audience doesn't know (ie. a risk) when coming to see your show:

- Will the show be any good?
- What is the show about?
- Have I been to the venue before?
- Is there somewhere to park?
- Will there be an interval?
- Have I heard of any of the actors?
- If I haven't heard of the actors, does this mean they're no good?
- Will my access needs be met?
- What will the rest of the audience be like?
- Is there a dress code?
- Will there be other people who look or sound like me there?
- What time will it finish?
- Will the story have anything in common with my life and interests?
- Will I be able to catch public transport after the show?
- What will I lose if I don't like it?

A long list indeed.

> **Task:** Taking the list above, draw up an action plan for each (add more if you think of them) specifically addressing how you could reduce some of the unknowns for a potential audience member. Different audience members will have different attitudes to risk, and those audience members who are used to seeing the work of new companies might be more up for the risk than others. But reducing the number of unknowns helps any audience member to make a decision to visit you. Remember: think of your audience from the perspective of your audience. How does each link with your vision, mission and values?

Let's for a moment consider the above list in the context of a new Netflix show. We can instantly remove any fear related to travel and venues as we'll be watching at home. Netflix will give me clues about the other work of the actors and will recommend similar films, if I'm likely to enjoy this one. I can see the run time, and can stop and start it as much as I like. There'll be subtitles if I need them, and I can control the volume to a level that suits me. If I don't like it, I can switch it off and I haven't lost any time or money.

This sounds like a support for lazy audiences, but that would be to misunderstand my point. It isn't so much that an audience for a Netflix show is lazy or less committed, but the level of risk has been significantly reduced. Visiting the theatre, by contrast can be fraught with risk. This is why audiences flock to well-known plays at established venues with big stars. It is not so much that this is preferable or that it has more artistic merit. But if people know the actor from something else, or have visited the venue previously, or are familiar with the play, the perceived level of risk is reduced, and their need to feel safe, enriched, and part of a community is more likely to be met. Of course, they may attend and hate your production of *A Doll's House*, and this may then reshape their perceived risk the next time they see a performance of *A Doll's House* advertised.

Target audience

Who is your work for? This can be a tricky question to answer when you're simply hoping that anybody will come along and like your work. But there is a difference between making something that will please everybody, and making something that everybody likes.

I always use the example of *Toy Story* when talking about target audiences. *Toy Story* is a fairly safe example of a universally loved film. Who doesn't like *Toy Story*? But if we look at *Toy Story* critically, a PG rated film about talking toys and the value of friendship and growing up, it becomes very hard to argue that this is a film targeted at my grandparents. Clearly, like all of Pixar's work, *Toy Story* is aimed at a very specific demographic: children between the ages of seven and ten. The fact that *Toy Story* is a film loved by children and grandparents speaks to the quality of the product.

When defining a target audience, be specific. I find it often helps to visualise one person – possibly somebody I know – who this work is for. Students often say to me that their work is for 'young people between thirteen and eighteen.' What eighteen-year-old do you know who looks and dresses the same as when they were thirteen? Who has the same interests? Who listens to the same music or hangs around in the same places? 'Sixteen to twenty-one' is another classic. A sixteen-year-old is still in school, likely still lives with their parents and has limited free time and money. A twenty-one-year-old, on the other hand, may live by themselves or with friends, and potentially works full time, with a degree.

The more specific you can make your target audience the more you will be able to define what your work is and judge your success in relation to that. Don't just think in relation to age and gender, either. Consider location, interests, personality types: the more specific you can be, the better.

But what about all those other people who love *Toy Story*, you might be crying out. This is where the target audience becomes so useful. By being defined with your target audience, you're not limiting who you appeal to, but instead visualising that one group who are *really* going to love your work. Everybody else falls into your secondary audience. Part of what makes Disney and Pixar so clever, and one of the largest and most fondly held brands on the planet, is their appreciation of the target audience. Young children can't visit the cinema on their own; parents and grandparents will accompany them. As will older siblings. Whereas some films for small children are irritating and garish, Pixar is romantic, colourful, and nuanced. There's jokes for adults. There's Tom Hanks. All of these things help to engage parents: parents who, crucially, hold the cash. Cash for return visits, cash for DVDs, toys at

Christmas, and visits to Disney Land. By appreciating secondary audiences, Pixar get a much more substantial and longer return on their investment per viewer.

Art that tries to appeal to everybody ends up failing everybody. We shouldn't make art specifically to sell tickets, but when our business requires us to sell tickets, it's vital to know who our art will appeal to and why they would want it. Only then can you think about growing and developing your audiences and taking them on a thrilling journey with you over the course of your company's life.

Remember that target audiences are a two-way process. You can, in theory, specify an audience and then focus all your energy on making work for them, but without those channels of communication, partnership, and listening, how do you know if this is the work they want or need?

Market segments

Although each person is unique and carries their own set of lived experiences, we often share characteristics, traits, and interests that can be helpful to understand from a marketing perspective. This shared *demographic* information, which might range from sharing a postcode to sharing an interest in Star Wars, can help us to group common interests and target our audiences effectively. To help make this easier, several organisations have profiled audiences into neatly defined categories of shared interests. There are differences amongst these systems and they're certainly not without their problems – how does one define 'low cultural engagement' for instance – but they can be useful when trying to articulate the difference between audiences. In England, the Arts Council publish an annual *Arts Audiences Insight*, but excellent alternatives to explore include the Audience Agency's *Audience Spectrum Profiling* and PurpleSeven's *Balanced Database*, all of which are linked in the resource section at the end of this chapter.

When thinking about target audiences and market segments, you are inevitably treading into the realm of stereotyping, which can feel awkward. This is the same path that implies that all girls like pink and all boys like Formula 1. You do need to be careful to check your stereotypes when thinking about your audience, but at the same time, a degree of generalisation is part of the game of audience development, where broad trends are as important as individual quirks in taste.

Once you have identified the segments of your audience, it makes sense that you will need to differentiate your marketing efforts in order to account for their differences. Visualising the different strategies you will employ and who they are designed to reach is a good way of seeing who you are including and who you might be missing. By far the easiest way of achieving this is to map your different initiatives (e.g. Flyers, Facebook ads, a trailer, a radio interview) against the main characteristics of your audience. In the example below, you can see how mapping wealth with cultural engagement helps me to ensure I have a range of initiatives to reach a wide variety of demographics.

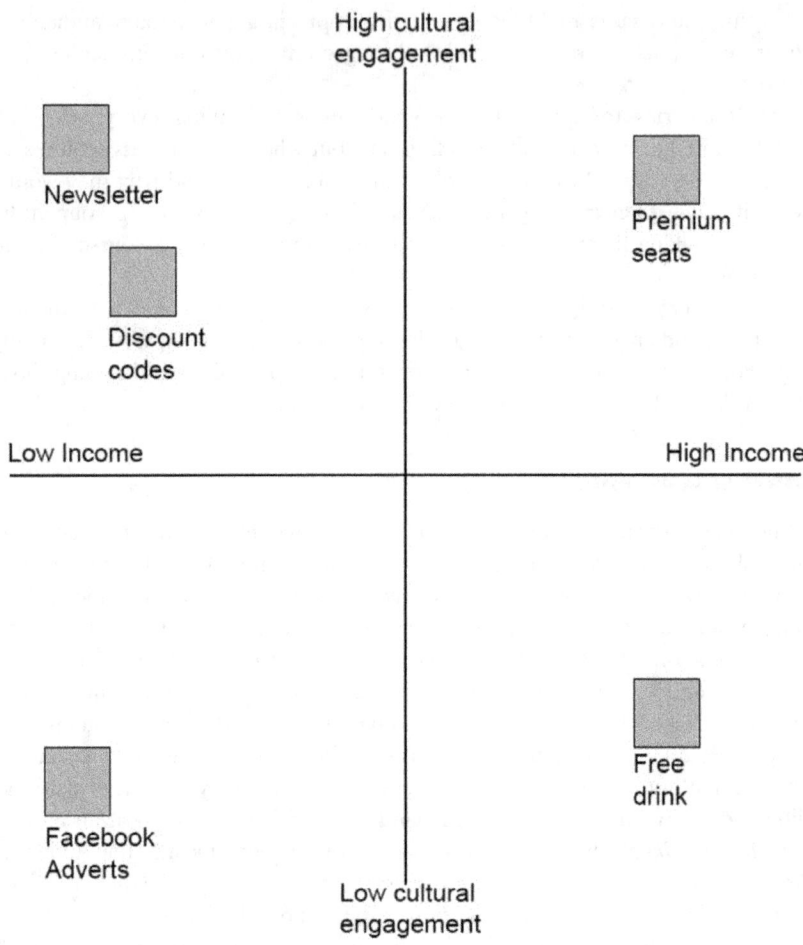

Figure 5.1 Mapping marketing with audience demographics

The audience journey and marketing strategy

Building an audience can feel daunting to begin with but following a few key principles can help to make this task a little easier. Audiences have many demands on their time and attention, so getting them to take notice can feel tricky, but as you stick around for future shows and word gets around that what you do is fantastic, this should continue to grow. Of course, major theatres employ entire teams of people to build and develop audiences, and I am not trying to imply that achieving this is easy, but progress can be achieved regardless of the size of your operation.

It is helpful to think of your *audience journey*. We make journeys with organisations all the time, although we may not be aware of it. When was the last time you went in and bought the most expensive product or membership a

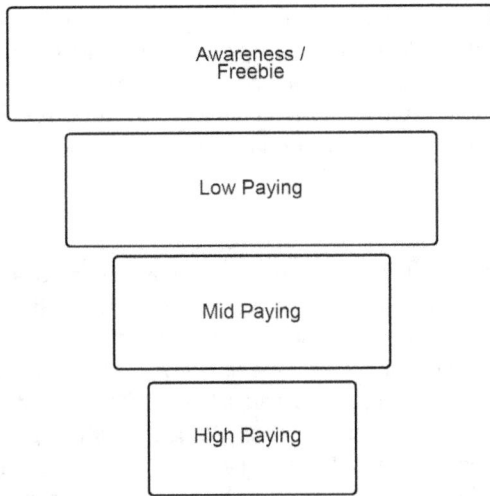

Figure 5.2 The audience funnel

company offered when you had only just found out about it? Your journey with a company begins from the moment you first become aware of their existence, right through to your last engagement with them. We discuss the idea of an audience journey, because our relationship with brands is never static. We are always in a flux between wanting to engage more, and the brand desperately trying to hold our attention. We can visualise the audience journey as a funnel.

At the start of the funnel, we have Awareness, followed by Freebie. These may be the very broadest ways in which a consumer hears about your company for the first time. It doesn't matter how much work goes on at the other end of the audience journey, if your audience don't know you exist, nothing else can happen. This level of audience engagement is non-committal, but by being so relaxed, customers can engage with your company in a way that reduces the risk for them.

After this, we have Low Cost, Medium Cost, and Premium Cost. Customers aren't going to jump to the bottom of the funnel without first building up trust and confidence in your ability to deliver. At the same time, you should be seeking ways to convert your low-cost customers into mid- and high-cost, because this is how you will get them to spend more money and time with you. Not all customers will come on the entire journey with you, for a variety of personal reasons. A helpful way to think about it is to imagine that 20% of the people you offer a freebie to will become a low paying customer. Of those 20%, a subsequent 20% will take the next step. And so on.

In order to start to think about our own brand and how we will reach audiences, we first need to think about market positioning. Simply put, positioning is the way we use our marketing to help our audiences define us from our competitors. A new type of mobile phone might position itself as the luxury item in a crowded marketplace, for example, whereas a competitor might position itself as the most technologically advanced. This is about understanding what makes our product or service unique within the given competition.

> **TASK:** Identify between three and five Unique Selling Points: things that make your work distinct. This can be anything from pricing strategy to artistic style. Why would somebody come to your work? Do the same thing with your competitors – for the time being, focus this on your most immediate competitors in your local area. Go back to your first list and tweak this in line with what you have identified about your competitors: are you offering something different? This may need you to go back and tweak some fundamentals about your offering, but remember that a Unique Selling Point can be almost anything. In a sentence, write down your positioning strategy to explain, briefly, what you are and why your work is unique. It might help to do this from the point of view of your audience.

Visualising the customer journey, and your own unique position in the market, is a helpful way to begin a *marketing strategy*. In the very early days of your company, your most important priority will be to raise awareness and to get the word out that you exist. Until you have done that, you have no chance of expecting people to join your membership scheme or to become a donor.

Remember though, you're not dispensing freebies for the good of your health. This is part of a coordinated strategy today to convert potential customers into – hopefully – the highest paying customers of tomorrow. So, when you're offering freebies, make it your mission to ensure that you at least get them to sign up to your mailing list. That way, they will be first to know about it when you do have something more premium to offer them.

Freebies are great because we all like things that are free. You might stand in the street with free food (always a good idea!) and use the excuse to hand out some flyers, chat to people and get some signups to your newsletter. Alternatively, you might offer a free performance, or put some archive videos up online. Anything you can offer, in the first instance, that allows potential audiences to judge whether you look good enough to spend time and money on, is effort well spent.

One of the problems with offering things for free is the negative ways we tend to assign quality based on financial value. We are conditioned to assume that something expensive is more worthwhile than something cheap. The very word cheap suggests its own, often negative connotations. A lot of research shows that 'free' tends to fall down when it is for delayed gratification. 'Come and see our show tomorrow, it's free!' sounds like a great offer. But when tomorrow comes my loyalty will be tested, much more so than if I'd committed some money in advance. So use 'free' to capture attention, but don't be ashamed of the fact that you are a business: your overall mission needs to be to turn as many people as possible into paying customers.

Use the idea of the customer funnel to direct your pricing strategy in the longer term. In the early days, when you are performing in small venues and have a lot to prove, you might choose to make your tickets extremely cheap. As the size of your performances and the reputation of the venues you perform at grows, increase the price. Depending on the contractual relationship with your venue you may or may not have input into ticket sales, but where you do, they are worth thinking about carefully. Don't launch your premium monthly membership a month after you've started your company: why would I sign up to that? Take your audiences with you. At the same time, don't close down avenues of potential income. Of your entire audience base there will always be people for whom finances are tight, but there will also be people willing to pay a lot more. Don't be afraid of tapping into that resource. Think about the benefit that donations and membership schemes can add to your bottom line.

It's important when considering marketing to be aware of your resources and what you have access to. Marketing budgets can be exponential and can include a baffling array of scale and opportunities. This is likely to be out of the reach of a company of your size, and not worth the expense, given the maximum profit you could return in ticket sales, even if you did have access to it. It's therefore super important to be aware of your opportunities and limits and to balance this against your time, finance, and logistical limits.

> **Task:** Before we think about the audience journey, it is helpful to visualise the audience. To do this, you are going to create three audience personas. An audience persona is a short paragraph describing an imaginary person, but who represents a potential member of your audience. An audience persona tries to imagine the realities of that person's life in as much detail as possible, so that our strategies for reaching that individual can be as tailored to that demographic as possible. Three should be enough for this, but if you need more, perhaps think about whether your audience is too broad. Similarly, if you struggle to visualise more than one or two, perhaps you haven't yet done enough work to think about who your work is actually for. I find that basing persona work from a person I actually know is helpful to help me move beyond the stereotypical and into the more specific, and useful.
> Example persona:
>
> **Jamie, 17, local student**
> Jamie doesn't engage with traditional schooling but has an interest in writing, which his school system doesn't allow him the opportunity to fully explore. Through a targeted Snapchat advert, Jamie joins our New Writers scheme, where he visits one evening every week, mixes with likeminded peers and is working towards a

> showcase. Jamie's family have never been to the theatre, but they are coming to see his performance and he is now considering applying for a creative writing degree at a local university. For the first time, he feels that his abilities are recognised and as a result, he has a sense of direction and investment in his own future. He also feels he has a community of likeminded peers with which to share his hobby and learn new skills.
>
> Once you have completed your audience personas, it's time to think about their needs. Map out the journey for your website and for each strand of your online content (videos, photos etc.) for each of your three profiles. Do the same for an audience member coming to your show. You can approach this in a range of ways, but you might find it easiest to visualise this as a workflow. What is the journey to purchasing a ticket, or watching a video, or sitting in a seat, and how does that change from one audience demographic to another?

The importance of evaluation

Often, we omit the part of the process in which we get to know our audiences. In the arts, this is so often incidental: hoping with each show that somebody turns up. While there will always be a degree of leaning in to the audience of venues where you perform, there is no substitute to growing your own engaged and interested audience who want to know more about your work. But in order to engage them, you need to understand them. Before your first show this is virtually impossible, but as soon as you begin to attract a crowd, finding out who is involved and who is not is important for building your audience and refining your future output.

Evaluation, combined with up-to-date market research, gives you a continued live snapshot of the effectiveness of your work and the interests and make-up of the people it is reaching. By doing this, you are able to assess who you are reaching, who you are *not* reaching and what they like and dislike.

Data types

When embarking upon market research collection, it is important to distinguish between the two primary forms of research, qualitative and quantitative data, as both have pros and cons.

Quantitative data (which you can remember easily by remembering the word 'quantity') is data that deals with numbers, facts, and figures. 'Our show attracted 700 people'; '54% of our audience are male'; 'Two-thirds of our social media following come from Spain.' These hard, cold facts are often useful for measuring change and demonstrating scale, but can lack context and personality. When presenting quantitative data, it is easy to manipulate, which can either be a pro or a con depending on which way you look at it. Saying that 90% of your audience want to pay more for your shows sounds great, but 90% of three people is very different from if you asked three hundred.

Qualitative data, on the other hand, is non-numerical data, such as interview transcripts and opinions. The broad benefit of qualitative data is that it allows for the human touch in ways that numbers alone can't communicate. A few snippets from audience members raving about your show can often sound more personable than saying '75% of our audience would return.' As a result of being more human focussed, however, qualitative data can sometimes be seen as less robust and more anecdotal.

Working with data

There are an incredible number of analytic tools available to business owners to help measure, analyse, and assess customer interaction with your work online. While this can feel overwhelming, and indeed, organisations have large teams to manage and track this, working alongside some key principles can help you to coordinate your effort and stand your ground in this increasingly competitive online space.

Key data

There are no hard and fast rules as to what data you should be focussing on, and in the very early days you might just be glad to get followers or newsletter subscribers at all. As you start to build, you will have an overwhelming volume of *analytic* information. In order to get most out of it, particularly when you don't have a team behind you, focus on the following themes:

- **HOW**: there is no point spending a lot of time and money on a website if people only access you via Facebook. Knowing how your audiences interact with your content is vital to understanding what they need from your online presence. Do your audience visit you via mobile or desktop? Which pages of your website do they visit? How much of your videos do they watch?
- **WHO**: numbers only tell you so much, so look for data that breaks down the demographics of your audiences. What is the age, gender, and location breakdown of your audiences and how do they differ across different platforms? Who are you not reaching?
- **WHY**: Why do people follow your page? Look at the content they engage with. An audience may be subscribed to your newsletter for a very different reason to following you on Instagram. Understanding this can help you to tailor your response.

- **WHAT**: related to the above, which content do your audiences interact with and what do they ignore? Experiment with posting the exact same content across different platforms – how do they compare? An audience on LinkedIn or Twitter might be engaging with your content for professional reasons, whereas popular content on Facebook tends to focus on human stories.

Data is only useful when we figure out the stories behind it. Look for the patterns of engagement and pay as much attention to what is missing as to what does well. Part of maximising success online is about giving our audiences what they want, and the key to this is in understanding that audiences are different and come to our content for different purposes.

Of course, we could ignore analytics and engagement data. This is a relatively new concept in some regards, although some funders will specify key metrics which they want you to obtain from your analytics, and they may also ask for evidence of you handling this data ethically (more on that below). If we have enough time and money to waste we can, perhaps, afford to ignore some of this. But effective businesses focus on the *return on investment*. If it costs you £100 and ten hours to design and print some flyers, but only one audience member comes to your show as a result, is that as effective as the Tweet with a discount code that brought in fifty people?

Measuring the return on our marketing efforts is essential in making best use of the time and resources we have. Companies will often be really keen to design flyers or to film a swanky trailer, but regularly fail to measure the impact of these measures. We need to know the marketing avenues that work and give us the best return on investment and we need to ruthlessly abandon those that are a waste of our precious time and money. In some respects, the theory here is quite simple: find out what works and give your audience more of what they want.

There are a number of methods for measuring return on investment (ROI). One simple method is to divide the return on investment (the money made) by the cost of the investment (the money spent). This is then multiplied by 100 to give a percentage, which is how ROI is usually communicated.

If you paid £50 for some flyers, for example, and another £20 for a designer, your total costs would be £70. If the result of those flyers resulted in £100 of sales, you could calculate your ROI as:

$$ROI = \frac{100}{50+20} \times 100$$

or

$$ROI = \frac{100}{70} \times 100 = 142.85 \text{ or } 143\%$$

If the ROI percentage is a positive number, it shows that the venture was profitable. ROI is deceptively simple, and it may be useful for you as a benchmark, but there are a few things to consider. Firstly, in the example above, it is likely to be very difficult in practice to measure that my flyers specifically resulted in those particular sales. We might instead do ROI for our whole marketing efforts at large, thinking about the total expenditure for all marketing versus the total income made through ticket sales. It's important to note that we are calculating net income, so make sure you have deducted all costs to ensure an accurate ROI figure.

At the most basic level, simply make sure you have methods in place to capture audiences who have engaged with your work. Usually this means making it easy for audiences to know about your newsletter and social media channels. Any extra signup you can get is a step towards our next goal: retaining audiences.

GDPR

A relatively recent piece of legislation from the EU, the General Data Protection Regulation (GDPR) centres around the collection and use of personal data. Although it might sound grand and something only for large corporations to deal with, it is something every company manager absolutely needs to be aware of, as it is likely that your activities will fall within its remit.

GDPR is an extensive and dense piece of legislation, but from it we can establish some key principles. As an organisation, you should not collect more personal information from your users than you need, and what data you do store should be appropriately safeguarded from being stolen, hacked, or leaked. Users are entitled to request a breakdown of the data a company has relating to them by submitting a Subject Access Request (SAR), which must be responded to within a month and cannot reasonably be refused.

The point of GDPR legislation is to offer control and the right for individuals to know what information a company holds about them. You particularly need to be mindful when sharing data about other people and whether this is necessary. Data, from the point of view of GDPR, is anything that can reasonably be used to identify a person, whether directly or indirectly (so items such as names and addresses, but less obvious pieces including IP addresses and cookie identifiers).

Get out of the habit of CC'ing groups of people in your email chain, unless they have consented to this, as sharing email addresses without consent could be seen as a breach of GDPR – particularly when you're sharing with people who may not know each other; if you're replying en-masse to a group who are coming to a workshop, for example. Before sharing somebody's personal information (when making a group chat or putting people in contact with one another), make sure you have the consent of that individual for you to do so.

GDPR can become tricky when dealing with venues, as it becomes tricky for them to share certain data relating to individuals with you. This has implications when discussing audiences, participants, and the press, to give three examples, and it is also something you must consider in reverse. Remember you must not share data that could identify an individual (such as names and contact info) with a third party without their prior consent.

> **Task:** Draw up a list of ways in which your organisation uses personal data. For each item on the list, provide a simple, clear action to ensure that your approach projects data and complies with your GDPR requirements. You don't need to overcomplicate this, but you equally should avoid leaving things to chance, as mistakes do happen and personal information can be used with malicious intent.

Methods of market research

Market research can be done in numerous ways depending on the scale of your operation. Key methods include interviews, focus groups, surveys, or questionnaires. Interviews are fantastic for collecting in-depth responses from individuals but take time to complete, whereas surveys are often useful for reaching a wider audience. However, the longer your survey takes to complete, the more people are unlikely to complete it. Focus groups can be fantastic as a way of exploring opinions in detail, but can be difficult to organise and often need to explore incentives as a way of persuading people to give up their time.

Who, how many, and why?

When conducting any research, you should always focus on the following questions, when deciding who your research is intended to reach:

- Who will you ask?
- Why them?
- Who are you excluding by asking that group?
- How many people will you ask? A survey of two people might not be representative of a wider group, but a survey of one thousand people might be very difficult to manage.

These questions are important to ensure you are capturing an accurate picture in your research. It is no point finding out that 90% of your audience would love to see you perform more Shakespeare, but you only had survey responses from white males over fifty. What about the people you didn't reach?

Question types

When conducting any type of research, it's important to ensure that your questions are best set up to provide the quality of information you are looking for. You should avoid asking *leading questions* which seem to imply a correct answer. 'Do you agree with me that Shakespeare is boring?' This is a leading question. Similarly, you should try to avoid *bias* in your questions that imposes a view or suggests a correct answer. It is much harder to be *impartial* than you might think.

Give thought to your language choice and ensure that you aren't using jargon which your audience may not understand. A range of open and closed questions is usually the best approach: closed questions usually imply a Yes or No answer: 'Did you have breakfast today?' On the other hand, open questions invite a more varied range of responses. 'Could you tell me what you had for breakfast today?' Both question types are valid in different situations and a range of question types often makes surveys more interesting for audiences to complete.

Consider the relative pros and cons of paper surveys vs e-surveys when collecting your market research and consider who may or may not have access to each. Don't always assume that digital is automatically better – there are communities for whom digital access can be a barrier – and think about how you can utilise a range of strategies to help reach the widest possible audience for your purposes.

Research timeline

The frustrating thing about market research is that it is only relevant for a short period of time. There is little point referring back to market research from five or ten years ago when trying to suggest an idea for the world *now*. Consumer habits and local competition change at pace, so make sure your market research is up to date. There is also no reason why your research should stop when your business opens: good businesses are regularly in conversation with their consumers to ensure what they are offering is what people want and need.

Hard to reach?

The term of 'hard to reach' in relation to audiences has long been thrown about in audience development parlance. If a company notices that it struggles to engage audiences from a particular age group or ethnic background, or from particular postcodes, it can often be decided that these groups present particular challenges that the theatre may be unable to meet. You may have similar problems when looking at your own audiences and you may be mystified about how you can diversify the people coming to see your shows.

Although the term 'hard to reach' suggests a nicely packaged problem, with the issue laying at the feet of those communities who are not currently engaging with your work, I would advise you to consider the implications of the term and whether you would ever constitute yourself as being 'hard to reach.'

The difficulty with this term is that it places the blame at the feet of the communities themselves and absolves theatre makers from their responsibility. I would argue that there is no such thing as a hard-to-reach community. We may need to consider different methods and approaches than what we are used to using as our default, and we may have to move out of our own comfort zones and if we want to begin a genuine and long-lasting dialogue with a diverse range of local communities. Does that make a community hard to reach? Is the problem that a community is hard to reach, or are our methods for reaching them unsuitable? Have we had a conversation with anybody from that group to understand their interests or are we assuming on their behalf and even, potentially, stereotyping? Often it is we who need to do the legwork, and blaming a community is often an easier strategy than taking the action and committing to the learning for our own part.

We need to reverse the conversation around so-called 'diversity' of audience development, which contains colonial implications and which continues to imply that certain communities would be educated, enriched, and empowered if only they knew about our life-changing work. Such entrenched views risk further developing a rift between intention and action and does little to resolve the problem. We also have to consider that communities may not want what we are offering: so often the dialogue around work by Shakespeare or in opera, to take two obvious examples, focusses around the need to diversify a generally white, middle-class, middle-aged audience, without due thought being given to the fact that those other communities may have taken a good look at what we are offering and have decided not to be interested.

It is much easier to lay the blame for a lack of audience diversity at the feet of the communities we are failing to reach, and much, much harder to interrogate our own systems and creative choices and unpack the implications of this. Instead, we should be asking ourselves what we have genuinely done to initiate a dialogue with other communities, to build trust and longstanding relationships around a culture of listening and action. If we do have those conversations, do we expect them to take place on *our* turf, or using *our* favourite coffee shop, or have we invited opportunities for the conversation to be a more equal balance of power? What is your own privilege in this, and what does your positionality imply? What work have you presented in the past and what have you done to interrogate and potentially decolonise this? The historical legacy of Western theatre has made it extremely likely that you've presented more plays by white men than any other group. There's nothing inherently wrong with this, but being aware of it and responding positively to it may be the first step towards making your theatre something which a broader spectrum of people feels invited to be a part of.

Audience development should not be seen as a one-way street. It should not be seen through the lens that people will enjoy your work if only they knew about it. All work has pros and cons and no work is entitled to an audience. Equally, your work shouldn't be about trying to please everybody, but about making sure that everybody feels able and welcome to participate if they choose to do so. There is a difference between being outpriced and intimidated from trying your first opera and looking at opera and deciding that it isn't for you. Remember that audience development and engagement is an ongoing process in conversation between venue, company, and audience themselves. It never ends but it should be constantly evolving as your relationships with both parties develop.

Working with customers

Building positive relationships with your customers should be your priority. You should develop a policy for customer service standards so that you can agree as a collective what your approach, tone, and methods for acceptable customer contact are. Whether you offer customers the opportunity to contact you via email or phone, for example, sends different messages, as does your speed of replying when customers make contact with you. When dealing with customers directly it is important to utilise active listening. This will help you to understand the customer's point of view and not jump to conclusions. Rephrasing the customer's question as part of your answer is a great way of demonstrating that you have listened to, and understood the question, and helps to build trust.

Customers can and do complain. Sometimes these complaints are legitimate, sometimes not. Online experiences provide ample opportunities for audiences to comment, praise, moan, or troll, and you should be prepared for this as your output grows. The more professional your work appears to be on the surface, the more entitled audiences may feel to critique what you are doing, which can be a struggle to deal with on your own.

Tools are slowly being introduced to control this, with Dislike buttons being removed or the option to block comments on some platforms, but you may also feel that this limits engagement and prevents a genuine conversation with your users. Being able to ban users may work on social media, but will be less effective against an angry member of the public wanting a refund after a show.

This is not to make you fear dealing with the public or to suggest that running a company will bring an unrelenting barrage of negativity. Hopefully this will never apply to you. While we can tend to demonise 'the public' as somehow 'other,' it's helpful to remember that 'they' are really 'us,' and we should deal with complaints fairly, humanely, and politely at all times. We are the face of our business after all.

In any conversation with a customer, take them seriously and be open to their needs and wants. Remember the power of 'Yes' and try to be open and approachable in your language, rather than jumping to conclusions or assuming you know better. 'Solutions not problems' is my mantra.

Retaining audiences

Getting an audience for a show is hard work – keeping and growing that audience is an entirely different challenge all together. Opportunities to work at different venues and to collaborate with different artists will always provide moments of growth as your work is shared across their channels, but this needs to translate into results in order for this to be effective for you.

Growing your own audience organically is a slog but well worth the effort. If people have seen your work and then decided to follow you, that shows a vested interest in continuing to follow your work. On the other hand, how many times have you gone to a show and felt utterly compelled to follow them on social media?

When you have an audience, it is important to ensure that you stay in contact with them so that they remember who you are and feel they have a relationship with you. Exactly how you choose to do this will depend on the specifics of your tone of voice and company ethos, but newsletters are only effective if they come with some degree of consistency. This can be a challenge both when you're busy (putting together a newsletter takes a degree of time) and when you're not (what do you put in it?), so you shouldn't underestimate the time potentially involved in this.

Audiences today want relatability, trust, and empathy from the companies they follow online. Audiences are savvy to the stereotypes and tricks that have grown stale on social media, and they are keen for stories they can emotionally engage in. The growth and rise of your fledgling company is a potentially gripping story, and the advantage firmly lies with you while you are small and people focussed. Large corporations often struggle to engineer a sense of relatability, when audiences know full well that they have huge marketing departments designed to produce content with the veneer of authenticity. You have that in bucket loads – the key is how to channel it effectively.

Similarly, as audiences become more digitally savvy, they are becoming more aware of disingenuous content posted on social media. There was a fantastic example of this on International Women's Day when, presumably to garner some goodwill and to promote their liberal credentials, hundreds of organisations tweeted their heartfelt support for the initiative. This would have been the end of it if it wasn't for the Gender Paygap Bot, which retweeted every post with statistics relating to the gender pay gap within those same organisations who were tweeting about how proud they were of their female employees. So if you're going to put content online, don't virtue signal and don't bullshit – people will see through it and they won't like it.

Wider audience trends

It is always helpful to appreciate audience trends beyond your own organisation. A recent example of this can be seen in the wider audience behaviour regarding the gradual return to theatres after the pandemic. Luckily, there are wonderful bodies such as the Audience Agency, PurpleSeven, and Indigo Ltd, doing a range of excellent research into audience behaviour on local and national scales, with insights that are both instructive and absolutely up to the moment. This can help shape your own output and behaviour, and is something worth spending your time engaging with.

Audience development planning

An *Audience Development Plan* brings together a lot of the work you have done in this chapter into a cohesive strategy for reaching and growing your audiences. It is a statement of intent and a plan of action, and can be a prerequisite for a lot of high-level state funding. What is the difference between an Audience Development Plan and a Marketing Plan? They're similar, on the face of it, but whereas marketing is about the selling of products you think the audience wants, audience development is about working in conversation with your audience, building relationships with the aim of them becoming more involved in your work. Audience development, as opposed to marketing, is a useful frame of reference because it again grounds your work in development with your audience, working with the community you are there to serve, and helps you to experience your brand from the perspective of the customer.

Creating an Audience Development Plan is a big task which is time consuming, but there are many excellent resources to help. The Audience Agency has compiled a comprehensive guide for the steps you should take when completing your plan and I have linked to this in the resource section. I have chosen to refer you to it rather than to summarise here, because audience development really is a key area which that detail, time, and skill, and you will find the guide incredibly useful in working you through this. They also offer a free online Audience Development Planner tool that you can work to complete alongside the guide and should be a first step for any organisation taking audience development seriously.

Audience Development Plans are big tasks, but if you have followed the work so far in this book you will find yourself a long way on the journey to completing this. Perhaps unsurprisingly, audience development goes hand in hand with all those essential questions about purpose, mission, and need, so the importance of knowing why your company exists and who it is here to serve are really useful in shaping your audience growth.

> **Task:** Read through the Audience Development Guide linked in the resource section, or find an alternative template if this doesn't work for your needs. Register for a profile and sign up to their Audience Development Planner tool. It is important that you do this as a company, and don't assign this task to the producer, as defining purpose and audience should be a job for your entire organisation.

Chapter Resources

Audience development

'Arts audiences: Insight,' ArtsCouncil, www.artscouncil.org.uk/sites/default/files/download-file/arts_audience_insight_2011.pdf
'Audience Insights,' Thrive, https://wewillthrive.co.uk/audience-insights/

Bernstein, Joanne Scheff, *Arts Marketing Insights: The dynamics of building and retaining performing arts audiences* (Jossey-Bass, San Francisco, 2006)

Bernstein, Joanne Scheff, *Standing Room Only: Marketing insights for engaging performing arts audiences* (Palgrave Macmillan, London, 2014)

Borwick, Doug, *Building Communities, Not Audiences: The future of the arts in the United States* (ArtsEngaged, Winston-Salem, 2012)

Culturehive, www.culturehive.co.uk/

Davies, Paul, 'Five ways to attract new arts audiences,' *Guardian* (13th October 2015), www.theguardian.com/culture-professionals-network/2015/oct/13/five-ways-attract-new-arts-audiences-manchester-camerata

'Have a poke around our brain ...,' Morris Hargreaves McIntyre, https://mhminsight.com/brain

'How to calculate Return on Investment (ROI),' Investopedia (11th August 2022), www.investopedia.com/articles/basics/10/guide-to-calculating-roi.asp#:~:text=ROI%20is%20calculated%20by%20subtracting,finally%2C%20multiplying%20it%20by%20100

'Market positioning,' Corporate Finance Institute, https://corporatefinanceinstitute.com/resources/knowledge/strategy/market-positioning/

Miller, Donald, *Building a Storybrand: Clarify your message so customers will listen* (Harper Collins Leadership, London, 2017)

Morris Hargreaves McIntyre, 'Changing arts audiences in the 21st century,' Culturehive, www.culturehive.co.uk/resources/how-c21st-audiences-have-changed-and-how-arts-organisations-need-to-do-the-same/

Newman, Danny, *Subscribe Now! Building arts audiences through dynamic subscription promotion* (Theatre Communications Group, New York, 1983)

'Creating an effective audience development plan: An introductory guide to audience development planning from The Audience Agency,' The Audience Agency, www.theaudienceagency.org/resources/guide-to-audience-development-planning

The Audience Agency, www.theaudienceagency.org

'The Space's online audience toolkit,' The Space, www.thespace.org/resource/spaces-online-audiences-toolkit

Walmsley, Ben, *Audience Engagement in the Performing Arts: A critical analysis* (Palgrave Macmillan, London, 2019)

6 Marketing and Branding

In the previous chapter we explored the importance of building an Audience Development Plan, and thinking about your audience at all stages of your company journey. This should lay the groundwork for all your subsequent marketing and branding efforts, and in this chapter we'll look at some of the specifics of how to achieve this.

Building a brand

You've identified who your work is for, now it's time to get the word out. Before we rush into marketing in the next chapter though, we need to consider our brand. Thinking about our brand might seem a bit corporate to some of you and might seem like an opportunity to create a fancy Instagram profile with all the bells and whistles to others. What is important is that our brand reflects our vision and helps in our journey to connect with audiences. Without that central DNA, we're just making beautiful-looking content that nobody wants to engage with.

Defining a brand is much easier if you have a fundamental understanding of your reason for existing and the sort of work you offer to the world. If your brand remains indistinct, you should go back to the core DNA of your company rather than rushing to redesign your logo, as this is the bedrock upon which good brands are built. Branding and marketing are the practical execution of your audience development goals, and we will explore this in detail in the next chapter.

> **Task:** Go back to your Vision, Mission, and Values statements. What do they say about you? Pick out five–ten key words that define you as a company. For example:
> - Value for money, new writing, female-led, local accents
>
> Try and stay away from hyperbole and avoid words such as 'innovative' and 'edgy' which are overused and don't really mean anything. In what way are you innovative? What might lead me to think of you as edgy?

DOI: 10.4324/9781003281726-6

> We touched on Unique Selling Points (USPs) and positioning earlier, but define them now and write down those qualities that make your work unique. Take this a step further and define, in a sentence, what positions your work from your competition. Why would an audience member choose you?
>
> - We are different to the local theatre because they only present work from the classical repertoire, but our work is all new writing.
> - We are different from the other local student company because their social media isn't well maintained and looks amateur.
> - We are different from other companies in our region because we are the only company integrating sign language into every production.
>
> Now do the same thing from the perspective of your three audience profiles. In their mind, why would they choose you? You might, in reality, be writing very similar things, but if so, this is good. If your USPs are clear and at the forefront of your audience's mind, this hopefully means that they are selling points that your audience are interested in. If you have a USP that you struggle to articulate from the audience's perspective ('we're the only theatre company blogging our daily lives on YouTube') it might be worth considering whether this is useful, and whether the audience care about this, at all. Remember: who you are and who your work is aimed towards should be one and the same thing.

These essential questions will provide the groundwork for your brand and should raise flags if any are difficult for you to define. You may need to revisit the work in Chapter 2 to better understand your reason for existing, or you may need to develop your audience research and analytics systems to better understand who your audience are and what they need.

Logo

An eye-catching logo may be the first step you ever take as a company, and while a theatre company logo doesn't carry as much importance as that of a product competing for attention on a shop shelf, it is still very important to help build trust and memorability.

Things to think about when developing your logo:

- Do you have the design skills to create a logo yourself or would it be better to employ a graphic designer? Just because you know your way around Photoshop, don't underestimate the skill it takes to design a truly eye-catching logo. If you can find a designer with a portfolio, you should.
- Simplicity is key. Don't cram your logo with lots of information, images, or multiple colours.

- Think about shape and colour. These will stick in the memory and audiences will come to associate them with your brand. Don't have more than two colours unless absolutely necessary. Brush up on the basics of colour theory and semiotics if you want to dive more into this and remember that audiences associate colours with meaning: there's a reason lots of fast-food chains have started rebranding in green!
- Does it pass the squint test? Your logo will often appear very small on flyers and on social media. Your logo should be simple with little detail. Try and look at it from a distance or squint whilst looking at it. Does the essential shape and colour still pop out? Is it legible?
- Consider whether to include your name. Increasingly logos don't tend to incorporate a company name. Consider McDonalds or Apple, for example. Brand names on logos can be difficult to read, especially when printed small, so consider having a logo that speaks to your name, rather than incorporating the name itself.

Making engaging content

Consumers face an attention overload and creating content that grips and captures attention is both necessary and daunting, especially when you are just getting started. The need to create a constant stream of content can feel overwhelming, and you should be strict with asking yourself how a particular piece of work will benefit your company before getting dragged down a rabbit-hole. Creating any content takes valuable hours, and sometimes this can be little more than a distraction, which doesn't actually result in a tangible increase in audience numbers. Don't put all your attention into building social media followers, as this is a very shaky way of measuring artistic or business success. In the early days it is unlikely that you will have the budget to outsource any of your marketing effort, but you should certainly seek out those with expertise and experience in marketing: these days everyone can create content, but creating engaging content that connects with an audience is a difficult and valuable skillset to obtain.

Here is a short guideline to creating engaging content online:

- Don't try to copy somebody else. It'll feel cheap and people will see through it.
- Don't try to reinvent the wheel. Not to contradict point one, but if you have seen or found something that works, go with it.
- Maintain a 'house style.' This gives consistency and recognisability to your work.
- Work within your means. Trying to create the feel of a movie trailer with your mobile phone is likely to leave you looking as though you're reaching. Focus instead on creating good work with the tools you have access to; rather like your artistic practice itself!
- Conduct basic analysis. Don't overwhelm yourself with analytics but try and tune in to the kind of content that gets the most engagement.

90   *Marketing and Branding*

- Think about accessibility. It's easier than ever to make content accessible, which usually generally results in better content anyway. Think about your choice of colours and add subtitles to your videos. You can conduct a quick and easy audit of your website's accessibility through a tool such as Google Lighthouse Audit. Lighthouse will give your site a rating out of one hundred for issues such as readability, load time, accessibility, and SEO rating, which you can use to measure your overall performance.
    - To conduct a Lighthouse search, open any web page in *Google Chrome* browser.
    - Right click and select *Inspect*.
    - In the box that appears (don't worry that it looks very technical!) select the double >> in the top right of the box.
    - Select *Lighthouse* from the dropdown menu.
    - Select *Go*. Google will run a quick report and the results will be displayed in an easy-to-follow visual breakdown.
- Start videos with a bang. Videos that start with a slow fade in or a dramatic title on a black background might be great for the cinema, but you only have the time it takes for someone to scroll past to catch their attention.
- Think about access points. If someone needs to visit your Facebook, to click on a link, to click a button, to click another link just to buy a ticket for a show, you're missing a trick. Find ways to make the customer journey's simple with as few friction points as possible.
- Keep your websites simple and fast. Website loading times are crucial for keeping customers engaged. Photos, videos, and other fancy features slow down loading time, which can be critical.
- Be consistent. It's a fine balance between not spending too much time, but out of date websites and social media platforms immediately scream that your company has lost its fuel, which can give out a negative impression before you've even started.

Analytics

We discussed the importance of analytics in the last chapter. The good news is, there are numerous ways to access a wealth of detailed analytical information, provided you have a business page on Google and your social media channels. Unfortunately, this is also its drawback.

Analytics tools provide a wealth of valuable insights into your audience's engagement online. Want to know the age breakdown of your followers on Facebook? Want to see which part of your video was most popular? Want to understand what part of your website audiences spend most time looking at?

To access these tools, you will need to opt into *business profiles* in your social media platforms. Having a business profile allows you to access a range of features that, at the time of writing, come at no cost, so is well worth looking into. Search online for the specifics of your platform of choice, as these are likely to change regularly.

Google Analytics is the major player in this area and is also freely available online. This focuses on website engagement, and you normally have to link your analytics account to your website. If opting for a free website option, look to see whether this feature is available to you.

Analytics contains a mind-boggling wealth of information that can be a game changer for organisations to understand how they operate online. One particularly useful feature is something called *A/B testing*, which allows you to trial different variations of content on your website to assess which audiences like best. For example, you might be torn between two choices of photo for your front page. A/B testing would randomly load one of the two images for every user who visits, which would allow you to see whether one was more popular, because it was clicked on most, for example.

Tone of voice

A tone of voice guide is a useful document to bring together as it can help to shape some of the specifics of your company, primarily how it communicates with others. A tone of voice guide sets out a series of guidelines for how you will produce content and engage with users across a range of platforms, including on your social media channels. What is your policy on using emojis in Tweets? How do you want to come across in your communication: are you friendly and familiar, or professional and remote? A tone of voice guideline helps to clarify this, to ensure that everybody is on the same page and that your messaging is consistent. This is important as you grow and build over time. Embedding a sense of consistency will help people to connect with and relate to your brand and recognise your work. By the way: emojis can be a nightmare for people with voice-assistance devices and other impairments, so think about avoiding them!

> **Task:** As a group, create a simple Tone of Voice document outlining your company's tone and style when communicating across a range of platforms. Think about social media but also consider other ways in which your organisation can be contacted. Remember to centre authenticity, and don't try to be too much like other brands.

Style guide

One thing is for certain: you will end up writing tonnes of information for your theatre company during its life. Whether it's writing copy for your website, producing flyers or show programmes, or adding descriptions to online videos, you will be called upon to develop a vast array of *copy* in your role as a company leader. A style guide helps to apply consistency to this process, to help define and maintain the idea of your brand. Style guides are incredibly specific: relating to the exact use of colour in your logo and communications, to the rules around spelling, language, and grammar. Your style guide may extend to having templates for things such as flyers and social media posts, so that your work maintains a stylistic consistency across many years of different shows.

In PurpleDoor's style guide, for example, we have rules clarifying that PurpleDoor should always be spelt as one word, always with capital letters for Purple and Door. Similarly, after some initial debate, we removed the word 'The' from our name, going from The PurpleDoor to just PurpleDoor. 'The' causes all sorts of problems, not to mention the fact that people will never remember to spell it with a capital T. These finicky details are the whole purpose of a style guide. Having one and making sure everybody sticks to it, including external bodies such as the press when writing about you, helps to strengthen your brand and add professionalism to your communications.

> **Task:** As a group, develop a style guide for your new organisation. Think about spelling, formatting, fonts, and colours. A style guide is usually created in a program such as Photoshop and represents its 'rules' visually, so approach it in this way if you are able. In photo editing programs, colours can be represented exactly using colour codes. Don't forget to seek permission if you are using privately created fonts from the web.

Copywriting

Copy is the process of writing content for a marketing purpose. Writing good copy is a really useful skill to have, and although anyone can do copywriting this doesn't mean that all copy is equal. Copywriting should hook a reader and tell a story, evoking an emotion that makes them want to find out more. Copywriting can take many forms, from loglines to social media posts, from show descriptions to blogs, and developing a knack for good copywriting is a skill that is really worth developing. Understandably, it's a skillset very much in demand!

Good copy should be:

- Proof-read and free from grammatical errors. This sounds obvious, but mistakes do give off a bad impression and are easy to miss when you're rushing to get a review quote on your poster before the print deadline and you don't notice you've made a mistake until you look back at it with fresh eyes later. Ideally you should get your copy checked over by somebody else who will be more likely to notice errors you have overlooked, or you can try printing your work and reading it out loud. Any way of

encountering your work fresh helps you to spot errors. Reading your copy is particularly useful for spotting poor sentence construction: if you trip over your words and run out of breath, maybe your sentence needs simplifying!
- Linked to purpose. Your audience, your purpose and your outcome should always be linked. Put yourself in the shoes of the reader when planning any copy: who are they and what do they want to know? Each piece of copy exists for a different reason and a slightly different audience, and failing to understand the purpose can lead to copy that is pointless and time wasting. Your reader may not stick with you for that long, and good copy gets to the point and knows what it wants to achieve.
- Linked to a strong call to action. See more on this below!
- Free from jargon. Related to the last point, don't assume your audience are experts on the same subjects you are. Subject-related jargon can confuse and alienate a reader – showing an image from your technical rehearsal, or mentioning iambic pentameter in your show copy, might make total sense to you, but might be utterly baffling to your audience. Furthermore, unless your copy is for a specific audience with technical knowledge, it is likely to be more effective if it makes sense and engages a reader with no prior knowledge, so try and find a useful outsider to cast an eye and give their opinion.
- Simple. Keep your sentences simple and easy to read. In line with your tone of voice, keep language accessible and engaging, and don't try and fill it with unnecessary big words to make it sound more intelligent or academic. You're not writing an essay! Such attempts to upscale yourself are likely to be off-putting to your average reader.
- SEO friendly. For more on SEO, see below.

> **Task:** Take your last show (or pick a show you have seen, or worked on, if this is easier) and create some practice copy for it. You might develop an example Tweet, a Blog Post, a Press Release, and a Brochure entry, for example. With each, specify the target audience and the purpose before you begin. If you are working in a group, share your efforts and proof-read each other's efforts. It is a good idea to see if you can guess the audience and purpose from the copy alone.

Call to action

How do you get a member of the public to engage with your content, whether online or in-person? A useful methodology is in the call to action, which is a technique used to snap audience's out of their passivity so that they feel compelled to engage. 'Click here,' 'Buy now,' 'Don't miss out' are all examples of a call to action. Telling me to do something makes it easier for me to understand what is in it for me and what I will potentially achieve.

> **Task:** Review your last five social media posts. How did they do? Did any of them have a compelling call to action, or a strong reason why a user may feel compelled to engage? If not, think about how your post could have achieved that and experiment with applying this to your next post. After some trial and error, make sure you measure the impact of this new change to see whether your engagement has increased.

Making a campaign plan

A simple yet effective step you can take in the journey of selling your show is to develop a marketing calendar or campaign plan. These are really simple to set up and help you to forward-plan and visualise your marketing strategy, which in turn can help you to manage your workload and ensure that your marketing is strategically planned to build momentum and interest in the lead-up to opening.

As we will explore later, marketing takes a lot of time, skill, and money, and we can sometimes lose track of why a particular piece of material was created, and what impact it had. To alleviate this, consider adding a small justification to each item you list in your marketing calendar. Who is it for and why is this the right solution to reach them?

Four weeks until opening:

Table 6.1 Four week marketing plan

dd/mm/yy	Poster	Blog, social media, website
dd/mm/yy	Press Release Email #1	Email
dd/mm/yy		

Three weeks until opening:

Table 6.2 Three week marketing plan

dd/mm/yy	Production meeting photo teaser	Social media
dd/mm/yy		
dd/mm/yy	Story of the author	Blog

> **Task:** Develop a marketing calendar for your next show. If you're not sure on exact dates for the moment, just use placeholders. The key is to ensure you have time to achieve the marketing you want, but also to think strategically about how to build momentum over a given period of time. Should you release your trailer before or after your poster? These are creative decisions that should be taken to build excitement and

> anticipation. If you aren't opening a show at the moment, you can apply this same idea to the launch of your company, or the launch of a new feature (such as a new website). Alternatively, you can retrospectively go back to a previous production and map how your marketing occurred. With hindsight, was it strategically rolled out to maximum effect? What could you have done differently?

Measuring the success of your marketing efforts is important to help you refine and target your content creation (for both your current project and more broadly) and you should consider how you will achieve this at the planning stage. Develop marketing matrices for each of your campaigns to track and visualise that campaign's success. Think of a matrix like a form of graph, where you can chart two or more benefits in line with your outcomes. If we decide, for example, that the two most important features in a car are the price and the fuel efficiency, we could add price to the horizontal line and fuel efficiency to the vertical line. Every new car we developed would sit somewhere on that graph. There are an endless number of metrics we could use to determine success (common examples include click-through rates, email opens, number of sales etc.) but a good place to start for planning your own marketing campaign would be to map out your different audience segments against each of your benefits and communication methods.

Established marketing teams work with metrices in great depth, using a detailed range of software to track all manner of factors. Although this will be out of your scope, and could quickly become overwhelming for an organisation of your own scale, applying the principles and thinking behind this will be a sure-fire way to holding your marketing to account, regularly tracking and assessing its impact to increase engagement, and ultimately driving more business.

Offline marketing

Not everybody uses the internet and offline marketing can still be beneficial, even in an age of social media and online content creation. Offline marketing is far from being antiquated, and picking up a flyer or seeing a poster are still effective techniques for attracting an audience, particularly when you know they are looking for such content, in the foyer of a theatre for example. Offline marketing works well when it speaks to your online marketing – if an audience member has seen an advert for your work on Facebook and then sees the same picture on a flyer in town, the gentle reinforcement helps to create a link and repetition for a potential audience member.

Newsletters

Newsletters are a cheap and easy way to maintain direct access to your audience. A newsletter demonstrates a level of interest in your work that still suggests a degree of loyalty somewhat higher than a simple follow on social media (which is both easy to do and easy to ignore). To revisit the idea of our audience journey train, we might consider a newsletter signup a step towards becoming a low-paying customer.

Newsletter signups are simple for audiences, usually involving just a name and an email address, and you can offer benefits or freebies for those who sign up, which creates a motivation for doing so. Analytics allow useful insights into how your content was engaged with, which helps you to provide content that you know your audience enjoy. However, they need to be maintained and to deliver on their promise, whilst not becoming spam that audiences want to unsubscribe from. Due to the unfair reputation of newsletters adding to the noise and spam of our inboxes, this can be an obstacle for some people when signing up, so think of ways you can put people's fears to rest at the sign-up stage.

Websites and social media

The most tangible metric we tend to be familiar with at the present time is the number of followers we have on social media. These free platforms allow an unprecedented level of audience–artist communication which can be used to potentially reach massive audiences. Increasingly, though, platforms are being accused of becoming toxic places and of existing in an echo chamber. Crucially, followers on social media doesn't really give an indication that your show will sell well, and you should not obsess over this as a metric of any measurable success.

As the age of social media begins to mature, audiences have also come to expect different nuances on different platforms. It is unwise to post the same content, in the same way, across different platforms. Audiences use Facebook very differently to Snapchat or TikTok, while video content on YouTube is formatted and consumed for a different purpose to video content on Instagram, for example. This creates an ever-changing landscape which can quickly become exhausting to keep up with. Larger venues and companies employ multiple people to monitor the content on each of these platforms, so it is more important than ever to prioritise your content online and not to get pulled into what can easily be an overwhelming amount of work. The first step towards dealing with this as a new company is to pick one or two social platforms and prioritise them.

Younger readers might wonder whether websites are still important in the age of social media. They have certainly dropped in popularity somewhat since the early years of the millennium, but don't discard the importance of a website, particularly for those audiences who may be new to your work. A website can act as an easy to digest repository of information, which serves as a useful way for potential new audiences to find out about you and what you do. Having a website and an email address still serves as a mark of professionalism beyond a social media direct message, as well.

Getting the most out of your website

There are good websites and there are frustrating websites! Websites do require a level of technical expertise, even if you use a free website builder such as wix.com, and there are additional resources at the end of the chapter to help you delve deeper into the technical aspects of website creation. You don't need a PhD in Computer Science to build a website by any means, but it is important to be realistic about the time and effort they take to make a good one, so that your audience is able to access the content they are looking for and so that they are more likely to engage with the rest of your work.

When building or re-designing your website, keep in mind the following principles:

- Make it mobile friendly. More and more of your web traffic will access your site via a mobile device, and if your website takes a long time to load or is generally inaccessible for a mobile user, you will be using a huge section of your potential audience. Bear in mind that a large chunk of your mobile audience will have come from, or will subsequently go to, your social media channels, so ensuring good integration will help to smooth that journey and convert those audiences into loyal subscribers.
- Keep it up to date. This is more effort than it appears at first, but in order to support your SEO rating and to keep your website at the top of search results (more below), your website needs to avoid feeling like a historical archive. News and blog updates are an easy way to achieve this.
- Consider the audience journey. What are users wanting to find out when they land on your home page? Make that journey as smooth as possible so that audiences don't leave your website feeling frustrated or uninformed. With the help of analytic tools, you should be able to find out which pages and areas of your website generate the most traffic. Use this same insight to cull information which is not getting looked at: your well-written five-page summary of your founder's biography may be interesting to you, but if nobody is looking at it, streamline your user experience and get rid of it.
- Don't clutter. Keep your design simple, avoid including too many items, which will slow your website's load speed down, and keep copy accessible and easy to read. Users are coming to your website for a different reason than when they look at your Instagram profile, so consider audience and purpose to design a website that helps your audience achieve their aims, whether that's to book tickets, to find out how they can engage with you more, or to get in contact with you.

Email signatures

If you pay to set up your own website, which is worth doing for the professionalism this implies, your hosting package will also offer you an email application, which I would strongly recommend going for. This will give you your own company emails with the name of your company at the end. For example admin@mytheatrecompany.com. This is great because it gives you a veneer of professionalism and helps to organise company contact from your own personal emails.

You can and should add a signature to your email communications. As a guide, this should include:

- Your name
- Job title
- Pronouns
- Contact info – phone and email
- Website
- Company name / number / logo / address

Some theatres put information about their upcoming shows in their signatures, but it can honestly become overwhelming quite quickly. Keep yours simple, but remember your legal requirement to put company info on all of your communications. This also applies if you are writing formal letters, where you will need to include a *letterhead* with the name, company number, and registered address of your business.

SEO

Search engine optimisation (SEO) is a method of making sure audiences can find your website when they search for you online. SEO is big business these days with many specialists charging high fees to ensure your work appears on the first page of Google, but the basics can be utilised by everyone regardless of budget. It is worth mentioning again that if your company name is very similar to others, particularly if those others have been well established for longer, you will struggle in the battle for this important resource.

Search engine optimisation refers to the algorithmic process that goes into deciding what search results will appear first when a user searches for something on a search engine such as Google. Imagine you are searching for a shop nearby to buy apples. There are millions of shops selling apples in the world and you want to know the most relevant search result for you. Are you really going to spend hours searching multiple pages of search results? Of course not! You're most likely to find the closest option to you from one of the top three search results. It's therefore important to make sure you can be found when users are searching for you. Users might be searching for you directly – which is one challenge – but they might also be yet to discover you. A user might search for something along the lines of 'theatre companies near me,' and you would hope to be one of the first options that pops up when they do so. Utilising search engine optimisation is how we try to make that happen.

Ensure that your website contains *key words* in its written copy so that search engines can return your page when users search for those terms. On a search engine such as Google, start to type a search phrase and you will see Google try and finish your sentence for you: these are commonly searched for terms and will help you to figure out the sorts of words and phrases users are searching for, so that you can include them in your own website copy. The greater the number of other websites that link to your own, the higher your web page will *rank* in search engine results, so never pass up the opportunity to make sure a venue has a link back to your website. Running a regular blog can give you ample opportunity for key words and for others to link back to your work, which can help with your SEO, but if you are going to do this, make sure it is updated regularly. Your website speed is essential to your ranking and SEO optimisation, as search engines are beginning to penalise websites that take longer to load on mobile or computer devices.

Your website is not going to appear at the top of Google overnight, especially if you are relying on organic SEO and not making use of paid advertising. Your website needs to earn its stripes, by being well established, running smoothly, helping Google to know what it is, and making sure it is updated regularly. It may take weeks, months, or even years, especially if your company name is similar to other, more established competition.

> **Task:** Complete a selection of popular terms searches in Google to find out what common phrases people are searching for in your area/sector. Try and think broadly about this – people might be searching for something obvious such as 'performing arts in Edinburgh' or they might be searching more vaguely for terms such as 'things to do at the weekend in London.' Although you need to think outside the box with this, you also need to stay accurate to what you offer, so don't try and invite people searching for acting classes if you don't do that, as length of engagement on your site is another key metric in SEO. This is to prevent spam and clickbait. Identify up to ten key words or phrases you can reasonably embed into your website and make sure they pop up in the content on your pages. Using a phrase like 'theatre company' or 'drama' can be so obvious that you don't actually include it, but see these as being like little flags waving to Google when people search for those terms.

Utilising key words can be a useful tool for increasing your SEO. Relevance is the name of the game here and you should first conduct some key word research to help you tap into this valuable resource. Make use of Google's autocomplete feature to see what popular words and phrases users are searching for when searching for companies like yours. How you actually add key words to your website will depend on the specifics of how you are building it, but every good website builder should have this feature somewhere.

Webpage speed

Ensuring your website loads smoothly and quickly on a range of devices is important to attract customer attention and improve your SEO. According to research from Kissmetrics, 47% of customers expect websites to load in less than two seconds, and 40% will leave a page completely if it takes longer than three seconds to load. You are potentially losing a huge portion of your audience before you've even started if your website runs slowly, and search engines are now indexing results to prioritise sites that load faster on both mobile and desktop devices.

The first place you should look if you are having website loading issues is the tools provided by your website host. There is an extensive list of tips provided in the chapter resources, but these are relatively technical, and you should make sure you are confident carrying them out before trying them yourself. One easy tip most people can follow, however, is to reduce the volume and size of content on your website. The more information your site contains, the longer it takes to load (in technical terms, the more HTTP requests it makes) and images, embedded social media, and videos can be huge culprits when it comes to sluggish performance, so be really strict about what an element adds before deciding to include it. Use Photoshop or an online compression tool to reduce the size of your image files, whilst trying to maintain quality. This step alone may provide the boost you need to get off the starting line. If you're wondering why this isn't the case for social media and places like YouTube – it is – they all add their own compression but it's taken out of your hands. There are several links in the resource section of this chapter with step-by-step guides for each of these areas, which I would advise working through within the context of your own site. They've been chosen for their accessibility, so hopefully they'll make your website better regardless of your experience level.

Of course, you can outsource almost everything related to websites, from the design and build to optimisation and mobile functionality. You won't be surprised to hear that this costs a lot, in the region of four to five figures, so only go down this route if you can be sure your website is having enough impact to warrant the expense.

Pay per click advertising

Most of the advertising online works on a pay per click (PPC) model, where you set a daily budget, and each subsequent click on your advert is charged from this. It can be tempting to think that spending more money will equal a broader reach, or that the relative simplicity of setting up PPC on platforms such as Google will be easy advertising. Unfortunately, services such as Google consider a number of factors when deciding where and when to place your advert, including the relevance of your key words, the past performance of your campaigns, and the relevance of the page you are linking to. In this context, the battle for eyeballs is not as simple as simply spending money and the field is not as democratic as it may appear.

With online adverts the key word is *relevance*, and you should ensure that you take the time to make adverts that are specifically targeted with a clearly defined target audience, a strong purpose, and a clear call to action. Google provide a range of helpful advice to understand and fully utilise PPC on their platforms, which I have linked to in the resource section of this chapter.

Google business profile

Nearly 90% of people use Google when searching online. Google offers services for business information to appear at the top of search results, which is a free and easy step to help audiences find you and increase your credibility. If you've ever searched for a business online and seen the logo and maps information at the top of the page, you'll be familiar with business profiles.

Sign up for a Google business account and make sure your information is completed and up to date. It is a relatively straightforward process, and you can sign up to receive regular updates, in which Google will let you know how many people searched for your business each week. As audiences come to expect this more and more, the simple process of setting up a business profile can be an easy win to increase credibility for your new business.

Posters: what to include

The best strategy to follow when designing a poster or flyer is to find an example that you like and copy the heck out of it. Large companies have refined their marketing through years of experience and skilled labour, so it is no bad thing to take inspiration from those elements that work well, providing, of course, that this fits within your broader brand and ethos. Obviously, I don't advocate copying carte blanche the work of another organisation, particularly not one on your doorstep, but do pay attention to those strategies and techniques that work. Similarly, before moving forward on any design work make sure you check whether your venue needs/wants one, and check what size displays are available.

It can be tempting to want to put too much info on a poster or a flyer, but the guide below can be a good place to start. Make sure your flyers and posters contain:

- The name of the show
- A graphic
- The venue
- The run dates
- Where to find tickets.

You might be obliged to include funding logos as part of your funding requirements, and the logo of the venue. Accessibility info is something to consider depending on context: if posting on your own channels you may want to make patrons aware of potential access issues they may need to consider, particularly if they aren't familiar with the venue. For posters to be displayed at the venue, you should check with the venue whether there is information to be included. You normally have to have your posters signed off by venues.

Avoid:

- Travel and parking information
- Run times
- Cast and crew information, unless a name is likely to be a selling factor
- Pricing information, unless the price of your tickets is likely to be a selling factor.

Posters need to capture initial interest and then inspire a potential customer to find out more. Overloaded posters can confuse and obfuscate the key information. Audiences may do no more than think 'that seems interesting' and take a photo or jot down a website, so make this process as easy as possible and don't assume that they will have the time and inclination to read an essay about your show there and then.

As with all graphic design you should consider your key principles when designing graphics. Make sure text is readable and that colours don't clash and consider accessibility when electing colours that some users may not be able to engage with easily. There is a comprehensive guide about colour accessibility provided in the resource section of this chapter.

Reaching audiences in person

In the good old days, we couldn't just post a Tweet and forget about our audiences, we actually had to go out and find them! One of the most enduring elements of being an emerging theatre company, particularly if you are taking your work to festivals (more on this in Chapter 11) is flyer-ing. The nature of live performance means that you may, on occasion, be thrust into places where you have no built audience, or where you are expected to find an audience 'on the ground.' While this can be intimidating for newcomers – there's nothing quite like the rejection of a disinterested public to yet another flyer-ing artist – it's also a great way to build resilience and to establish a powerful connection with those few people whose interest you do pique.

Flyer-ing is difficult and thankless and can feel very awkward at first. The fact that most people look past you as if you're invisible is both a blessing and a curse. It can knock your confidence, but when you realise that this is nothing personal, it can be an empowering way to get the job done.

Of course, this isn't the only use for flyers, and you should look for opportunities in your local area to display them. The venue will usually display flyers for upcoming shows, as will local shops and places of interest. Remember that it is illegal to flyer through people's letterboxes!

Freebies and discounts

When it comes to getting bums on seats, a producer's gotta do what a producer's gotta do. When setting your *pricing strategy*, have a look at other shows playing at your venue and work to an average of the different prices. Most venues will have a range of work from different sizes and styles of companies, so it is likely that prices will vary, but working out where to position yourself will be important to catching an audience's attention. Depending on the type of venue and the nature of your contract, you may or may not have a say in pricing strategy, but for straight-hire venues and fringe it is likely to be your choice. You obviously don't want your tickets to be so expensive that your audience are outpriced – remember, early on they will be taking a lot of *risks* by coming to see you – but you equally don't want to sell yourself short on ticket sales when you could easily have made some more money.

Consider a range of tactics when it comes to generating a buzz for your show and getting those tickets moving:

- Offer *discount codes* to selected groups or cheaper tickets on less appealing performance days (Mondays and Tuesdays, I'm looking at you!). Don't do this without first discussing with the marketing department of a venue though.
- Conduct flash mobs or other attention grabbing stunts near the theatre.
- Partner with another company to offer bulk discounts if audiences come to see both shows (this is known as *cross-selling* – if you've ever worked in hospitality you might be familiar with up-selling; these are both useful techniques).
- Give away free tickets by running competitions. Limit numbers to encourage engagement, for example, by making it only open to people who subscribe to your newsletter.
- Add special codes to flyers to give audience's reduced prices. This makes them feel special and reduces wastage as they feel incentivised to keep the flyer.
- Explore subscriptions and loyalty discounts where possible.

There are a million ways to sell tickets and your options are only limited by your imagination.

Contacting press and the press release

Generally speaking, you will want to contact press for two reasons. Firstly, newspapers and radio stations will often run features on their local arts offerings and will cover shows before they open. This is a really valuable opportunity to reach a wider audience who may not be following you on social media and is something you should always include in your marketing strategy. Speaking with the press can also be an opportunity to book in a review.

Press previews are great because they are essentially free promotion. Reviews, especially good ones, can be helpful in building momentum and word of mouth around a show, but only if the show will run for long enough after the review is published for its impact to be felt. Where this isn't possible, legacy reviews of past productions can help to create a kudos and seal of quality around your work.

To contact press you will need a *press release*. A press release is a short document which radio producers and newspaper editors will look at before deciding whether you are *newsworthy* enough to cover. This really is about grabbing attention and you are always going to be competing against all the other shows, big and small, vying for the attention of those same editors.

A good press release needs to be short and snappy: anything over one page is too long. Format it nicely in a Word document beforehand but get into the habit of copying your release into the body of the email itself. Editors tend to prefer this as it saves them having to download your file and open it, which in turn clogs up their inbox and becomes easier to lose track of.

To catch the attention of the press, you need to give some thought to your story. You are trying to sell a show, but journalists are trying to find stories with local resonance, so think about the newsworthiness of your show before writing your release. It really doesn't matter if your show is good, you need to remember that the press are trying to make sure *their* story is good. If you are using local actors, telling a local story, or you have garnered attention from a celebrity, anything that can help your story become newsworthy to their readership is a huge help for editors and will be much more likely to make your press release a success.

Find your hook and focus on that. The plot of your show and its production quality are likely to be incidental at best. Finding a hook is much more difficult than it sounds, especially when you remember that you're competing against all the other shows with paid publicists and marketing departments competing for the same airtime or page space.

The press are very unlikely to print your logo or show poster, but an engaging rehearsal or production photo can be a big benefit to getting your story printed and to attracting eyeballs. Make sure you finish any press release with a summary of dates, times, prices, and where people can buy tickets.

Although it can be extremely tempting to spam every local journalist you can find on Google and email them en masse with a generic 'Hi there!' it is important to remember that (a) journalists are human beings and (b) they can see right through that tactic. It does take more time and effort but taking time to try and establish a relationship between you and a press contact can be the difference between getting a reply or not. For the love of all things Holy, when contacting journalists (or anyone for that matter!) take the time to spell their name right, use the correct pronouns, and avoid 'Dear Sir/Madam.' Depending on the openness of the venue and your relationship with them, you may be able to gain access to their press list. This is obviously beneficial to you, but also something to be treated with respect, as you don't want to annoy your venue by being dismissive or unprofessional with press contacts. If you have access to these, see that as a privilege and not a right and treat it with respect.

There is a fine balance to emailing press to maximise the opportunity for exposure. Too early and they will see no relevance in running your story yet, too late and it'll be too short notice for people to take the opportunity to come and see your show. While there is no golden rule for this, a few weeks before you open is a good time to make contact, leaving yourself time for a polite chase up email a week later if you still haven't had a reply.

Digital theatre and online work

Theatre can be filmed for a variety of reasons, both for posterity or to extend an audience beyond the physical space. Some practitioners are vocally against the filming of theatre, arguing that it goes against the ephemeral essence of the form. A filmed show is not the same experience as a live production, but I believe audiences are intelligent and digitally savvy enough to know this and to appreciate the bigger picture. Such conservative attitudes risk sounded outdated and pretentious. Filmed theatre doesn't change the fact that there was a live experience which audiences could engage with in the first place.

Filmed shows can be made available via a range of platforms, and you may be aware of the worldwide cinema screenings that large organisations such as the Met or the National Theatre have been producing for several years now. The Covid-19 pandemic created further opportunities for utilising the power of services such as YouTube to reach a much wider audience.

Streaming online

Streaming online on platforms such as YouTube has a range of benefits. These services can be utilised to host live performances in real time, or to archive productions, with options to make work available for limited time periods or for much longer. Although there are services you can pay for, I would recommend that for most readers free accounts with YouTube would be sufficient.

Streaming: technical considerations

In order to stream work live, you will need a device with access to YouTube (or an alternative streamer). This could be as simple as a mobile phone, but I would advise against this as phone cameras and microphones are still not as reliable as more advanced equipment, especially for the wide range of volume and light levels typical of most theatre productions.

You will need camera and sound equipment in order to capture your performance. In most cases this will mean, as a minimum:

- A camera
- A microphone
- A tripod.

Each extra angle you want to capture your show from will require additional cameras and tripods. Cameras should have batteries that will last the duration of the show (or have spares ready) and should ideally be good at filming in low light. Theatre productions have huge *contrast* in their visual images (contrast relates to the difference between dark and bright parts of an image) and consumer quality cameras can result in either fuzzy dark images or overblown 'overexposed' bright sections.

Microphones are a tricky question to consider due to the number of options, and each presents its own problem. With microphones, the general rule is that the further away the microphone is from the mouth of the person speaking, the more background noise it will also pick up. You could hang several microphones above your stage space: this can be a cheap and easy way of broadly capturing the whole space, or you could consider lavalier mics which will attach to each individual performer. You can source invisible versions of these mics, which can be taped to actors' hairlines (similar to mics used generally in musical theatre) but these need time to ensure actors are comfortable rehearsing with them without hitting them. Be careful not to place a microphone too near to a speaker, as this will create a *feedback loop*, which does not sound pleasant!

When you have your cameras and microphones, they need somewhere to be plugged in to. If you are working with a single camera and nothing else, you might be able to connect this directly to your laptop via USB or similar. Not all cameras and laptops will support this, so check online before you buy.

For more advanced setups, you need an interface. An interface takes the signals from your different sources and organises these before sending them to the laptop. For sound, you will need a mixing desk (this is exactly the same process as using sound in your production), which can control the individual mic levels before sending these to the laptop. If you are already using mics for your production for amplification purposes, you can plug into this system. Usually mixing desks will have an output connection where you can connect a *jack* or *mini-jack* to the desk at one end and your laptop at the other.

If you are using multiple cameras, you need a system to *cut* between them. This is called multi-camera, and is the same system that you see any time you watch a live-TV show like a gameshow or the news. TV production companies will pay tens of thousands of pounds for advanced multi-cam setups, including features such as live-greenscreen and digital sets. Until recently, this was an impenetrably expensive industry, but recent years have seen the rise of many consumer 'video switchers' primarily to support YouTubers and other content creators. These switchers will then plug directly into your device, with the feed going straight to your YouTube stream.

The link to your live-stream can go live in advance as a holding page. On the day, audiences are able to interact with your show in a range of ways, but spend time setting parameters around this, as you do have moderator privileges to control the level and type of audience engagement. You can, for example, turn off the live comments chat altogether.

Increasingly, you can integrate your stream with a range of payment options so that audiences can donate money to you directly. If you don't want to charge money for a digital ticket, this can be a good way of receiving direct support in a method that is consumer led.

Obviously, a successful stream relies on a strong internet connection, both for the sender and the receiver. You will place a great deal of strain on your internet connection if you are streaming live and you should never do it over mobile data or Wi-Fi.

Captioning and access

Streaming services increasingly offer options for making your work more accessible via captioning. For pre-recorded material, you can upload your own captions, or live shows can be transcribed automatically via an algorithm. Although the technology behind these services is improving all the time, they're not great to rely on, and any unusual or highly specific words can come out horrifically wrong!

For any other video upload – trailers, interviews, pre-recorded shows – get into the habit of adding captions unless it is physically impossible to do so. Editing software such as Premiere Pro and Davinci Resolve have advanced features for adding captions quite easily, or you can add these to your YouTube uploads through their portal. This is really quite an easy gesture to help ensure that your work can be widely appreciated, so do try and build in time to add these when producing any video content for your company.

Price and access

Most streaming services allow free and open access for anyone to access your stream. You can limit this (by making the link private, for example) but you may need to explore options for a paywall (a private link or password protection, for example) if you need people to pay before viewing. Some services embed this feature directly, or you might operate through a separate e-commerce function on your website, with people receiving the link once they have paid. Of course, you need to consider the fact that people could simply share that link with others who have not paid.

The pandemic saw many new audiences engaging with theatre digitally. The essence of this technology helps to support and increase diversity and accessibility, and it is arguably difficult to defend charging large sums for digital screenings. For many, accessing theatre for free on platforms such as YouTube might be the start of a longer-term relationship, where that same audience member may come and see the show in person or may feel comfortable to visit in the future, where they might not have done before. Consider who you include and exclude through your online streaming strategy.

Remember the bigger picture

It's a useful time to remind you again of the effort-to-output ratio that you should always bear in mind when thinking about marketing. It can be super easy to get dragged down rabbit holes, sometimes very productive and exciting rabbit holes, only to later realise that the effort didn't result in much return. Arguably, it can be just as easy not to realise how ineffective something has been, if you don't have a system for measuring impact. If you produced some flyers, did a radio show, launched a Twitter page, and made a video trailer, can you say with any certainty how many tickets the flyers helped to sell?

Videography might be the worst offender here, simply because of the amount of time it can take to produce. Here's where you should take advantage of the wealth of social media data available to you: focus on content that gets engagement. A trailer or a behind-the-scenes documentary might seem like a great idea, but in reality it is much more likely that it will get a lot of views and not a lot of click-through. It can be easier than you think to be really self-indulgent with your marketing, and when your time and money are short, you need to keep laser focused on what will produce a good return for your investment.

Chapter Resources

Theatre marketing

'Create a theatre marketing plan that drives revenue,' Spektrix (29th May 2019), www.spektrix.com/en-gb/blog/how-to-create-a-theatre-marketing-plan-that-drives-up-revenue-us

Griffin, Caroline, 'This way up: A flat-pack guide to marketing the Arts,' Arts Marketing Association, www.culturehive.co.uk/wp-content/uploads/2013/04/This-Way-Up2.pdf

Hill, Liz, *Creative Arts Marketing*, 3rd edition (Routledge, Oxon, 2018)

Kaiser, Michael, *The Art of the Turnaround: Creating and maintaining healthy arts organizations* (Brandeis University Press, Lebanon New Hampshire, 2008)

Mabbit, Clay, 'The big list of theatre marketing tactics,' Sold Out Run, https://soldoutrun.com/theatre-marketing-tactics/

O'Donnell, Trevor, 'Marketing the arts to death: How lazy language is killing culture,' https://trevorodonnell.com/books/

Copywriting

Scorfield, Hannah, 'Copywriting tips and tricks: a complete guide,' Salt Agency (14th January 2022), https://salt.agency/blog/beginners-copywriting-a-guide/#styles

Websites

'5 ways to get the most out of your website,' Snapshot, https://snapshotinteractive.com/5-ways-to-get-the-most-out-of-your-website/

McCormick, Kristen, '39 ways to increase traffic to your website,' Wordstream (3rd September 2022), www.wordstream.com/blog/ws/2014/08/14/increase-traffic-to-my-website

Mission statements

Wadeson, Ivan, 'The relationship between mission statements and the people they serve,' Culture Hive, www.culturehive.co.uk/resources/17116/

Access

Black, Aymie, 'A 10-step guide to making your social media content accessible,' Big Blog Scotland (15th April 2020), https://bigblogscotland.org.uk/2020/04/15/a-10-step-guide-to-make-your-social-media-content-more-accessible/?utm_source=The%20Audience%20Agency&utm_medium=email&utm_campaign=11559283_Digital%20Snapshot%20109&dm_i=1X0O,6VR77,WS4JY0,RMPD6,1

Fitzgerald, Anna, 'How to identify web accessible colours for products & websites,' HubSpot, https://blog.hubspot.com/website/how-to-identify-web-accessible-colors-for-products-websites

Read, Alice, 'Our web accessibility journey as a 'visual arts' organisation,' Medium (14th October 2019), https://medium.com/digipaul/our-web-accessibility-journey-as-a-visual-arts-organisation-83b0ac1faf51

RSC, 'Visual story for the relaxed performance,' Royal Shakespeare Company, https://cdn2.rsc.org.uk/sitefinity/access-pdfs/dream2016visualstory.pdf?sfvrsn=2

'The difference engine: Discrete new tool for making events and performances accessible,' Difference Engine, https://differenceengine.talkingbirds.co.uk/audience/

Online audience building

'20 ways to speed up your website and improve conversion in 2022,' Crazy Egg (30th September 2021), www.crazyegg.com/blog/speed-up-your-website/

Google, 'Google ads help,' Google.com, https://support.google.com/google-ads/?hl=en-GB#topic=10286612

Google, 'Stand out on Google with a free business profile,' Google.com, www.google.com/intl/en_uk/business/

'How loading time affects your bottom line,' Kiss Metrics, https://blog.kissmetrics.com/wp-content/uploads/2011/04/loading-time.pdf

Pacuet, Miranda, '5 SEO mistakes that will hold your business back,' Constant Contact (8th February 2022), www.constantcontact.com/blog/seo-mistakes/

Streaming

OBS Studio, https://obsproject.com/

Inclusivity

Cameron, Dawn, 'How diverse are we really?' Culture Hive (July 2021), www.culturehive.co.uk/wp-content/uploads/2021/09/How_diverse_are_we_really_CPP_research_September_20211.pdf

Gladwell, Holly, 'Putting inclusivity front and centre,' Culture Hive, www.culturehive.co.uk/resources/putting-inclusivity-front-and-centre/

Audience development

'Arts audiences: Insight,' Arts Council, www.artscouncil.org.uk/sites/default/files/download-file/arts_audience_insight_2011.pdf

'Audience Spectrum: The most powerful segmentation tool for the cultural sector,' The Audience Agency, www.theaudienceagency.org/audience-finder-data-tools/audience-spectrum

'Creating an effective audience development plan,' The Audience Agency, www.theaudienceagency.org/asset/2157

Jarboe, Greg, 'What is a content marketing matrix and do we need one?' *Search Engine Journal* (12th January 2022), www.searchenginejournal.com/content-marketing-matrix/431529/#close

'Online audiences: Resources,' The Space, www.thespace.org/resources

'Understanding audience segments,' PurpleSeven, https://purpleseven.screenstepslive.com/s/11891/m/90064/l/1145042-understanding-the-segments-in-detail

'The immersive audience journey: An overview of audience insights and perspectives on immersive art, culture and entertainment,' Audience of the Future, https://audienceofthefuture.live/wp-content/uploads/2020/07/Audience-of-the-Future_The-Immersive-Journey-Report_July-2020.pdf

7 Logistics of Production

It is finally time to create work. It can often feel as though actual creativity comes at the bottom of your priority list when working in a company, but this is what it's all about, and when it goes well, there is nothing more enjoyable.

Although every creative process will be different, this chapter aims to take a fly-by look through a typical production process for the type and scale of work you are likely to be creating in your early years. It does not aim to replicate the wealth of excellent reading material already available on creative process, and I have linked to many of these in the resource section. As with everything, there are many pressures that impact your ability to create the perfect rehearsal process and balancing your production's artistic integrity with the many pressures of real-world logistics is one of the big challenges of artistic creation.

Rehearsal space

Every production needs somewhere to be rehearsed. You will already have experience of rehearsal studios from your college or university experience, and often it can be a helpful first port of call to see if you can take advantage of these as graduates of the institution.

Regrettably, high quality affordable rehearsal space for theatrical performance is somewhat rare. University spaces can often be the best spaces due to the money and size of space available. Although most major cities will have a creative hub of rehearsal space, much of this is often tailored towards bands and music production, and on the occasion that they are of respectable quality, they are often, by their nature, much smaller than you will need for rehearsing a show.

It is usually unlikely to find a perfect rehearsal space; indeed, many major theatres struggle with this, also. But it is important to have an understanding of what an ideal rehearsal space should have, so that you can make an informed decision of where to compromise when looking at the options available to you.

A rehearsal studio should ideally be:

- *Light*: We focus and retain our energy for longer in well-lit, open spaces. Artificial light can vary wildly and can cause significant strain to actors when it is patchy and below ideal levels.

- *Ventilated*: A similar point, this also helps to create an environment that is fresh and pleasant to work in. Essential when doing more physical work!
- *Temperature regulated*: Rooms that are too hot can be very inhibitive towards energy levels and focus. Rooms that are too cold often necessitate wearing additional layers, which makes any sort of intimate, connected rehearsal very difficult to achieve.
- *Spacious*: You should ideally have enough space to 'mark out' your whole performance area, with enough room for your creative team to sit apart from the show to offer some perspective. This is often difficult to achieve in practice, as larger rooms tend to cost more in hire fees, but it is something to work towards.
- *Secure*: Your cast need to feel safe and relaxed, and need to feel comfortable with leaving their belongings, including at breaks etc.
- *Easy to access*: Nothing creates a bad start to a rehearsal more than actors arriving in a bad mood, especially when they've travelled halfway across the city to get there. Think about the journey of all your team and try to split it if possible.

Casting

Draw up a list of characters and any important information needed for each. Casting is an essential part of any production process and getting it right can make or break a production.

Some roles may require specific demographic requirements, but you should remain open to the possibility of alternatives. Always think inclusively and openly about your casting choices, particularly in older plays, where white, male casting has been taken as 'correct' for too long.

You must decide whether you will hold an open call or whether you would like actors to audition for specific roles. Both have pros and cons, but an open casting can be an excellent way to see ideas and partnerships that you would otherwise have overlooked. Our production of *Hamlet* cast a female in the title role only after a successful audition. This changed the entire concept of the production and made all the other castings more exciting and meaningful, entirely because we were open to the possibility of who walked through the door.

Whichever way you choose to audition, you must be clear and transparent with your potential actors about what is expected and what is offered in return. People are time precious, and actors will spend a lot longer than you realise thinking and preparing for your audition, so it is entirely appropriate that you are clear and communicative with them about the process. You can run your casting however you like but putting the actor's experience at the centre of your thinking is a great way to help them to give you the performance you are looking for.

There are numerous ways you can run a casting, not least driven by personal preference and the needs of the specific production. If you would like a monologue, decide in advance if you will provide a specific text or if you'd like the actor to select their own. Either way, aim for between two and three minutes. Remember that some actors perform better than others under audition pressures, which, after all, is a very artificial setup for them to deliver good work. Ideally, your audition space should be quiet and welcoming, with a separate area for people to wait before being seen. If you're able to provide water and easy to access toilet facilities, taking time to be courteous now will pay off in numerous ways for you later.

If you're able to give people an audition slot, aim to stick to it and be respectful of the time people have taken to visit you. People will be nervous, and some will be inexperienced – neither of these things equate to a lack of skill. When an actor first comes into a room, introduce yourself and your team members, welcome them briefly and then jump into the first audition speech. Don't drag out too much conversation at this stage, and certainly don't overload the actor with information about the production – all they will be thinking about is the audition! Much better to start with this so that you can engage with the actor after they have performed.

In the audition itself, you should be looking for openness, integrity, and good communication. You want to know that the person auditioning for you has technical skill and can respond well to direction. You are looking for a good listener, who has flexibility and spontaneity. It is typical to give the actor some pointers after their first reading to see how they take direction. You should approach this process exactly as you would in rehearsal, as it gives the actor a chance to see a glimpse into your process. Remember though that these actors are new to you, so keep any feedback and direction positive and supportive. If there was something the actor did that you weren't sure about, don't address it directly as this could make them uncomfortable. Instead, be creative with your pointers to see if you can conjure something different from the performer to help you make a well-judged casting.

In the wake of the pandemic, some auditioning has moved online, and although this brings benefits, I would draw your focus to the many benefits of the in-person casting which you may be missing out on. Particularly for theatre work, casting online or requesting self-tapes can be limiting, as it does little to give you a sense of the actor's presence, their whole body or their voice. These might be useful first-stage auditions, however, with an in-person audition to follow, but when working online do try and get a sense of more than just head and shoulders and be respectful to the fact that people will feel drained quickly and potentially more restricted.

Depending on the scale and size of your auditions, you may plan to operate recalls, where you invite a select group to audition with you again. There is no set method for recalls, but I would advise trying to see something different a second time round (rather than repeating the same audition), whilst being respectful of the actor's time. You should have been clear about the stages of audition at the time of posting the casting call, but do remind the performer of the plans for recall and when they should expect to hear from you, as a courtesy.

Finally, make your decision as quickly as practical and make a point to let the actors know. There is nothing worse than not being told the outcome of an audition, or worse, finding out through a social media announcement that you didn't get a job. Actors have given you time and attention and they deserve the respect of a timely response to your call. Even if you weren't impressed, even if you didn't think they'd tried, don't assume that you know what's going on in their lives and give them the respect of a timely, grateful follow-up.

Venue communication

In Chapter 12 we will look at the specifics of finding a venue, getting programmed, and signing contracts. For now, let us focus on what happens once you have a performance space in mind. Communication with your venue(s) is essential to ensure things run smoothly on both sides, and to avoid any unnecessary hold-ups on the day. Your time at the venue will likely be very brief before your performance, so you should make it a principle aim of rehearsals to ensure that everyone knows something about the space they will eventually be performing in.

You may be able to get a tour around your venue in advance, but this is not something they are obligated to provide and the general level of activity in a theatre can make this difficult to accommodate. However, anything is better than going in blind, especially if you are completely new to a venue, so do see if this is possible before signing a contract. Failing this, going to see a performance at the venue can give you a limited, but nevertheless, helpful perspective on the venue's quirks, its benefits, and its limitations.

Venues will usually be proactive about establishing key lines of communication between you and the appropriate departments. Of particular importance at this stage is to receive the key technical information for the performance space and any information regarding performance limitations. Many venues won't allow naked flames or smoking on stage, for instance, and it is better to know this now rather than on the day of your get-in. Anything that has the potential to cause a health and safety issue for the cast, the venue staff, or the audience, is something the venue will need to know about and approve in advance. Although you may not have all the answers regarding your finished piece at this stage, out of respect and courtesy you should ensure you're familiar with the contract guidelines and not expect a venue to permit you to use water or cigarettes, for example, with very little notice. Apart from the obvious health and safety implications, venues have their own legal obligations to maintain, and they may need to get permission from the local council or another body, which is another reason to respect their systems and time frames. On a related note, don't try and hide issues like this from the venue technicians. It can seem like a headache or a creative blow to have your impulses interrogated and restricted at this point, but breaching health and safety with an unannounced live flame is reckless and irresponsible, and the venue are well within their right to halt your show mid-performance if you do this. This can also extend to things like strobes and smoke machines, so always triple check your contract or speak with the venue technician directly to avoid issues later.

The technical information supplied by the venue will also allow you to mark out your rehearsal space. Again, there are excellent resources elsewhere regarding the preferred way to lay out a rehearsal room, but it is helpful to consider this pragmatically from the perspective of a small touring company. You are very likely to be sharing or hiring a rehearsal space. You may be touring to several venues with wildly different stage sizes and layouts. Your rehearsal space is likely to be too small to fully mark out your stage, as you would like. All of these very real challenges are part and parcel of working in small-scale theatre, and you should approach each of them head on for the clarity and security of your cast and crew. Even if you have seen a performance space, your cast may only have your words to go on, which can be incredibly frightening, especially when technical time before performance is likely to be short.

Ideally, you will mark out your entire stage space and any key elements of the set with tape, so that your cast and crew have a to-scale overview of the stage and their *blocking*. If this is not possible, consider where you can make changes and communicate this thinking with your cast. You may not want to introduce this until later in the creative process, especially if you aren't sure what shape your finished performance will take. If this is the case, it is still important to share the bricks and mortar specifics of the stage space with your cast so that they understand the framework they are performing in. Your own photos and videos, venue photos from the internet, and *technical plans* can all help with this. Your time in the venue before your opening night will be limited, so you need to mitigate against any unnecessary surprises for yourself or your team.

Finally, as you move into the development stages of production, don't let your contract with the venue sit in a drawer forgotten. The contract will lay out a range of important dos and don'ts, which you will need to build into your artistic plans. There may be restrictions on what you can do on stage (for issues of health and safety) and there will likely be specified technical, marketing, and facilities contras which you may have to pay for. As always, speak to the venue if anything is unclear.

A note on technical plans

Every venue should be able to provide you with technical plans to show the size and layout of the space and the positioning of the *lighting rig*. For more advanced venues, this will be a multi-page venue document containing multiple Computer Aided Design (CAD) drawings and lots of technical graphs you may feel overwhelmed by. For smaller venues, this may be little more than a rudimentary list of the kit available. While this can be overwhelming, this document has been developed to support every possible show that may ever come into the space, so the first step is to filter out what you don't need to know. At the most basic level, you may only need to be aware of the available entrances and exits, the stage size and the lights available. If you have a technician in your team, their expertise will be invaluable, but if you don't, make sure you spend the time to understand the important information from the venue so that you are prepared. You can always communicate directly with the venue technical team, but remember, they will be busy and are often part-time or freelance at smaller fringe venues. Their obligation to you may only begin when you arrive for your *get-in*, so do what you can before pestering them.

Scheduling

Scheduling a rehearsal process is a fine art. The greater the number of components (scenes/actors/rehearsal times), the more impossible this task can feel. A good producer will understand that a schedule is a live document and subject to change, but creating one is incredibly important to ensure that the production will be ready on time and for your cast and crew to know when they will be needed.

It is always helpful to start with the scenes and the availability of your actors. Print a blank calendar as a rough draft and write down the dates when certain actors aren't available. After that, it's a game of trying to maintain the integrity of your ideal rehearsal schedule as much as you can.

Be mindful of your actor's time and try to work with them where you can. How long a scene will take to rehearse is a question you will gain a judgement for with experience, but don't ever get an actor to attend a rehearsal that you won't end up using them for. In film, different scenes that share the same location are often filmed on the same day for ease of logistics. This is a good approach to take with scheduling, and the more you don't waste the time of your actors, the more they will work with you.

Ideally, you would want to build up your play gradually, starting with a read through, then text work, improv, and getting it on its feet. You will then move to a rough block, before refining the play scene by scene and working towards run-throughs. This is not always possible when working around an actor's availability, and it is a difficult balance to strike. However, I would encourage you to be imaginative with your scheduling, and to see the pros and cons in different structural approaches. How would it help your cast and the production if you didn't have a read through? Or if you had a run-through halfway through rehearsals? Or if you explored the end of the play first? When an ideal may not be possible to reach, it is up to you to be creative in finding solutions to get the most out of the time that you have.

If you are devising a piece or working with a text that is not traditionally scene-based, try and find similar ways of delineating chunks for the purpose of your schedule. Sometimes it can be helpful to start backwards. When is your performance date? What do you need to have achieved by that date, etc., etc.

Call times

In rehearsal and during production, the show producer or stage manager will need to allocate call times so that actors know where to be and when. If you are working in a fringe/un-paid context, you can operate this in a way best suited to the availability of your cast, but when working professionally with paid actors you will need to ensure that these times (including the allocation of breaks) are in line with contractual and union guidelines. Going over these times – if a rehearsal has overrun, or if you need to schedule an extra week – can be very expensive, as this will trigger overtime payments. You don't need to be in the dark about this though as there are lots of resources to guide you through the specifics in your territory, but it is important when scheduling to think carefully so as to avoid this at the outset.

Good rehearsal practice and inclusivity

Each director and company will have their own style and artistic approach, based on their values and the type of work being created. This is to be encouraged, and is an inherent part of the creative process. However, directorial vision or creative methodologies should never be used as an excuse for poor people management, safety, or respect. Almost every creative urge or impulse can be better fed and supported through *effective* rehearsal practices that place the well-being and needs of the company at its centre. Be wary of anyone or anything that seeks to suggest otherwise, in the name of art.

On a similar note, make sure to take time to consider the content of your show and how it may impact your cast in rehearsal. Shows can often explore a range of difficult topics, and ensuring there are trigger warnings and systems in place to support cast members who may be affected is important for you to consider. Shows are increasingly making use of intimacy coordinators to support the direction of scenes requiring physical intimacy or nudity between performers, and you should view the staging of such content with the same precision, choreography, and focus as you would a fight scene or a dance. Issuing trigger warnings to your cast and building in time for de-briefs, effective warm-ups and sensitive scheduling, can all make the world of difference to ensuring the creation of a safe space where your performers are able to create their best work. Don't ever put your performers at risk of physical or emotional harm for a show, and where such an outcome is possible, seek advice and think very carefully about the way to approach such a topic.

Structure

Have structure to your rehearsal process and share that with all present. Starting with a warm-up can be an effective way to bring everyone into the space physically and mentally and can be a helpful way of engaging actors who may not be used in a scene for quite some time. By running all rehearsals in the same fashion, you will generate a sense of rigour and structure which can be conducive towards creating a hard-working environment. You may want everyone to stay for a whole rehearsal, but being tactful and respectful of people's time can only be a good thing: if someone won't be used for three hours, for example, can they join later? Such practices may well be rejected in other formal aspects of theatrical training, but we are working with real people who have real lives. Especially if our actors are working for very little, we owe them the dignity of respecting the time they are giving to us.

Breaks

Breaks are essential and you should set out expectations for breaks early on. Can actors pop to the loo in the middle of a scene or when they're not needed? Again, it is worth reminding yourself that actors may need rehearsal breaks or toilet trips for a whole host of reasons, and it really does no harm to remember this in creating a safe and welcoming environment for everyone to perform to their best.

Warm-ups: cool-downs

Warm-ups can be incredibly effective for a whole host of reasons. I like to think of rehearsals in the same way as I would think of a lesson at school. Without a starter, students aren't prepared to plunge right into the depths of a lesson and have little context with which to appreciate it. Similarly, a lesson that ends mid-flow can feel unresolved and inconclusive. Spending some time planning your rehearsals and selecting your warm-up, structure, and cool-downs with a specific aim of achieving your creative goal, is a sure way to make a more productive and cohesive rehearsal experience with a sense of forward momentum. A good warm-up or game can also be a brilliant way to break a creative deadlock!

Etiquette

Although you should aim to be flexible with many areas of your rehearsal process, one area that you should be rigid with is your expectations around etiquette and respect. This can feel difficult to broach, but it is harder to impose retrospectively if you don't establish some ground rules early on. Explain whether you welcome other people's ideas (hint: you should!) and explain how and when people should give them. A creatively engaged ensemble is an incredible thing, but what happens if someone else starts directing a performer mid-scene? Or if someone laughs during the rehearsal of a vulnerable scene? A seemingly shared set of responsibilities and lack of 'rules' can easily slip into something harder to manage. Dealing with this doesn't require you to be dictatorial, by any means, but even something as simple as sharing directing responsibilities requires some moderation if you both have conflicting ideas. Never get into a situation where your actors are afloat and exposed due to your lack of creative control.

Time management and adaptability

You will face a myriad of challenges to your original schedule which will require you to constantly improvise and use your initiative. An actor may be five minutes late. Another may have to leave earlier than you expected. Whereas you had previously planned a meticulous rehearsal schedule, suddenly you may not have enough time to run a warm-up if you are to rehearse that key scene with your lead actor before they have to dash off.

Such things are frustrating and can be difficult to deal with. It can be disheartening to know you had a fantastic plan and, through no fault of your own, it wasn't executed as planned. However, adaptability in the face of difficulty is an incredibly useful skill to have, beyond running your company, and it isn't unheard of that looking for alternative solutions can lead to better plans and more creative ideas that you may never have considered.

Working with children

We all have a responsibility to protect vulnerable people in our care, never more so than when working with other people. Safeguarding is the action that is taken to protect children and vulnerable people, whilst in your care. Every organisation that works with young people should have a safeguarding policy in place, and it must be updated regularly and known to all appropriate parties. If your organisation is of appropriate scale, you will need to designate a Safeguarding Lead, and you should have a system in place for users to raise concerns about any member of your team. You should also give consideration for hierarchy, to make sure that concerns can be raised about those in leadership positions, to ensure that your organisation has safe processes against the abuse of power.

Safeguarding applies equally to everybody your organisation works with, be they full-time members of staff or one-off freelancers. You have a duty to ensure that your users are safe and that you have conducted appropriate checks on those you work with, and you should also make sure that your safeguarding policy and processes are transparent and available for all to access. This makes it much easier to ensure that there is a consistent system and less likely that mistakes will be made.

In the UK, you will require a Disclosure and Barring Service (DBS) check in order to work with children. A DBS check is a way for employers to check your criminal record, to ensure that you are safe to work with and to employ. While a whole range of employers can choose to request a DBS check, it is a legal requirement for those wanting to work with children and vulnerable service users. There are four different types of DBS check, which vary in the level of detail they produce:

- Basic DBS
- Standard DBS
- Enhanced DBS
- Enhanced DBS with check list.

When working with children, you will require an Enhanced DBS check. The process of applying for a DBS check is relatively straightforward, and often an employer (if you were working in a school, for example) will operate this process for you, but you do have to pay.

A freelancer, member of staff, or member of the public should not be left unsupervised with a group of young people without a DBS check.

You generally require a new DBS check for each new employment you undertake. A relatively recent development allows for an annual payment of £13 to join the *DBS Update Service*. For the annual fee, your DBS check will be kept up to date automatically.

Safeguarding doesn't just apply to children. Safeguarding is everybody's responsibility and you should take time to look at your own organisation through this lens. It is very easy to fall into the trap of saying, 'that sort of thing happens to other people,' but unfortunately this is overwhelmingly likely to be the attitude that creates problems and makes it harder for abuse to be detected. Everybody running a company should be vigilant to it and clear, accessible channels should be created to ensure that concerns can be raised and dealt with.

There are specific rules for working with children in theatre or on a film set, including rigid restrictions on the number of hours they can spend in rehearsals and the timing of breaks. To keep children safe, they must be accompanied by a *chaperone*, a trained professional whose sole responsibility is to ensure the child is being looked after and treated fairly and safely whilst in rehearsal or performance. Chaperones will be accredited to their local council. Sometimes this role can be fulfilled by a child's parent. Chaperones aren't volunteers and are a cost you need to consider in your budgeting. If you are working with multiple children, and you have both boys and girls, you will need to employ the services of multiple chaperones.

In order for a child to be permitted to perform in a show, you are required to obtain a *performance licence* from the local authority where the child lives, not the authority where the performance will take place. Council websites will have a page dedicated to this, with forms and contact information. Performance licences should be applied for early; councils often specify up to twenty-one days in advance. It is your local authority who creates the rules on working with children from their area, and it is they who will approve or reject your application for a performance licence for that child.

It is important to ensure that you are on top of the rules and requirements when working with children, for obvious reasons. However, it is equally important to remember that systems are in place for a reason, and despite what you may think, people are available to help and support you if you have questions. Don't be afraid to ask – building relationships with the key people in this area is a huge benefit.

Disclosures

Your organisation should have a clear, transparent, and simple system for people to make a complaint or disclosure, and for incidents of all kinds to be addressed. If an incident or a disclosure takes place in your company you should complete an *Incident Report* as soon as possible, while the details are fresh in your memory. If an incident occurs whilst working with another organisation, they may require you to complete this for their own paperwork, but it is essential that a paper trail exists in case it is required. An Incident Report details the full information regarding the incident, and could serve as a vital piece of evidence, so it is essential that it is detailed and accurate. The Incident Report should detail exactly what happened – not what you think happened, or what you wish had happened – and give full details of the people present and the actions taken.

There should be an identifiable chain of authority right up to Board level, so that there is somebody for the report to be given to. This person is then responsible for ensuring that appropriate action is taken in a timely manner, where needed.

Tips and tricks

Every show will require some combination of set, props, and costumes. You may be working with designers and have the budget to exert full creative control over these aspects, but below is a quick list of tips and tricks if this area falls under your responsibility:

- Charity shops (and similar) are an excellent way of securing costumes cheaply. A skilled seamstress could adjust and upscale charity shop finds, if needed, and they can be a treasure trove of ideas. However, they are unlikely to be as size appropriate as if you were making them (or buying them) yourself, and any requirement for matching costumes would be almost impossible to fulfil.
- Always start from the cast themselves, where you can. You will save yourself a huge amount of time, effort, and cost by asking the cast to source their own props and costumes. Especially for generic items such as white shirts, black trousers etc., this is a really easy way to save budget.
- Charity shops selling furniture are also a great place to look for set. Sometimes they will even let you pay a small fee to lend the item and return it after your show, saving you the headache of what to do with it after the show has finished.
- Create a shared document listing every prop, costume, and set piece, with the name of the person responsible for purchasing and bringing it to

performance. This is a good way of dividing responsibility and a helpful way of tracking logistics.
- Every item you take into the theatre needs to be taken out again. Your final show will likely finish late into the evening: where will you take those six mirrors, that prop coffin, and the charity shop sofa?
- It is extremely easy for your green credentials to take a hit during this part of the process – try and coordinate where you can. It may take a bit more time and effort, but coordinating deliveries and relying on more energy-efficient methods such as click and collect will help you to ensure you keep your carbon footprint low.
- Van hire is a really beneficial way of transporting a set but beware that you usually need a driver who is over twenty-five years old in order to be given permission to rent one. Van hire can be competitively priced, but this usually comes at the expense of an eye-watering refundable deposit, with some very draconian terms and conditions. Often these holding deposits need to be placed on a credit card and *not* a debit card: red tape it is usually much better to know about in advance!

Reviews

It is a great idea to get your show reviewed. Despite the various protestations of many actors, who claim not to read them, there is no denying their importance in helping to sell a show to an audience. Particularly when your work is starting out, a good review can act as a strong indication that your performance is worth the cost and effort of attending. Yes, it is only a single person's point of view and no, a review shouldn't be indicative of the quality of performance, but they do hold weight with audiences and should be rejected with caution.

However, not all reviewers are equal, and there is a fine balance to be struck in the age of the internet blogger. It is, perhaps, easier than ever to get your show reviewed. Social media and the internet have encouraged a huge number of alternative and amateur reviewers to set up shop, which makes the chance of securing a review in your early days a lot easier. A good reviewer is like gold dust, however, and you should be cautious about inviting people calling themselves reviewers without any real credentials. There is an art to being a good reviewer, often completely unappreciated by those of us who create work and live in fear of their judgement. It can be instructive to start to read reviews, not just for theatre, and to begin to consciously consider their building blocks. Very soon you will discover why effective reviews hold weight and learn to be more critical of those that lack the correct underpinnings.

Amateur reviewers can tend to fall into two categories: the overly positive reviewer who writes gushing praise about everything, and the wanna-be scary critic who criticises without an underpinning ideology. Although the former might, with your marketing head firmly on your shoulders, be a positive for selling your show, you really want to seek reviewers who will enhance your practice and provide a solid, objective overview that you can be proud of. You don't have to agree with them, but at least they've invested the same diligence into their review as you have in creating the show. Similarly, sharing a glowing review quote from a blog or publication nobody has ever heard of can undermine its intended impact.

When contacting reviewers, you will need to provide them with key information about your press night, show info, and a photo. This can sometimes be a hurdle, as you're unlikely to have any photos of your show until after it has opened!

A quick note about press nights. Clearly, this is a different ball game than for a large-scale show, which may have many weeks of previews before opening officially and hosting a press night. More often than not, your press night and opening night are the same thing – if only there were time for previews! It is canny to think about the *purpose* of your reviews when your run is so short. Will your reviews be published in time to make a tangible difference to your ticket sales? Perhaps, if you are being reviewed by a key player for a run at a large festival. However, if necessity requires your show to be reviewed on its very first performance in front of an audience, will the show be at its best? Sometimes it can be more prudent to review your show later during its run with the aim of collecting a positive review for posterity. Your next flyer will always look better with five stars on it!

Regardless of your approach, it is important to share a strategy for your reviews with your company. You cannot control their outcome and you must be prepared for any eventuality. Respect that some people will read reviews and some won't and be mindful of the fact that reviews can have both positive and negative consequences for your show and the individuals within it. This isn't limited to bad reviews. Positive reviews can provide an inflated sense of self-confidence, which in turn results in less focus in subsequent performances. Poor reviews can focus on the entire production, or on an individual company member, including yourself. Never will you be required to show leadership more than in the aftermath of poor reviews.

Having had the full spectrum of reviews, from five to a personal low of half a star(!) – sometimes for the same show – it can be too easy to reject them as having failed to grasp the concept of your show, particularly when trying to rebuild morale within a company. They are only a single person's perspective, but I find it helpful and healthy to try and understand their perspective, and to use this to help. Whether I personally agree with their point of view or not, something has led to them having that point of view, and it can be instructive to think about what that something could be. I often find myself agreeing with reviews more and more after the show has ended and after I have stopped being so defensive about it, but if you try and consider them as feedback, even if they aren't delivered in the most constructive or helpful way, the experience can become a useful method for helping your practice.

Paper tech

A *paper tech* is an idea that has been slow moving in the UK but is a fantastic way of making your venue tech much smoother and less cumbersome. A paper tech should take place towards the end of the rehearsal process, and is an opportunity for the director, stage manager, and tech team to sit and work through the show and ask any questions. It gives the whole creative team an opportunity to name cues, describe what they do, and ensure the *book* is up to date. Paper techs are an incredibly efficient way of ensuring that your stage management and tech team go into a tech knowing the show inside out, which aids communication and saves time. It is well worth trying to find the time and resource to fit this into your schedule, and for a show with smaller tech requirements, your paper tech might only take an hour.

When things go wrong

Things can and do go wrong, and when they do it is important to know what steps to take. Things can go wrong from your perspective, but also from the perspective of the venue, and in the most extreme case this may result in a show being cancelled or postponed. If a venue needs to cancel a show it is important that you consult your contract so that you know what, if any, compensation you are entitled to. A key phrase to be aware of is *force majeure*, which is a technical term for things outside of your control. A venue isn't obligated to reimburse you if they've had to close the theatre because of a flood or – and this always makes me laugh – 'an act of god.' In those cases, it's tough luck, which is not much comfort to you. Hopefully these are events that will never occur, but having just gone through a worldwide pandemic, I would treat that sentence cautiously!

If you need to cancel, your contract with the venue will lay out the terms and consequences. As with a lot of cancellation clauses, you are likely to be better off the earlier you cancel – if you are hiring the venue outright, the portion of the fee you will still need to pay will depend entirely on how much notice you provide. If you have been forced to cancel the performance due to no fault of your own (such as widespread cast illness, for example), the venue may be able to reschedule or postpone your performance, but obviously this comes with a lot of implications for ticket sales, marketing, and scheduling, as they will likely have a packed program, of which you are just one part.

It may be the case that you need to cancel a performance, or a series of performances, mid-way through the run. Consult your contract, which should specify what to do, who to inform, and what will happen in such an event.

Depending on the nature of your agreement with the venue (whether you are hiring/whether you have been programmed etc.), the consequences for payment will be specified in your contract in the event of cancelled or delayed performances. It is vital for you to know whether you will still receive any payment if a show is cancelled or delayed by either party.

At the venue

What happens at the venue will depend on several factors. If you are hiring the space, then the venue is yours for the length of the period of hire, meaning that it may be up to you how much time you want to spend before a performance opens. Alternatively, the venue may have carved out predetermined times: arrive at 10.00am, first show by 7.30pm, for example.

If you have been programmed by a venue, you will have a pre-agreed schedule of everything from get-in to first night, in consultation with a producer at the venue. If you are then touring to subsequent venues, you are unlikely to have the same luxury again, as both you and the venue are losing money for any night the auditorium isn't open for business. As such, arriving at a touring venue is likely to be much quicker than what is listed above. In most cases, you will be expected to know your show already, with your prep-time at the venue given for fit-up, rigging and focussing, programming your cues, and running a quick cue-to-cue before opening, maybe on the same day.

Whereas large-scale shows can have days of technical rehearsal, you may be arriving at your venue within a few hours of performance, which can often cause the most pressurised part of the entire process. It can be helpful to view this process from the perspective of the venue as a way of getting the most out of it in the smoothest way possible. It can be very easy, at this stage, to bash heads with venue staff or crew members, as your long-held creative plans get harshly rejected and overlooked in the mad dash to opening. Remember, everyone's aim is to get a show in front of an audience, so go into it with an open mind and be ready to compromise where necessary.

Depending on the venue, when you arrive, their in-house technical staff or venue manager will want to give you a brief overview of the space and get things moving as quickly as possible. You might be given a welcome pack with the key information you will need. Despite everyone's excitement, it is essential that cast and crew are respectful of this tradition and listen carefully to any health and safety advice. Technicians are often overlooked and poorly treated by creatives, but they can be your greatest allies: remember, they're in charge of making your show look good!

Your first job will be to allocate the dressing rooms. It is perhaps easiest to have a male dressing room and a female dressing room, but this might not work for the balance of your cast. If you're at the stage of working with performers with a level of fame and reputation, dressing room allocation may well have been stipulated as part of their contract with you.

I always tell my cast one simple rule when approaching tech: this process is not about them. After weeks of rehearsal, it can be difficult for actors to let go of the process to the technical team, but this is not the time for character work or difficult attitudes. The tech is about making sure, at its most basic, that your performance happens, and that the action can be seen and heard by the audience. Yes, it can be frustrating. Yes, actors have to spend a lot of time waiting around. Yes, it is always rushed. But an awareness and appreciation of the process can make this stressful period more harmonious for everyone.

Technical rehearsals will often start with focussing. This involves a rough positioning of the lights needed for your show. Sometimes venues will ask for technical information in advance, and in the case of fringe festivals, you may be restricted to using a fixed rig. If this is the case, you should have received this information far in advance so that you can work with it. In order to plot, you need people to stand on stage in the correct position so that they can be lit by the technicians – this is a thankless job, so get someone happy to do it without making a fuss!

After focussing, plotting is the process in which lighting states and cues will be set. If you have the time, these can be programmed into the lighting desk. This means that during the show, you can move from cue-to-cue easily and repeat the process nightly. You are likely to come across *QLab* (or one of its alternatives), which is widely used as a technical plotting programme for your sound, lights, and video. Luckily, you can hire short-term licences for QLab for the duration of your show, so you don't need to be prohibited by the software cost, although it is still exclusively available for Mac only. QLab allows you to programme cues for light, sound, and video, and you can start to prepare this in advance of the technical rehearsals, so it is well worth looking into. You don't need to be an expert on QLab, but a familiarity with the process, and its positives and limitations will make you much more popular with your technical team! If you are at a venue with its own technical team, you are unlikely to be doing these elements yourself, but understanding the language of technical theatre and what can be achieved, and the time and complexity involved, will make you a much more efficient partner in the race to get your show ready for performance.

Most venues will have a lighting and sound desk, but they may not necessarily have a machine loaded with QLab for you to use. This is worth clarifying, as you may need to bring your own Mac for this purpose. Most fringe venues tend not to have this piece of kit, so although QLab is an option, you need to provide the infrastructure to be able to have access to it.

The purpose of a technical rehearsal is to rehearse the technical aspects of the production. This may sound obvious, but it's important to hold this thought in your mind so that you can keep on track and deal with unrelated issues afterwards. Some cues may require several runs to get right and you won't be able to move on from a particular cue until the technical team are happy that it can be executed safely. If you are pushed for time, you may want to do a *cue-to-cue* rehearsal, where you skip over the parts of the show where nothing is happening technically, and jump straight to the next piece of tech. Your cast should always be ready and prepared for their entrance when doing a tech: it's unprofessional to hold up a tech rehearsal because someone didn't know they were needed.

An important trap to avoid – often the worst nightmare for a lot of festival creators – is forgetting the need for your set to be safe for fire purposes.

Working in theatre requires a level of familiarity with fire safety, and you'll make venue staff respect you a lot more if you have a basic appreciation for the need to keep everyone, including yourself, safe. There will be specific fire safety clauses in your contract, but one that can trip up companies regularly is the requirement for flammable materials in your show to be *flame proofed*. This will rule out some materials altogether, but you can buy flameproofing which coats your set in a protective shield. As with many things, there are different levels of quality here, and some venues will be more rigid with this than others. Ultimately, your venue staff want to make sure that your set can't catch fire and, given the substantial number of fire risks in most theatre productions, this is a very real concern. If in doubt, check and ask. They will respect you much more for doing so.

A dress rehearsal is usually the final piece of the puzzle before opening. In fringe theatre, this is often the first luxury to be dispensed with, and if you think this might be an issue, you should focus your attention on the specific parts of costuming that may create issues. Characters walking in heels, wearing glasses or hats, or carrying props and weapons are all high priority for a dress rehearsal. In the absence of a dress rehearsal, I always find five minutes to get my cast to run through each of their entrances and exits at speed. Entering and exiting from the darkness into an unknown space is a recipe for disaster!

Because tech time is so limited, I often try to dampen expectations in advance, so that the cast know that it is unlikely they will get a full dress rehearsal, or whatever it is I think we may have to rush. That way, if we do suddenly get the time, it feels like a bonus, rather than people going into the first performance terrified that they haven't had time to test out their heels or to see how much their Renaissance dress makes them sweat under the lights!

Be aware that any delays or anything running over agreed time is likely to hit you in the pocket, either as a blank fee or as it relates to the technical contras specified in your agreement.

Electrical items

If you plan to bring electrical items into the theatre for use in your show – a TV or a projector, for example – they will need to be PAT tested. Portable Appliance Testing (PAT) checks the electrical integrity of any electrical item that can be considered to be portable. PAT testing is not a legal requirement but is something venues will often insist on. PAT tests need to be carried out by a trained person, and usually need testing again once a year. If you are hiring equipment, it is likely to have already been PAT tested, but if you are planning to bring your own electrical items you should discuss with the venue before you arrive for their advice. They may be able to conduct a PAT test on site: it's a quick process but you do require the correct tools and training to be able to do it.

Front of house

Prior to the opening of your first night, the front of house manager will want to grab you for ten minutes to run through some essential audience information. This is often ten minutes that you don't have, just before the house is about to open! These questions will talk about audience management: whether there is an interval, how many tickets have been sold, whether there are any pre-show announcements, etc.

Before the performance

Ideally, you should spend some time doing a warm-up and a quick, focussed session prior to performance. If you are pushed for time, it is even more important to try and squeeze in some form of this. Yes, it brings focus and can unite the cast, but more importantly, it is very important to ensure bodies and voices are effectively warmed up and prepared before the show begins. It is your responsibility to make sure that your cast perform safely and take care of themselves, so making time for a quick stretch and vocal warm-up is something you should always try and prioritise. If you expect that you won't have time for this, at least try and facilitate there being space for the individual cast members to warm up for themselves.

Feedback

You may want to collect audience feedback or communicate directly with your audience after a performance. This may not be a regular feature of professional theatre but there may be several reasons that make this necessary for your company. If you do need to communicate with an audience, make sure you're clear about how this is to be managed. For example, if you want to hand out a questionnaire, this should probably be done as the audience enters the house, but will there be front-of-house staff to do this, or do you need to do it yourself? Can you leave these on the seats? Who collects them in? What about pens to fill them in? It is often easier for audiences to fill in forms once they have left the auditorium, which tends to be too dark to write clearly.

You may also want to appeal directly to your audience for donations and support. This isn't something most people relish, but it may be a financial necessity, and if you do need to do this, make sure you give some thought to what you want to say (note, be brief!) and have something for people to put their change in. Don't expect people to put their money somewhere where it could easily be picked up by somebody else.

The curtain call

No one will remind you to block the curtain call until about three minutes before the house opens, so try to set yourself a reminder! Although it can be easy to rush, this is the final statement from your production and a sloppy curtain call can look amateurish and lazy. Remember to thank the technical team and agree on a policy for ovations. If you are in a thrust stage, or in the round, it is traditional to acknowledge all sides, but if you don't have any audience on one side, omit it. How you fashion your curtain call will say a lot about your company values: avoid individual bows and don't milk it.

Also, give thought to who stands where and how people will enter and exit the stage. To coordinate timings, assign someone to lead the bow, who the other cast will take their direction from. Cast can understandably be emotional at curtain calls, especially as they see friends and family in the audience but maintaining the standard of a professional bow will do wonders for the overall finesse of your evening. Remember, your cast must stay silent when they exit for the last time!

After the performance

You did it! After all of the time, focus, and hard work, your production has opened. Well done! You should always remember what an achievement this is, in and of itself, and celebrate the fact that you have got this far. Naturally you will want to dwell over every detail of the opening night but remember to always take a moment to celebrate your achievement in getting the show this far. The hardest step is out of the way now: everything from here is about improvement.

If you are simply directing the show and not also appearing in it, it is customary for you to sit in the auditorium and watch the performance. You will want to make notes but be mindful of the audience around you who may be distracted by this. It will be dark, so you will either want to bring a light or get used to writing in the darkness: both can be very irritating for audience members to deal with. You should alter your position throughout the run so that you aren't just observing from the best seat: often you will only spot problems when you sit in a more restricted position.

If you are also in the show, it can be a challenge to get a relatively objective view of how the space looked and felt. You might resort to a camera as a reasonable compromise, but make sure this is discrete and out of the audience's way so that they don't feel as though they're being filmed, and so that there's no danger of them sitting in front of it or tripping over it. You might enlist the services of a friend to take notes for you, but you need to trust that they have your eye to pick up on the things you'd notice if you go down this route. It is at this point more than any other where the challenge of both creating and being in the same show will present itself, and it is worth brainstorming solutions in advance so that you can take full advantage of those early performances to shape and refine.

Before leaving the theatre, make sure everybody knows the *call-time* for the following day. In the euphoria of a post-show celebration, it can be easy for this information to be lost, and if you want to work through notes and changes it is particularly important for people to know when they will be needed. If you want to work through changes, make sure you know when you can access the venue from. You might want to be back at 7am to work on things but it doesn't mean the venue will let you! In fringe festivals, you may not have access to the space much at all outside of your performance times.

It is almost always beneficial to run notes to improve your piece, and it is a skill every director should harness. It is usually better to run through notes the following day, when your cast are rested and focussed on preparing for the next show. Bear in mind that actors can only be expected to take on board a certain number of changes at this stage, and the time may be too late for sweeping adjustments. You can also work on technical cues or change them altogether, but make sure you do this cautiously so that you don't affect the rest of the tech for your show.

The second show curse

After the excitement and nerves of an opening night, second nights are almost always less focussed and energetic. It's a strange phenomenon, but one widely recognised, and the key to dealing with it is to address it head on so that your subsequent performances reach for something more and continue to grow. Booking reviewers for your second night is always a good antidote to this!

The final performance and get-out

Agree on the process for get-out before your final show. Emotions will run high once the curtain drops and people will want to be with their friends and family after the performance ends. This leaves you in the unenviable position of taking down the set and cleaning up: the joy of being in charge! It is not a venue's responsibility to clean up after you, and nor should you expect them to. Your contract will require you to return the venue how you found it, and you should not underestimate the time and effort this can take. On more than one occasion I have found myself driving a van moving set at one or two in the morning, on my own, long after the cast have gone off to enjoy themselves.

The best approach is to agree on a strategy in advance and coordinate a plan as ruthlessly as you did for your get-in. If the whole cast commits to stay for ten or fifteen minutes to *strike* the set, this can be a huge benefit to you, whilst allowing them to still go and join their peers in the bar.

Make sure you have a plan for where everything will go, including litter. Venues should not be left with rubbish from your performance, and it is very unprofessional to suddenly ask them to look after a chair or other piece of set until the following day. Don't be surprised if you don't get a warm response to this. Avoid this situation by only taking to the performance what you know you can take away.

The debrief

The show is over and life goes on. If you are touring to more than one venue the process will be a copy and paste of the above, with each venue and audience bringing its own perks and challenges. But eventually the journey will be over, usually when you have returned a van to the hire depot and not been charged any extra!

You may have reviews or production photos to share and admin to wrap up with payments and contracts. Make sure you complete these obligations in a timely manner and thank your whole cast and crew, regardless of the emotional and personal journeys you may have gone on throughout the run. It is important for everyone involved to have a conclusion to the experience and to be able to draw a line under it.

It is always incredibly helpful to reflect on your practice and your work and to do so in a manner that is constructive and developmental. Developing a good habit with this will make you a better reflective practitioner, capable of acknowledging your own strengths and weaknesses, and using this to build on them. Immediately after a show is too soon for such judgements, and you should avoid jumping to rash conclusions or straight into another project in this way. Typically, somewhere between three weeks and three months after a project is a healthy, objective framework to work from. I would avoid getting the whole company back together for this. They are likely to have moved on to other things, and this can quickly become an unhelpful distraction, particularly if elements of the show hadn't gone as well as planned. This is where your mentors and confidants become important. Going for a coffee with someone whose feedback you respect, but who has no emotional connection to the show, can be a great way of going through the process of reflection for yourself.

Chapter Resources

Tech

J.S., 'Paper tech, Q to Q and tech,' Puckermob (25th May 2022), www.puckermob.com/moblog/paper-tech-q-to-q-and-tech/

Price, Lindsay, 'How to run a tech challenge in the drama classroom,' Theatre Folk, www.theatrefolk.com/blog/run-tech-challenge-drama-classroom/

QLab, https://qlab.app

'Tech considerations,' Edinburgh Fringe, www.edfringe.com/take-part/doing-an-online-event/tech

Toth, Claudia, '"Can we tech this?": Tips for small theatre companies,' On Stage Blog, www.onstageblog.com/editorials/2019/12/22/can-we-tech-this-tips-for-small-theatre-companies

Logistics

Bradford, Wade, 'Curtain call: Dos and don'ts,' Live About (4th April 2017), www.liveabout.com/curtain-call-dos-and-donts-2713056

Capital Theatres, Edinburgh, 'How does a get-in/get-out work in a theatre? Join us behind-the-scenes,' YouTube (28th May 2020), www.youtube.com/watch?v=ly5DXA6SFNY

Cocumelli, Tina, 'Theatre on a shoe-string: The #1 secret to a great, low-budget show,' On the Stage, https://blog.onthestage.com/theatre-on-a-shoestring

'Glossary of technical theatre terms – Beginners,' Theatre Crafts, www.theatrecrafts.com/pages/home/topics/beginners/glossary/

Scooter, Pandora, 'How to bow (and what your bow says about you),' Performer Stuff (3rd August 2017), https://performerstuff.com/mgs/how-to-bow-and-what-your-bow-says-about-you/

'Your ultimate guide to Portable Appliance Testing (PAT testing),' PHS Compliance, www.phscompliance.co.uk/news/ultimate-guide-portable-appliance-testing-pat/

8 Legal and Safety

There are several legal responsibilities to keep track of when running a company of any kind, and several specific requirements for those in the entertainment business. This chapter will provide an overview of your responsibilities and how to ensure your activities are above board, before exploring in more detail the best practice for running a company that is ethical, held to account, and clear on its responsibilities.

Legal responsibilities: an overview

Your legal responsibilities will change from month to month and from production to production. Some of these will come with flexible deadlines, while others can be severe in their punishment for late compliance. Ensure you add dates to a yearly calendar and set reminders at least a week in advance so that you don't overlook anything important.

Legal requirements will vary by country; however, it is likely that the broad principles will remain the same, regardless of territory.

Company policies

It is a good idea, and in some cases, a requirement, to have company *policies* outlined and available for your users to access. You should familiarise yourself with those statutory policies you need to include for an organisation of your type, in your region, and prioritise developing these first. At the same time, make sure you are familiar with the rules surrounding these policies, as statutory policies usually need to be made easily available to your staff and/or the public. Policies may be wide ranging and highlight an organisation's strategy, approach, or attitude to a given issue, such as Safeguarding or GDPR. Having a written policy increases transparency and demonstrates a commitment to a fair and robust system. It also shows that you have given the issue enough thought and priority to create a policy in the first place.

There is no correct number of policies to have, as large organisations can have hundreds of policies on everything from printing to human trafficking. It can be easy to fall into the trap of having a policy for policy's sake, and you

DOI: 10.4324/9781003281726-8

134 Legal and Safety

Table 8.1 Overview of responsibilities

Activity	Category	Deadline	Extra Info	For Review	Purpose
File Company Accounts	Company Management	Company specific	Balance Sheet Profit and Loss	Annual	To ensure financial compliance
File Company Tax Return	Company Management	Company specific	Tax Return	Annual	To declare and pay company tax
File Confirmation Statement	Company Management	Company specific	Costs £13	Annual	Confirms that information relating to company address and directors is correct and up to date
Data Protection	GDPR	Company specific	Costs £40	Annual	Ensures the company is adhering to its GDPR requirements
DBS for Practitioners	Safeguarding	Before undertaking any work with children	Complete appropriate DBS form Register with update service for ease of renewal	DBS checks don't expire – but it is best practice to need a new one for each subsequent employer	Ensures safe practice and safeguards children and vulnerable adults, by screening candidates for any convictions
Public Liability Insurance	Insurance	Required before conducting any work with the public. Can be project specific or annual cover	Search online for a quote: insurers specific to the entertainment industry are best suited	Check policy – usually annually	Protection for your business in case an external body is injured as a result of your operations
Employer's Liability Insurance	Insurance	Required for any business employing people, which in this definition includes students/unpaid volunteers	Cover of £5m required by law as a minimum in the UK	Check policy – usually annually.	Protection for your business in case anyone working for you is injured or made ill at work

Activity	Category	Deadline	Extra Info	For Review	Purpose
Trademark	Company Management	Takes four months for approval	£170 – not refunded if you get rejected	Needs renewal every ten years	Helps protect assets such as your company name from being copied by others
Performance Rights	Performance	Varies but usually takes several weeks – needs to be obtained *before* starting rehearsals	Price varies wildly depending on play. Charged per performance	Per production	To ensure appropriate permission has been obtained to perform a play and for authors to be paid as required

should ensure that the policies you do have are well considered and able to be actioned and regularly reviewed.

Some policies, by their nature, contain sensitive company information, while others are in the wider public interest to remain visible and accessible to all. Several theatre companies have a policy section on their website, which is something worth exploring, particularly if your work involves children or vulnerable groups.

> **Task:** Look at the websites of several producing theatre companies and access their policies, or at websites such as the Independent Theatre Council. You don't need to read through them, but use this to compile your own list of policies to create. You should avoid writing more than ten at this stage, and it would be a wise idea to start with those policies that are required by law (rather than simply best practice). If you know you will work with children in the future, for example, there is nothing wrong with writing a policy for this now, but your policy needs to be specific in order to be useful, so focus your attention on the work you are doing right now.

Never copy and paste someone else's policy without working it through, in detail, for your own circumstances. They can be dense and some of the language can be obscure, but as soon as you publish a policy, you're holding your actions against this for future reference. Never publish a policy that can't be enacted if the circumstances arise.

Policies should be updated regularly to ensure that the information contained within is still appropriate, and to make sure that the expanding work of the company is covered. It is a good idea to establish a schedule for updating each of your policies on an appropriate basis, and where you have expertise within your Board, ensure the most appropriate person is responsible for approving it.

> **Task:** From your initial list, place these policies into a table. Your table should list the policy name, who is responsible for updating it, and when the next date for renewal will be. This should be shared with everyone necessary in your organisation. Although it can be fair to spread the workload, make sure you are assigning policies to people with the expertise and knowledge to be responsible for it.

A *Document Control Sheet* at the end of each policy helps to evidence when the document was last updated, and who by. Below is an example of how to chart this:

Document Control Sheet

Document Name:	Policy Name
Issue Number:	1
Document Owner:	Company Name
Date:	XX 20XX
Review Date:	XX 20XX
Document History:	Issue 1–1st formal issue
Document Approved by:	Name
Date Approved:	Issue 1 – XX 20XX
Document Authorised by:	Name

Insurance

You will be all too aware of the purpose and need for *insurance* in the rest of your life, although you've probably only encountered this from the perspective of a consumer. As a producer, you are responsible for ensuring the correct insurance is provided for the duration of your activities. There are numerous optional insurance packages available to you, but here we outline the types you're most likely to need.

Public liability insurance

As somebody staging an event, you have a responsibility to keep people safe. When you visit a shop, or a museum or a theme park, you assume that the owners of that space have done everything possible to keep you safe, and you would probably expect to blame them if you were injured, through no fault of your own, whilst on their premises.

Public liability insurance covers claims made against you by the public, clients, and your cast and crew for accidental injury or damage to their property. Your public liability insurance will help to cover the costs if you are found to be responsible, including for compensation pay-outs and legal fees.

When working with any sort of venue they will have their own public liability insurance. However, venues should always make it clear whether their own insurance protects your activity in the space (unlikely) or whether you need to provide evidence of your own insurance to cover you for the duration of your time on their premises. In this way, if an accident occurs in their space because of your activities, the host venue is indemnified, and you are responsible.

Like all insurance, public liability insurance can be bought for a single day or for longer-term annual options. If you are doing a number of projects throughout a year, it may well be better value for money to take out an annual policy. Public liability insurance will come to a certain value (how much the insurance will pay out to cover costs), usually with options starting from £5 million. When venues ask for evidence of your cover they will usually stipulate the minimum value that the cover must be for.

Employers' liability insurance

Employer's liability insurance relates directly to claims against your business by employees. It safeguards your business from legal or compensation claims – for example, if they fall ill as a result of working for you. By law, most businesses in Britain are required to have a minimum of £5 million employers' liability insurance from the moment you take on your first employee.

Health and safety

When creating events and working with the general public, there are a number of legal responsibilities you need to be aware of with respect to keeping everyone safe and avoiding unnecessary harm. This is a legal obligation but also a moral obligation, and you should make sure you are up to date on the latest requirements in your territory. Your national Health and Safety regulator (The Heath and Safety Executive in the UK) is a helpful first point of call for getting to grips with this topic. Generally speaking, in addition to the insurance requirements laid out above, you are obliged to keep yourself, your employees, and members of the public safe, and to have appropriate policies in place to ensure that this is done properly. This applies regardless of whether you have paid employees, or whether you are working with unpaid volunteers.

Risk assessment

Risk assessments are important documents that you will come across throughout your time running a company, and while they can look intimidating at first glance, the guiding principle is actually very simple. Risk assessments consider all of the potential risks in a given scenario and then highlight the opportunities to mitigate those risks. The aim of a risk assessment is to both identify possible problems and to find solutions, and if risks remain likely after mitigation, questions need to be asked as to whether that activity is safe and responsible to proceed.

You are quite likely to be asked to provide a risk assessment when working at a venue, or you may fall under the risk assessment of another organisation when working in their space. Often, risk assessments form part of the legal requirements of a venue to keep people safe, and you should ensure that all of your company are aware of and follow any health and safety related rules presented to them when working with a third party. You should feel confident to ask venues for a copy of their risk assessment if you feel a need to check it over.

When completing your own risk assessments, there are numerous templates of varying complexity available online. Most will follow the same basic formula: presenting a list of the problems and any mitigations put in place, followed by a rubric calculating the final risk level.

When identifying problems, it is important to consider a whole range of eventualities – there is often an endless list of unlikely things that can go wrong, and you should put your hypochondriac's head on when completing a risk assessment to ensure that you have considered all bases. Hopefully none of these problems will ever happen and you'll go through life filling in risk assessments for them never to be needed. Good. Remember, often a risk assessment is a legal requirement and if something does go wrong, this would be the first document higher authorities would want to cast their eye over. If you did everything possible to mitigate risks and to keep your cast and crew safe, but an unfortunate accident did still happen, that is a very different scenario than facing an accident that had been caused by your negligence.

When assessing the level of risk, risk assessment templates will often give you a guide to follow. You will need to think about the severity of the risk if it did happen (bumping into the corner of a table, for example, might leave a nasty bruise, whereas failure to secure lights to a rig properly could cause danger of death) and the likelihood of that risk occurring. Likelihood is often measured on a numbered scale from one to three or one to five, and severity is often listed as either Severe, Moderate, or Minor. Different risk assessments will employ different calculations for arriving at your final risk level. In most cases, it'll involve a variation of multiplying the severity level by likelihood to determine whether an activity is safe.

You can't always guarantee complete safety, so don't panic if you face risks that you're unable to lower. You can't do much to stop somebody willingly sticking their fingers in a plug, but what you can do is make sure that everybody is aware that they need to keep fluids and conductible objects away from plug sockets and ensure they're switched off before plugging things in. In this way, the potential severity (electrification, burns, or death) is high, but the likelihood is low.

If an activity remains both potentially severe and extremely likely to happen, it needs to be reconsidered.

First aid

Depending on the scale and specifics of your business, first aid training might become a requirement – if you become responsible for a building, for example. First aid training can be quite pricey and needs to be updated every couple of years, and while it isn't about turning you into a health professional, it does give you a set of skills to be able to deal with a range of emergency situations and is something well worth investing in. We never know when we might be called upon to assist in such a situation and it is a great comfort to know that those skills are somewhere in a company repertoire.

Copyright

Copyright is the protection of your *intellectual property*. This encompasses a wide range of created content and is a term you are probably already familiar with. It protects our own work from being copied by others and prevents us from reconstituting somebody else's work as our own creation.

Copyright protection gives us the ability to sue if we believe another party has stolen our ideas, although it can be quite difficult to prove in actuality. The fine line between copying and being 'heavily inspired by' is very difficult to define.

The more practical issue surrounding copyright in the 21st century is the ease with which we can reappropriate work online. When we use a typeface on a poster, that typeface has been created by someone. When we apply music to our trailers, that music has perhaps been created by a whole group of musicians. When we download an image for our website, that photograph was captured by a photographer. Each of these people deserves recognition and/or payment for their work, and we should not use their products without permission. The speedy rise of platforms such as YouTube and Spotify have blurred the boundaries relating to copyright significantly, with platforms generally being slow to address copyright issues. On the one hand, platforms such as Facebook and YouTube are getting better at reacting to copyrighted material – usually by muting clips with licensed music. On the other hand, platforms such as TikTok have further increased copyright complexity by actively licensing popular songs for use on their platforms.

Amidst this rapidly changing landscape, it can be difficult to know where to place your work. However, the rules remain simple: if you're not sure whether you have explicit permission to use something you haven't created yourself, don't use it.

Some useful pointers to be aware of:

- 'Royalty free' content is content that is freely available for you to use. There are a range of websites offering royalty free video footage, fonts, photos, and music, sometimes for a fee.
- Work doesn't remain in copyright forever. Check your local territory for this, but as a guide, work goes out of copyright in the UK seventy years after the death of the creator. This is why you can do whatever you want with a Shakespeare play!

Permissions and release forms

You will probably want to film and photograph a large portion of your work. If you do this, you own the copyright as the images belong to you. If you employ an external photographer, they will likely get you to sign an agreement, which will either pass the copyright on to you, or will give you permission to use their images as long as the images bare their watermark and aren't cropped. If you're working with anyone else to get promotional images or footage, make sure you're clear about the usage agreements so that you don't come unstuck at a later date.

When filming or photographing people yourself, it is always a good idea to ask them to complete a consent form. Many templates are available online, and they broadly require the user to agree for you to use the image however you like. This is important, especially when filming interviews, etc., as it gives you the right to edit and adjust what somebody has said. This shouldn't be as sinister as it sounds! Editing is a natural part of all photography and videography work – obviously this is a privilege that can be abused, and you need to respect this boundary when working with images of other people. Getting talent to sign a consent form will also futureproof you in case you want to use the imagery later down the line.

The simple rule to remember with permissions is that you basically need to get permission for everything, particularly when filming. Location permissions (for public property), music permissions, talent permissions – the list can feel endless. YouTube have excellent videos about filming laws in different countries, so search in your own territory for advice.

Performance rights

If you are making your own work, you can ignore this section. If you're staging pre-existing work by other playwrights, the chances are that you will need to explore performance rights. This doesn't apply if you're dealing with work that is out of copyright (see above), but it does apply if you're working on an adaptation that is in copyright. A translation of a Greek Tragedy or Chekhov, for example, would require performance rights as the work is, from a rights perspective, essentially a modern play.

Performance rights ensure that the author of a work is appropriately acknowledged and remunerated for performances of their work. In many cases, however, it is also a system of permission granting, giving you the blessing of the author or their estate for your production to go ahead. You must not start work on a play until you have obtained permission, and you are not allowed to stage a production if permission is refused. Every playwright has different attitudes to their cannon, and often you will find a breakdown of the performance rights situation within the first few pages of the printed script. In most cases, any changes to the script – gender swaps, cut lines, etc. – will need to be laid out and approved as part of the process of applying to obtain rights. There may be logistical or artistic reasons for doing this but some authors do exercise infamous control over their play texts (it is their work, after all!). Why does this matter? Artistically, audiences coming to see your version of a play will take away an impression of that work, for good or bad. Some authors may not want their work to be staged by students, or amateur companies, while publishers can sometimes block performances based on clashes (is a professional production running simultaneously?), location, or proposed changes (good luck trying to change the gender of characters in a Becket play!).

Performance licences vary based on venue size, play type, and length of run. However, the process is usually the same. The company who holds the rights to performance (such as Concord Theatricals – previously Samuel French – in the UK) will have an application process that must be carried out several weeks before rehearsals are due to begin. This is often tricky as you need to apply early enough to recover in case of an issue, but late enough so that you have the information about performance dates that you will need to apply. Typically, performance rights are granted on a per performance basis. So, for example, if the amateur performance rights for a particular show were £100 for a venue with a capacity of less than one hundred seats, three performances would cost you £300, and so on. There is no standard performance rate, so it is always worth checking before embarking on a particular production as you may discover you can't afford to stage a particular show!

For musical theatre, a similar process applies. You must first deduce whether the rights for a musical are available by obtaining written confirmation from Music Theatre International (Europe), as rights may currently be withheld for amateur performance for any number of reasons. Musical licensing works in roughly the same way as for theatrical plays, but there can often be quite draconian restrictions about how the work is to be presented, and as with theatrical plays, you are obliged to perform the piece as written, without any cuts, changes, or swaps of things like gender, without prior written permission. Musicals are very rarely available with backing tracks, meaning that live musicians must be used, even if this is as little as one person and a piano. You are usually not permitted to create your own backing tracks or to source them from elsewhere, which can create obstacles to your performance based on the skills of your crew. You also usually have to hire the scripts and scores from the licence provider as part of this process and, in most instances, you are not permitted to use ones you have obtained yourself (from a local library, for example).

Music licensing

Just as you need permission to perform the work of a playwright, the same principle applies when using music in your show. Unless you wrote the music yourself, there will be an artist somewhere who should be paid for your use of their music in your production. In some cases, depending on the thematic and contextual plan for the use of the music, permission may also need to be sought. There are a number of high-profile cases of political parties trying to use the music of popular bands who have objected on the grounds of not wanting to be associated with them. Artists should be entitled to object on the basis of association: for instance, if you were performing a play about a taboo subject, would an artist be happy for their work to be used as part of that production?

PPL PRS is the slightly clunkily named organisation for your music rights queries in the UK. Merged from the separate PPL and PRS into one body dealing with all music licensing requests, their website contains a comprehensive breakdown of the costs and systems to apply. When planning to use music you have to be incredibly specific about the duration and part of a track you plan to use, which can be quite tricky if you haven't thought about this yet, but need to obtain the licence in time for performance.

Music for performance falls broadly into two categories. Incidental music is music not heard by characters, such as that used for scene transitions, and is usually automatically covered by the venue's music licence. Interpolated music is music that forms part of the world of the play – the characters can hear it – and usually requires a specific licence to be obtained.

There are complexities with copyright to consider, and finding the correct body to approach or discerning who actually owns the rights to a piece of music can sometimes prove tricky. Often this difficulty is outsourced if you list your music use through a venue's system (below), but if you do run into difficulties, speaking to PPL PRS (or your regional equivalent) would be an advisable place to start. If a particular piece proves tricky it might be an easier solution to change the track!

Venues will have their own performance licence to cover the vast range of musical performances in their venue, and incidental music within your performance will come under this. Where this is the case, venues may ask you to complete a form on their behalf detailing the use of licenced music in your show, and will apply a blanket percentage fee from your box office to cover licensing payments and admin costs. This can be quite a substantial hit to your takings, and you should look to see if a clause exists in your contract to circumnavigate this by paying for the music rights yourself. This means added work but is likely to be cheaper for you.

You might not be planning to use music by Beyonce in your show, but your friends who are in a band might have given you permission to use their music. Usually this still has to be declared, as the music licensing bodies will want to be satisfied that the artists have given their consent and have had the opportunity to be paid. In these instances, it is worth checking with your appropriate licensing body and contact them if you are unsure. You may still be required to declare the music use.

In America you should look up the American Society for Composers, Authors and Publishers (ASCAP) and in Ireland you should search for the Irish Music Rights Organisation (IMRO). All local territories will have their corresponding body for music performance rights, which you should consult before beginning rehearsals.

Dance performances also fall under this category, relying, as they do, on the use of copyrighted music. You must follow a similar process as with plays and musicals, to discern whether permission can be obtained from the publisher before proceeding. Remember that recordings of classical music are likely to still require permission, if that recording itself is still in copyright. As with all music use, music that is out of copyright in one country may not necessarily be out of copyright somewhere else, and you should always seek to obtain permission to use a track before you begin rehearsals. As with plays and musicals, there may be restrictions put on the use of music (whether it can be used for choreography or edited, etc.).

Ethics and trigger warnings

What you can and can't show, or should and shouldn't show, on stage, is a perennial discussion with strong arguments on both sides. Here I want to focus not on the individual creative choices of a company, but on some of the wider infrastructure to consider when dealing with potentially sensitive issues and themes.

It is unusual for this to be the case, but it is worth revisiting the contract for your venue to ensure that there are no restrictions on what you can produce artistically. Rules around nudity and swearing may need to be considered, and this may be linked to performance times. If there are likely to be clashes between your artistic choices and the rules stipulated in your contract, always discuss this with the venue in advance and act on their advice. Don't try and ignore them – not only would this be a breach of contract, but it's also an unnecessary way to create bad blood for something that could be resolved more amicably.

If your production does contain sensitive material, you may want to consider the potential benefit of informing your audience in advance. Venues will often ask for an age rating for their website. There are all sorts of arguments around the validity and potential censorship of age ratings, but again, these need to be considered from the venue's perspective and you should be upfront and mature about the content's potential to cause offence. Again, the inclusion of any violence, nudity, and swearing are the key considerations, but you should also think thematically if your play deals with potentially triggering or upsetting subjects.

Trigger warnings are a safe and sensible way of raising awareness about the content of your play. There is no standard way to present a content warning, but you might present it in your show program or announce it before the show begins. If you think your production does require a trigger warning, it might be worth considering whether a warning that comes twenty seconds before the show is about to begin is the most appropriate form of warning: could you, for example, raise people's awareness before booking? Could it be included in your marketing copy and in the venue's season brochure? What about the people who don't follow you on social media? Otherwise, a warning risks being good in principle, but lacking in real usefulness.

An important thing to consider in supporting your production in this way is to step outside of your own experience and recognise that audience members will come to your production with a whole host of life experiences, traumas, and obstacles that you may not have personal experience of or may not have even considered. We are in a privileged position to bring any work in front of an audience, and we should recognise and celebrate the diversity of experience that makes up this essential part of our creative process.

You may believe the art itself will be compromised by such advanced warnings and that you don't want to pre-empt the audience's expectations by making them aware of things that will happen in the show. There is validity to this argument, and getting this right is something of a balancing act, but it's equally worth remembering that there are a range of ways to present a trigger warning that can potentially improve the experience for those few without needing to disrupt the artistic aims of the piece at large. Ultimately, you should want your audiences to feel safe in your space and we can all afford some creativity and time towards achieving this aim without necessarily having to spoil our artistic integrity.

Chapter Resources

Safeguarding

'DBS check – Employer's guide,' Gov.uk, www.gov.uk/find-out-dbs-check/y
Mind, 'DBS checks and your mental health,' mind.org.uk, www.mind.org.uk/information-support/legal-rights/dbs-checks-and-your-mental-health/overview/
NSPCC Learning, 'Safeguarding children and child protection,' NSPCC, https://learning.nspcc.org.uk/safeguarding-child-protection

GDPR

Burgess, Matt, 'What is GDPR? The summary guide to GDPR,' *Wired* (24th March 2020), www.wired.co.uk/article/what-is-gdpr-uk-eu-legislation-compliance-summary-fines-2018

Music licensing

ASCAP (US), www.ascap.com/
IMRO (IE), www.imro.ie/
PPLPRS (UK), https://pplprs.co.uk/
'Theatre Royalties,' PRS for music, www.prsformusic.com/royalties/theatre-royalties-and-grand-rights

Insurance

'What is employers' liability insurance?' Hiscox, www.hiscox.co.uk/business-insurance/employers-liability-insurance/faq/what-is-employers-liability-insurance
'What is public liability insurance?' Hiscox, www.hiscox.co.uk/business-insurance/public-liability-insurance/faq/what-is-public-liability-insurance

Copyright

'Copyright basics,' Copyright Society of the USA, www.csusa.org/page/Basics
'UK copyright law: the basics,' Out-law guide, Pinsent Masons, www.pinsentmasons.com/out-law/guides/copyright-law-the-basics

Health and safety

'First aid: A minute can make a difference,' Red Cross, www.redcross.org.uk/first-aid

'Policy Statement Template,' Health and Safety Executive, www.hse.gov.uk/simple-health-safety/policy/policy-statement-template.pdf

'Prepare a health and safety policy,' Health and Safety Executive, www.hse.gov.uk/simple-health-safety/policy/index.htm#article

'Theatre,' Health and Safety Executive, www.hse.gov.uk/entertainment/theatre-tv/theatre.htm

Royalties

Broz, Matic, 'What does royalty-free mean?' Photutorial (17th May 2022), https://photutorial.com/royalty-free/

Concord Theatricals Performance Rights, www.concordtheatricals.co.uk/

'Performing rights and royalties,' Arts on the Move, www.artsonthemove.co.uk/youth-theatre/rights-and-royalties.php

Ethics and responsibilities

'ADC theatre content warning guide,' ADC Theatre, www.adctheatre.com/media/4273/adc-theatre-content-warning-guide.pdf

'Easy read artist contract,' FACT, www.fact.co.uk/resources/2022/03/easy-read-artist-contract

Mayer, Sydney Isabelle, 'Responsible theatremaking: Content warnings and beyond,' Howl Round, https://howlround.com/responsible-theatremaking

9 Finance

It may not be much of a generalisation to predict that funding and finance are two of the words you feel most intimidated by: it may even have been a substantial factor in your motivation to buy this book. Creative people can tend to shy away from finance, thinking it complicated or boring, and while I don't expect you to be signing up to the algebra fan club by the end of this chapter, I at least hope that I can persuade you to take control of this subject and see the advantages of doing so.

You may tend to discuss funding and finance interchangeably, but they are two distinct steps on your journey. Understanding your day-to-day finances, including your profit and tax requirements is a crucial facet of running any business. Before we can think about fundraising, we must ensure that our own financial systems are set up and that we understand their role and purpose. The good news is, it isn't half as scary or as complicated as you might worry, especially in your early stages.

It is beyond the scope of this book to cover every possible step and likely scenario, so my focus here is to break down the key terminology and first steps so that you feel empowered and knowledgeable enough for appropriate action, as dictated by your particular situation. This chapter alone could fill several books, and I have listed a number of additional resources at the end of the chapter. One of my frustrations with anything financially related, however, is that it can rapidly feel as though I've opened Pandora's jar, so even though these resources are provided here, the basic building blocks within the chapter itself will be enough to get you started without the need for extra homework.

Although I want readers to leave feeling as though they have a grasp on their financial requirements, it is also important to reiterate that this should not be underestimated, and severe consequences can befall companies that get this wrong. Furthermore, ignorance is not excusable as a reason for making errors in financial reporting. As such, readers are advised that the information in this chapter is provided as an introductory guide only and is not to be taken as independent financial advice. Likewise, you are strongly advised to seek advice and services from those with appropriate skills and expertise, particularly in relation to accountancy and bookkeeping, and to have this process overseen by your Board.

DOI: 10.4324/9781003281726-9

Your financial journey

Bookkeeping. Accounts. Tax returns. Profit and Loss. Margins. Gross profit. Equity. Corporation Tax. There is a seemingly endless list of technical terms wrapped up in the world of finance to confuse and trick us. But how do these things work together and where do we even begin?

Key to unlocking this system for me was in understanding how the different elements relating to finance speak to one another and work together. I am indebted to Embrace Finance for the inspiration behind a version of this, which visualises the different processes inherent within financial planning and their relationship to one another. Although all these elements are required for a fully functioning and healthy financial system to be in place, using this representation to strategically build your system will help with your workload and will make the connections between the different elements clearer and more understandable as you build them.

Financial systems work like every other system in the world: there is little point worrying about what a car's paintwork will look like until you have designed the engine. By approaching finance this way, we can break up a seemingly huge mountain of work and focus on establishing the key components needed to begin our financial journey.

At this stage, we don't need to be thinking about those higher-level tasks such as financial constraints and strategy: that will come later. When we reach that stage, we'll likely be able to bring in extra expertise or pay for others to help. That is not to say that those strategic, high-level steps are not important,

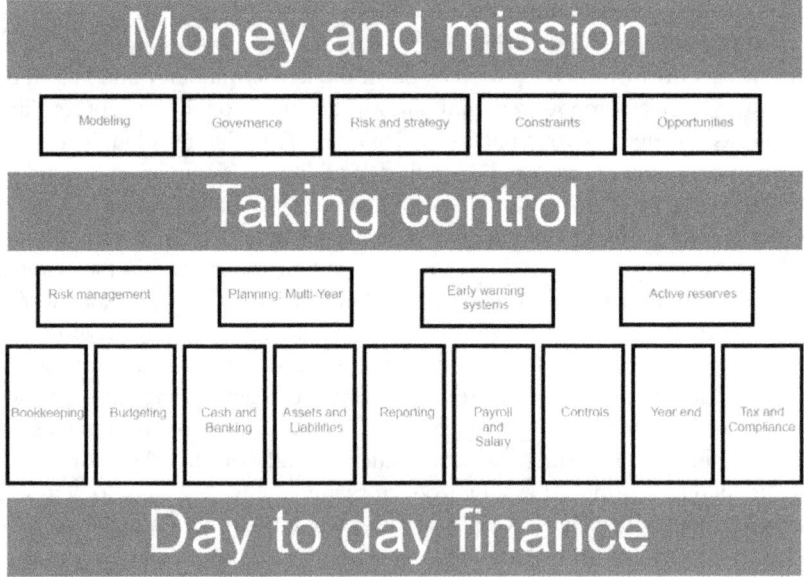

Figure 9.1 Financial management system overview

or are not things we should be concerned with as business leaders – they absolutely are, especially if you want to lead your company with vision and growth in mind – but as a way of feeling empowered in a perceptively difficult arena, focussing on the basic controls makes a lot of sense to get started.

Bookkeeping

How do you know how much money you've spent and how do you prepare for your annual accounts? This process is known as *bookkeeping*, and it's surprisingly easy if you stay on top of it. As a small theatre company, you'll probably be handling a small number of similar transactions every month, which means you don't necessarily need to become an accountancy expert to understand it. When you do have to account for something new – for example, if you've received a grant for the first time – there are plenty of helpful websites and resources to point you in the right direction. Again, hiring an accountant can make this process vastly quicker and easier and can help avoid costly mistakes.

You can set up your own processes for bookkeeping, using Excel or Google sheets, but for added benefit and ease of use, there are numerous cloud-based digital services available which automate this process for you by directly linking to your business bank account. This saves a huge amount of time and stress. Many offer reduced rates for smaller businesses as well as cheaper membership fees for the first six months, which should give you enough time to get on your feet. Using software such as this can also make working with your accountant quicker and easier, which will ultimately save you time and money.

One final note on accounting, which we have taken a whistle-stop tour through here, is a reminder to always keep your receipts. Amongst other things, receipts act as evidence that you spent your money where you said you did (which is especially vital when using public funds from places such as Arts Council England, etc.) and companies are obliged to store their receipts for up to six years (some documents need to be kept safe for up to ten). Set up a document on your computer and a folder in your office and be fastidious with this process. As either a sole-trader or a limited company, there are a small amount of important business records you are obliged to keep, as evidence of your business activities, so ensure you do a search before you start trading so that you know what needs to be kept. HMRC can ask to see your business records, so ensure you have these safely stored and, crucially, separate from your personal accounts.

Receipts and invoices

In principle, each *transaction* should be logged daily in your bookkeeping system. Each transaction needs evidence to prove that the amount was as stated. In most cases, this will either be a *receipt* or an *invoice*. You will be familiar with receipts from everything you've ever purchased, and when running a business you are required to keep hold of those receipts for much longer than you will be used to. As a general rule of thumb, small businesses must store their receipts for at least five years, so it is really important to establish an orderly system for your own business, where these can be kept safe and in date order. In most cases, a digital receipt is acceptable, as long as it is legible. The important thing is that the value on your receipt matches what you have entered into your bookkeeping log.

An invoice, on the other hand, is a request for payment. You may have sent invoices yourself if you have ever done some freelance work for another company. An invoice is sent prior to payment. Therefore, an invoice is a request for payment and a receipt is proof of payment.

In the UK, you only legally need to send an invoice if your customer is *registered for VAT*.

Bookkeeping systems

Traditionally, bookkeeping could be a tedious process, but there are numerous cloud-based services available today such as Quickbooks and Xero, which help to make this process much more streamlined and simpler. These are worth exploring, but they do tend to come with monthly costs.

Double-entry bookkeeping

We're going to get a bit mathematical for a moment, so stick with me. Let's imagine that you've made three payments this month, as listed below:

- £60 – fuel costs to travel to work
- £200 – a desk for your company office
- £16.50 – second hand books.

You've also had a payment for a workshop you ran:

- £100 – workshop ticket sales.

Fantastic. Each of these payments now needs to be logged into your bookkeeping software. Although they are all relatively small and simple payments, did you notice that they're all for very different things? The desk you bought was a great bargain, and you've potentially got it forever now. On the other hand, the fuel you just bought ran out at the end of the journey.

Because there are a million different ways we can spend or earn money as a business, and because things like fuel work very differently to things like furniture, we need to categorise them into different *accounts*. Think of different accounts like different buckets, dividing up the different aspects of your business. In one bucket you might have all of the money you have spent on travel, in another bucket you might have the loan you took out from the bank. By categorising the money we spend and earn, we are able to figure out how much profit we have made and how much tax we need to pay.

Because every business is different, we have standardised shorthand to help clarify this process regardless of your size or industry. This is where *debit* and *credit* come into the equation.

Simply put, debits record all the money flowing *into* a particular account, while credits record all the money flowing *out*. If we return to our workshop ticket sales listed above, we can imagine £100 landing in our cash bucket. To use accounting terms, we are *debiting* the cash bucket by £100. In our bookkeeping system, the transaction might look something like Table 9.1.

When money leaves the bucket, we record that as a credit. So, for our examples above, we'd list these as shown in Table 9.2.

It can be confusing to get your head around this, because you might have had a debit and credit card for many years and associated both with spending money. If you had £50 in the bank, you might say that you were £50 in credit. If you withdrew £10 your bank would say that they had debited your account. The slightly confusing thing here is that the bank is looking at these transactions from the point of view of *its* finances. If you put money into your account, the bank owes you that money. Without getting too wrapped up in this, this is why these terms can appear to contradict what you've been taught previously, but the important thing is to remember the difference when thinking about this from your perspective.

The examples above aren't quite right at the moment. Money doesn't just appear or disappear out of nowhere. It has to come from somewhere and go somewhere. This is the principle behind double-entry bookkeeping.

Let's focus again on that example of the desk. When we bought it, it is right that we credited our cash bucket for the value of £200, because we now have £200 less than we did before. But we've also gained £200 worth of desk. Our business may have less money to spend, but it now has a desk with value. So, as well as crediting our cash account, we also need to debit our furniture account, which lists the value of all the furniture your company owns. You debit your furniture account because value is flowing into it.

In this case, the entry would be as shown in Table 9.3.

Table 9.1 Cash debit example

Account	Debit	Credit
Cash	£100	

Table 9.2 Cash credit example

Account	Debit	Credit
Cash		£60
Cash		£200
Cash		£16.50

Table 9.3 Debit and credit example

Account	Debit	Credit
Furniture	£200	
Cash		£200

It's worth taking a moment to make sure this makes sense. We can't just say that we have spent £200 without thinking about what we have gained in return. Otherwise, we'd incorrectly report that we were £200 worse off without considering the fact that our company now owns a swanky new desk, which it could one day sell and make money from. The desk has its own value. Double-entry bookkeeping balances this transaction.

Assets and liabilities

When we bought the petrol, the desk, and the books in the example above, our business now owns these. We can therefore refer to these as *assets*. Assets help to show how much your business is worth. In brief, if you own it and it has a value, it's an asset.

As this is such a broad category, assets are broken down a bit further. *Current assets* include cash (including in the bank) and anything that can be converted into cash (such as stock) within a year, plus any money you're owed from your debtors. *Fixed assets*, on the other hand, relate to things such as land, computers, vehicles, and trademarks.

Liabilities are things we owe: essentially, *debt*. Debts might take the form of bank loans, unpaid bills, IOUs, mortgages, or any money that you owe somebody else. As with assets, we break liabilities into two primary categories: *current liabilities* are debts that you expect to be paid back within the next twelve months. Long-term liabilities are debts that aren't due for another twelve months.

Why is this important? Assets and liabilities tell you what your company has, what it owes, and what's left over. It's the essential ingredient for understanding the health of your business.

Depreciation

We paid £200 for our desk, but is that how much it is worth? If you were to sell it, even the day after you have bought it, it is likely that it's value will have decreased. Alternatively, if we held on to the desk for five years and sold it on at a later date, it's likely that we'll get a much smaller sum for it. If the leg breaks and we're forced to take it to the recycling centre, we may get nothing for it at all.

Accounting has systems in place for all these eventualities, which are referred to as *depreciation*. As an item falls in value, it depreciates. This is important because even though we're currently claiming that we have gained £200 worth of desk, it would be inaccurate for us to still be claiming that in a year, or ten years' time. Balance Sheets (which we'll come to soon) have an area to account for this.

Taking stock

So far, we've introduced the notion of bookkeeping, debit and credit, assets, and liabilities. Even these simple starting points can seem overwhelming, so it is important to take the time that you need to really digest this information. It can feel difficult at first, but the essential principles are quite simple once you adapt to this way of working.

This is a useful point to take a step back and consider the broader picture, so that you can develop an appreciation of exactly why all this matters and how it fits together. Companies need to know how much money they're spending and what they're making so that they can make profit, detect errors, and inform others. Although it might be nice for each company to do this in their own way, there is also a legal requirement for companies to pay tax and be transparent and open about the money they have made. Bookkeeping is the first stage of this process, with the *Balance Sheet* and *Profit and Loss accounts*, as we'll explore in a moment, formalising these records so that the *story* of these transactions can be understood.

Help! It's all too much

Although getting a grip on numbers can be empowering (how would you know if you were spending more to make a product than you were making by selling it?), it can be a seriously persistent hurdle for many. The pressure of not making mistakes, as per your legal requirements, can similarly be a big headache on top of the day-to-day running of your business. It is important to remember that help is available, although unfortunately this does come at a cost. The previously mentioned cloud-based accounting systems are worth looking at, as they help to automate much of this process, cutting down on the time investment and helping to direct your steps and spot errors. Many also come with fantastic bank account integration and additional support.

If you are financially able to, you should seek the services of an accountant at your earliest opportunity. Not only will this save you time and money in the long run, the worry of getting it wrong will be reduced and, as you start to grow, their expertise will help to make sure that you are streamlining your operations to be tax efficient. Because accounting can be so complex, it is recommended that you find an accountant who deals with your sector (entertainment, leisure, etc.). If you are in a position to afford an accountant, remember to take the time to scope them out and get a feel for them: they're being paid to work for you, so make sure they work *for* you. The relationship with your accountant will be crucial going forward, so finding somebody who you can work with will really pay off.

Tax and VAT

Any limited company must pay *Corporation Tax* on its business profits. At the time of writing, the rate of Corporation Tax is 20% in the UK, though this can change regularly, so check your government website for the latest rate. You don't receive a bill for Corporation Tax, so you have to work it out yourself, and payment is usually due nine months after the end of your accounting period (so if your annual accounts are due in August, for example, any payment will be due in May). Unfortunately, this can be a headache-inducing stage for many companies, with the process not being incredibly user friendly. Again, the services of an accountant are highly recommended, and you're advised not to self-complete your tax return unless you feel confident in doing so. One slight silver lining is that the less profit you've made (or even if you've lost money) the easier this process is to complete! You must pay Corporation Tax on profit your company makes from doing business, or 'trading profits' as it's officially known, and this can all be done online via the Government Gateway.

You may have heard that companies don't pay *VAT* on purchases in the same way you and I do when we buy things from shops and restaurants. You *must* register for VAT if your 'taxable turnover' is greater than £85,000, or you can voluntarily register before this threshold. Registering for VAT means that you can reclaim any VAT that you are charged when you pay for goods and services, but you must also charge VAT to your customers for things like business sales. If your *'input tax,'* the amount of VAT you pay, is greater than your *'output tax,'* the amount you collect from your customers, you can collect the difference back, which can save you money. It also comes with increased paperwork and, by charging VAT, higher prices to your customers. If you're thinking about registering for VAT before reaching the threshold (at which point it is mandatory), take time to research the potential pros and cons before making any major decisions.

Statutory requirements

You need to exercise good financial management to protect the health of your organisation, but there are also a few elements which you are required to keep by law. The specifics of what this includes depends on your territory and tax requirements, and this can often be broken down further by company size. For example, in the UK, small and micro companies are able to produce streamlined financial accounts, which do not contain the same level of detail as their larger counterparts. Usually though, the foundational elements of these accounts will include a version of a Balance Sheet and Profit and Loss accounts.

You are required to submit your annual accounts to the government and relevant tax authorities, so that you can be taxed appropriately for any profit you have earned. In the UK, this authority is known as HMRC, although if you're ever unsure, a quick search for 'submit annual accounts' will always point you in the right direction.

My Theatre Company
BALANCE SHEET
As of Today's Date

	TOTAL
FIXED ASSET	
Tangible Assets	
Books	80.02
Accumulated Depreciation	-16.00
Total Books	**64.02**
Costume Stock	500.00
Accumulated Depreciation	150.00
Total Costume Stock	**350.00**
Props	2300.00
Accumulated Depreciation	1300.00
Total Props	**1000.00**
Total Tangible Assets	**£1414.02**
Total Fixed Assets	**£1414.02**
CASH AT BANK AND IN HAND	
Business Bank Account	11140.00
Cash	0.00
Total Cash at Bank and In Hand	**£11140.00**
DEBTORS	
Debtors	0.00
Total Debtors	**£0.00**
NET CURRENT ASSETS	£0.00
CREDITORS: AMOUNTS DUE FALLING WITHIN ONE YEAR	
Current Liabilities	0.00
Accruals and Deferred Income	0.00
Total Current Liabilities	0.00
Total Creditors: Amounts due Falling Within One Year	**£0.00**
NET CURRENT ASSETS (LIABILITIES)	£0.00
TOTAL ASSETS LESS TOTAL CURRENT LIABILITIES	£12554.02
TOTAL NET ASSETS (LIABILITIES)	£12554.02
CAPITAL AND RESERVES	
Opening Balance Equity	0.00
Retained Earnings	100.00
Profit for the Year	1068.02
Total Capital and Reserves	**£1168.02**

Figure 9.2 Balance Sheet example

Note

- The accounts have been prepared in accordance with the micro-entity provisions.
- The accounts have been delivered in accordance with the provisions applicable to companies subject to the small company's regime.
- Grants have been recognised using the Accrual basis - grants for current and future expenses, where income is recognised when the expenses occur.
- For the year ending mm/dd/yy the company was entitled to exemption from audit under section 477 of the Companies Act 2006 relating to small companies.
    - The directors acknowledge their responsibilities for complying with the requirements of the Act with respect to accounting records and the preparation of accounts
    - The members have not required the company to obtain an audit of its accounts for the year in question in accordance with section 476
- The financial statements were approved and authorised for issue by the board and were signed on its behalf on dd/mm/yy.

....
Name, Director

Figure 9.2 (Cont.)

Balance Sheet

A Balance Sheet brings together much of the information we discussed above. It summarises what the company owns (assets), what it is owed (liabilities), and the value of your investment (equity). The Balance Sheet is a legal requirement as part of your annual accounts, and it is an essential snapshot of the value of your business at the moment of time when it was created.

Profit and Loss accounts

The Balance Sheet shows the overall health of your business at the moment it was created. What it gains in breadth of information, it lacks in helping to show exactly where your money has come from and gone to. The Profit and Loss account brings in the information from your bookkeeping system to summarise where you have spent your money and where you have generated income over the last accounting period. This information hopefully will reveal that you have made more than you have spent this year, hence generating a profit. The Profit and Loss account is another of the key financial documents usually required by law as part of your company accounts.

Profit

Making profit is one of the main goals of any business, but you need to appreciate the different ways in which profit works to really understand where your business stands. If you sold £30,000 worth of tickets this year, you might be tempted to say that you have made a £30,000 profit. While this isn't incorrect, we also need to think about the fact that you spent £23,000 on all the various costs associated with creating a show. When we take this into account, you only actually have £7,000 more than what you started with.

My Theatre Company
Profit and Loss
1st September 20XX - 31st August 20XX

NOTES	Yr 2	Yr 1
INCOME		
Discounts Given	0.00	0.00
Sales of Product Income	341.33	595.86
Services	100.00	0.00
Total Income	**441.33**	**595.86**
COST OF SALES		
Cost of Sales - Materials	0.00	0.00
Furniture Hire	20.00	0.00
Makeup	30.00	0.00
Set Hire	100.00	0.00
Set Raw Materials	0.00	0.00
Total Cost of Sales	**200.00**	**0.00**
GROSS PROFIT	441.33	595.86
EXPENSES		
Advertising / Promotional	0.00	0.00
Bank Charges	1.20	3.00
CPD	0.00	0.00
Entertainment	0.00	0.00
Fuel	0.00	0.00
Insurances	0.00	0.00
Legal and professional fees	0.00	0.00
Music License	0.00	0.00
Office/ General Administrative Expenses	169.10	0.00
Printing, Postage and Stationery	0.00	0.00
Studio Hire	99.80	216.18
Supplies	1400.00	168.80
Theatre Hire	171.80	0.00
Travel and Accommodation	0.00	0.00
Travel meals	0.00	0.00
Bad Debts	0.00	1055.68
TOTAL EXPENSES	**1840.70**	**1443.68**
NET OPERATING INCOME	-1399.37	-847.80
OTHER INCOME		
Donation Income	0.00	0.00
Government Grant	1400.00	0.00
Other Miscellaneous Income	0.00	0.00
TOTAL OTHER INCOME	**1400.00**	**0.00**
OTHER EXPENSES		
Depreciation	16.00	12.00
Loss from Disposal of Assets	0.00	0.00
TOTAL OTHER EXPENSES	**16.00**	**12.00**
NET OTHER INCOME	16.00	12.00
NET INCOME	-1383.37	-835.80

Figure 9.3 Profit and Loss Account example

Gross profit

The two terms we must consider when discussing profit are gross profit and net profit. While turnover is the total number of sales made, gross profit is the total profit made minus your *cost of sales*. Cost of sales appears in your Profit and Loss account and is a summary of the costs associated with producing your product or service. Imagine you are selling a chair for £100. It might cost you £50 to buy the parts from a supplier, plus £5 for delivery. Your labour cost might be £20. Sold at £100 − £45 − £5 − £20, your gross profit would = £25.

Net profit

Net profit, on the other hand, shows your total sales minus all the costs of running your business. In addition to the above, you would include rent, bills, salaries, and bank charges. If you have a gross profit of £5,000, rent of £1,000, salaries of £3,500, £100 of software, and £20 bank charges, then your net profit is £5,000 − £1,000 − £3,500 − £100 − £20 = £380. Linked with this, it is always really useful to know your break-even figure. This number details the point at which your sales cover your expenses, and often represents the minimum number of sales you need to achieve to return a profit.

Paying yourself and others

Paying yourself and eventually paying others is a fantastic mark of success for any business person. As with many financial components, there are a lot of variations and region-specific complexity involved with this, so always do your own research into the specifics of your own situation and seek financial support if you are unsure. Payroll systems automate the paying of staff wages and the complexities of tax deductions, student loan repayments, and whatever else may come out of a person's pay packet. In the UK, this is referred to as PAYE (Pay as you earn). The complexities of having a payroll of staff is probably beyond your current stage and is outside the scope of this book to explore fully, but you do need to be aware when choosing to pay yourself, either as part of your profits or with money from a successful grant, as you cannot simply dump money into your personal account and then move on.

You should seek independent advice about the best way to pay yourself, as there are a range of complexities regarding tax thresholds, whether or not you have another job and how much you must pay in tax. I have linked into several excellent resources at the end of the chapter to support with this when you reach this stage. If you are already registered as self-employed, this is arguably the easiest situation for you to navigate, as the earnings can be sent across to you in a lump sum for you to work out the deductions as you would on any other income, but again, please check your own situation and seek advice where you can.

Cashflow and automation

As a business owner you have a significant number of financial concerns to keep on top of. You have your budgets, your annual accounts, your daily, weekly, and monthly performance and your bookkeeping, to name but a few. It can be easy to lose track of the purpose of each of these processes and even harder to stay in touch with how they help and what links they have to each other.

As somebody who found finance daunting, it was very useful for me to take the time to break down each of these constituent parts to understand how they worked and then develop an appreciation of how they spoke to one another. Often we are expected to discuss an entire system of financial management, which can make it very difficult to get a foothold when we are building our confidence in this area. For me, having the time and permission to ask what felt like stupid questions about each of these individual areas was of huge help to developing my confidence in the process as a whole. You may find it helpful to visualise all of these steps in the form of a chart or calendar, both to keep track of your workload and to communicate how one piece of work informs another.

While it is really important to understand how the individual building blocks of financial management work, it is a relief to know that there are tools to help automate key parts of this. I put it this way, because the tools available are not there to plug a gap in your own knowledge but to make your workflow easier, and so you do still need to do the homework rather than hoping that a system such as an online accounting software will do the work for you. This can be an easy path towards not understanding your numbers at all, which could be disastrous. Feeling empowered by your numbers is a really healthy way to understand your business, and the key to doing this is clarity and storytelling. Clarity comes in the way the data is presented to draw attention to the important details, and storytelling comes from how we interpret that data into something useful.

When you are confident with your numbers, those stages of automation that make life easier can be a blessing. If you run a business with a point of sales (POS) or e-commerce system, make sure you link them up with your online accounting software. Similarly, with your business bank account, do your research to find out which banks communicate with which accounting software. These time-saving tips can make the whole process simpler and can also reduce the chance of mistakes, both of which will be of comfort to you. When you're in the daunting but exciting position of creating your financial ecosystem from scratch, finding ways to make sure those processes speak to each other should be a big priority.

Budgeting and forecasting

Budgeting is a mindset as much as a skillset. You will most likely come to budgeting when you're applying for your first funding grant, but it is something you should be doing – and doing well – from the very first project you run.

Budgeting allows you to predict costs and ensure that you are on top of what you are spending and how much you are making back. After the event, budgets allow you to review what parts of your operation took up the most resources and which were the most profitable.

The broad and granular mindset

Budgeting effectively requires two simultaneous mindsets. On the one hand, you have to be super obsessed with detail and make sure you have covered every possible eventuality so as not to be surprised further down the line. On the other hand, there are always a number of unknowns when budgeting any project, which can make it almost impossible to estimate accurately. So where do you begin?

Firstly, recognise which of the two areas (detail or estimation) you are generally more comfortable with, and spend some time honing the weaker of the two for you. I am a stickler for detail and I will often start budgets by digging away at minute details down to the last penny. What I'm less efficient at is taking those broader strokes to envisage the project at large. Sometimes this means that I can't see the wood for the trees, but it does mean that my budgets tend to be relatively accurate. On the other hand, many people are really good at estimating broad costs and absolutely hate adding detail. Recognising your own preference, and the fact that you do need competence in both, is the first step on this journey.

Starting to budget

There is no perfect guide to budgeting, and you could approach this in multiple ways, so experiment to find a system you like.

When budgeting you are often trying to establish how much money you will need (costs) and how much money you hope (or need) to make (profit). These are linked, but they are two separate calculations, so for the time being we'll focus on costs.

Start by compiling a list of broad costs for your production. For now, these can be fairly generic. Where you have the information to make a reasonably informed guess, put that in, and where you don't, leave it blank.

In the example in Table 9.4, I have used really broad headings to begin my budget. I know that the performance licence for this production costs £50 and

Table 9.4 Simple budget expenditure example

Cost	£
Performance Licence	£200
Studio Hire	£375
Props and Costumes	£500
Transport	

I know I'm performing for four nights. £50 x 4 = £200. Similarly, I know the hourly rental rate for my rehearsal studio and how many times I need to rent it, so I can fill in this cost accurately.

When it comes to props and costumes, I'm entering into a grey area. I don't know this for sure and costs could vary. I have ten cast members who will all need some level of costume and props, so I've taken an educated guess, based on my past experience and a bit of research, that each cast member will cost about £50. Of course this will vary: some cast members will cost a lot more and some hardly any, but this feels like an estimate that I am comfortable with.

For the time being I have left transport blank. This is the kind of cost that has a lot of variables. How many people am I transporting? Where to? What method of transport are they using? Suddenly this can start to feel complex. Let's break it down.

We'll imagine that we've agreed to pay train fare for ten actors to travel from Liverpool to Manchester. A cost of a ticket is, on average, £13. One actor has a car, though, and wants to drive, so we'll cover their petrol. They said they'd be happy if we could just give them £10.

With a bit of research we can start to dig into these unknown sums a bit, to reach a figure that feels reasonable. Nine actors x £13 = £117 + £10 petrol = £127. At this stage, we can round that up to £130.

To begin with, budgets are about estimation. In the above example, if we were applying for £100,000, we might decide to round up the fuel cost to £200, to cover us if needed. Budgeting, particularly to begin with, is about guided, defined guesswork, backed up by research or past experience. By the time you budget your tenth show, you won't need to necessarily estimate so much, as you'll have a wealth of experience to fall back on. Your aim, in the first instance, is to arrive at a rough figure so that you understand the ballpark you are operating in. Are your costs £1,000 or £10,000?

Contingency

Costs always fluctuate and every project will contain unexpected savings as well as unpleasant surprises. Contingency is the budgeting word for 'a safety net' and it's almost always necessary. Funders like to see that you have taken this into account as well, so it's useful to incorporate this into any bids for external funding. Usually between 8% and 10% contingency is seen as a respectable level of safety net. Any less might be too small to weather unexpected changes and any more might be seen as needing more discipline.

Risk management

When thinking about any financial matters, it is also important to consider risk. Your board are responsible for ensuring healthy financial management, but it is up to you to recognise risks and initiate a process for dealing with them. Risk is obviously not related specifically to finance – there are risks in all aspects of running a business – but it's particularly worth mentioning here because of the obvious implications for failing to mitigate against financial risk.

Every risk management process involves the following steps:

- Identify the risk
- Assess its impact
- Prioritise its importance
- Find a way to mitigate
- Monitor the ongoing progress.

The easiest way to evidence this is through a risk register, shared with the board. A risk register, as shown in Figure 9.4, highlights the potential risks and assigns a score based on their likelihood and potential severity. It's the same format as a risk assessment in health and safety, which you may be familiar with.

A risk register helps to demonstrate to yourself and others that you have been responsible with your governance and that your financial plans have been developed through a robust process, in conversation with the board of directors.

Risk	Risk Details	Impact (1 - 5) 1 = Lowest 5 = Highest	Likelihood (1 - 5) 1 = Lowest 5 = Highest	Impact x Likelihood Overall Score	Action Required	Owner	Updated: Date
1	Failure to secure funding to support core activity	1	3	3			
2	Failure to secure funding to support business development ambitions	2	5	10			
3	Landlord serves us with an eviction notice	3	5	15			
5	Inability to generate sufficient unrestricted income to use as match-funding on applications	5	4	20			
	1 – 8 = Green	Green - minor or insignificant risks			Low level monitoring required		
	9 – 14 = Amber	Amber - moderate or major risks			Remedial action and senior level monitoring required		
	15 – 25 = Red	Red - major or extreme / catastrophic risks			Urgent remedial action required		

Figure 9.4 Risk register example

Budgeting process

If you earn money and have bills to pay and manage to do that each month, then you know how to budget. Budgeting for a large-scale theatre tour is exactly the same process, but just with more numbers.

Budgeting should not be scary, and taking ownership of your numbers empowers you creatively because you know what you can and can't achieve. With this knowledge, you're better prepared to ensure the production meets its potential with the resources available to it.

When budgeting, it can be helpful to find a template and work from that. However, in my experience, these templates can often be more advanced than you require and their added complexity can cause confusion. A very simply budget could be knocked up on Microsoft Excel in less than fifteen minutes. So by all means look at some templates as examples, but it may be easier in the long run to define your own set of rules.

The rules and formulas behind a budget are generally going to be fairly simple, so don't feel as though you need superior knowledge to be able to create your own. The only place you may want to make an exception for this is when it comes to layout. Budgets are notorious for growing as you remember more and more things you need to budget for, and before you know it a simple sheet can be hard to follow. There is no right and wrong way to lay out a budget, but you may want to spend half an hour brushing up on your Excel formatting skills to recap how to colour cells, add tables, thick lines, and different font colours, etc. Remember, though, this is most definitely not an exercise in making a budget look pretty: it needs to be clear and easy for anybody to follow. Formatting should help with that; it does not need to look pretty. In fact, depending on who the audience for your budget is, such an approach could unwittingly end up counting against you.

The general expectation is that a budget will indicate both the income (how much you are going to make) and the expenditure (how much you will spend) for your production. If you plan to spend more than you will make, your budget needs revising as your production will currently run out of money and make a loss. Your aim is to ensure that your budget balances: that your level of income matches your level of expenditure.

Budgets should always balance. A budget is said to be balanced when your income is equal to or greater than your expenses. In simple terms, there is little point in putting together a project that is going to cost more than you plan to make back – on this basis, you are guaranteed to lose money, and in practical terms, you will run out of cash before the project is completed. A budget can be balanced, though, from many different sources. In the example in Table 9.5, this

Table 9.5 Simple budget income example

Income	£
Money from savings	150
Expected ticket sales	300

project would be contributing £150 from savings and expecting to make a further £300 from ticket sales (which is in the future, and therefore an estimate). This gives a total projected income of £450, so if the costs of the project were less than this, the project will be financially healthy.

When detailing your costs and income sources, your budget will become pretty unruly if you list every single item you plan to buy and sell. Therefore, use categories to make this budget more user friendly. You may be travelling by train to rehearsal, flying to one of your performance venues and hiring a van. All of these could come under the budget heading of Travel. You want to strike a balance between being concise and giving enough detail. Having separate headings for Train Travel, Air Travel, Petrol, etc. might be too much. Equally, you need to avoid ambiguous headings, or headings that make it confusing as to where something would fall. Look at examples of other theatre budgets to help find standardised categories that make sense to everybody.

Predicting how much something will cost is probably the hardest part of a budget. How do you know what your set build costs will be when you're only at the budgeting stage and haven't got a design or a designer yet? Spoiler alert: you aren't expected to know. The best you can aim for is an educated guess. You could do some research into the cost of raw materials to settle on an estimate that feels right. Could you ask a designer for a quote for their fees? As you become more experienced, you'll start to know that 'we budgeted X for our set last time and it was nowhere near enough,' and your past experience will help refine your budgeting skills more accurately.

The important thing to remember with budgeting is that it is your best guess. The key is being able to back up those figures with some reasonably informed knowledge to show that you haven't plucked those numbers out of thin air. When applying for grants, lenders may sometimes ask you to justify your figures, and your application will often be being judged by somebody who has more experience of projects at this scale, so the more confident you can be that your numbers are more or less in the right area, the better. What you don't want to do is estimate that a budget item will only cost £100, when some research would easily have told you it'll cost £10,000. This looks unprofessional to funders who will doubt your project management skills, and more importantly, if the project did go ahead, you'd quickly find yourself with a big financial headache.

So far, your budget will look something similar to Tables 9.6 and 9.7.

Table 9.6 Project income

Ticket Sales	1000
Donations	250
Grant Money	1000

Table 9.7 Project expenditure

Costumes	200
Set	500
Accommodation	1000

Income

Expenditure

You may notice that I have presented conveniently rounded up numbers. This is the good old broad and granular mindset in play. Whether to round up or not all depends on the audience and purpose of your budget. For yourself, you might find it more useful to present your incredibly specific calculations, but for budget applications it is usually easier to round it up so that it looks a bit tidier. A rounded up figure of £400, also creates room for a margin of error that conveys more confidence than if you have budgeted £345.22, for example.

Your budget should indicate your Income and Expenditure, but following this simplistic approach will create some difficulties as your project expands. It is therefore advisable to break down your Income and Expenditure into clearly defined budget lines. This helps to visualise the different categories contained within Income and Expenditure, for example, Props, Set, and Costumes, so that you can see on a line-by-line basis what the budget is for each. Apart from helping with the overall comprehension of a budget, which could quickly become unwieldy, budget lines are essential to separate so that you can respond efficiently when your project begins. To appreciate this fully, let's add some additional headings to our budget.

All good budgets will contain variations of the three columns seen in Table 9.8.

Budgets aren't just for the beginning of the process, and they become most useful when they are regularly checked and updated throughout the life of a project. The three headings in Table 9.8 help to visualise this, so that you can keep a regular check on how much things actually cost and what this has done to your finances overall.

This is where visualising your separate budget lines becomes an essential step in your budgeting process. Budgets are always interlinked, so a purchase from one budget line which costs you £200 more than you expected needs to be found from somewhere else, either by borrowing from another budget line or by raising more cash.

Table 9.8 Budget costing headers

Predicted Cost	Actual Cost	Difference
£20	£16	–£4

Support in-kind

A term you will become familiar with, particularly when submitting budgets for funding, is in-kind support. In-kind support is a technical term for being given a favour, and attributing a financial value to that favour.

For example, if your university gives you permission to use their rehearsal studios for free, this would be classed as in-kind support. If that same studio would normally cost £20 an hour to rent, you are able to estimate the rough value of this in-kind support by estimating how much you have saved.

Support in-kind is something to consider when calculating your budgets because this usually serves as an income line. It can therefore help to show that you have raised more income for your project, even though it is not necessarily cash based.

Spreadsheet tips

The overview of your project's projected Income and Expenditure is referred to as your *top sheet*, because it would traditionally be the sheet presented on the top of a printed budget, which briefly outlines everything a producer or investor needs to know, without going into all of the nitty gritty detail.

However, the above section is not to imply that the detail is not important: it absolutely is. The detail, i.e., the thinking behind those nice, clear figures in the top sheet, is where people will make judgements about your process and where you will keep track of actual spending. The simplest way to do this is to use other *sheets*.

If you haven't used other sheets in your spreadsheet program before, they're very simple to get to grips with. Think of them as another page: when you add another sheet you'll be greeted with another blank spreadsheet. You may find it instructive to create a separate sheet for *tracking* income and another for tracking expenditure. This can be broken down further, by creating a separate sheet for each budget line. It's all about what works best for you. Using sheets allows you to do the hard calculations, and to show that you've done them, while also keeping that out of sight, so that your basic financial picture can be understood by whoever is looking at it. Spreadsheets need to tell a story, otherwise they become a mass of numbers and headings that mean nothing to anybody, except perhaps the person who made it. This is not a good habit to get into. In your life as a producer, it will be a rare occasion when you are the only audience for the budget you are creating.

Three formulas are particularly useful to be familiar with when budgeting. Let us imagine that we need to buy three boxes for our show. We could log this in our budget as shown in Table 9.9.

Table 9.9 Spreadsheet items listed individually

Box	24.50
Box	24.50
Box	24.50

Obviously this is a waste of time and space. But we could simply combine these costs as in Table 9.10.

We lose the important detail of how much the boxes cost individually. This is important, because if we later decide we need five boxes, we're making work for ourselves to figure this out.

A much better strategy is to add some columns and a formula to our spreadsheet, as in Table 9.11.

In order to make this work how we want, we need a basic formula. In the Total column, we need to tell our program to multiply the Unit Price (24.50) by the Quantity (3). To do this, we would type:

=SUM

This is the technical language that indicates to your spreadsheet that we are about to enter a formula. Now we need to look at which cell our information is contained within. All spreadsheet programs contain *rows* and *columns*, each of which is listed with a number or a letter. These work alphabetically and numerically, so the third cell along on the first row will be cell C1. The fifth cell along on the fifth row will be E5, and so on.

Going back to our table, we need to find the cell with the Unit Price – in this case, it's cell C2. The cell with the Quantity value is cell B2 (Table 9.12).

We can now add these to our formula to give us:

=SUM(C2*B2)

Notice that I have used brackets to contain the part of the formula where the sum actually takes place. This is part of the language your software uses to

Table 9.10 Spreadsheet items accumulated

Box	73.5

Table 9.11 Spreadsheet layout example

Item	Quantity	Unit Price	Total
Box	3	24.50	73.5

Table 9.12 Spreadsheet cell identification

	A	B	C	D
1	Item	Quantity	Unit Price	Total
2	Box	3	24.50	73.5

know that I want it to do a calculation at this point, and the important thing to remember is that you must always close your brackets once they have been opened (a sentence such as this one which has an open bracket at the start but no bracket at the end looks very much like a mistake, right?

The second thing to notice is the asterix *. This is the sign for multiplication. What we're asking our program to do is to multiply the value in cell C2 by the value in cell B2.

This may seem like a lot more work than whipping out your calculator and asking it to multiply 24.50 by 3. But budgets are always changing by their very nature. By placing this formula here, the computer will do all the work for us now if we decide to change the quantity, or if the price of the boxes increases. It will now take me a matter of seconds to update this in the table and the program will do the calculation for me.

When you have listed all of the costs in a category, you will need to figure out the total. You could use your calculator to do some adding up, but as your budget grows, this will quickly become cumbersome. To make life easier, we need to add formula. Take a look at the example in Table 9.13.

We want to calculate the total cost of our expenditure from the calculations.

I have deliberately added larger and more complex numbers here to demonstrate the point. It would be simple to pull out a calculator and total these up to reach £22,500. But imagine that between budgeting and starting this project, minimum wage increased by £0.10. Now our staffing costs will be completely inaccurate. We'll need to go to our Staff Cost sheet and total all of our figures up again. Let's imagine that our new cost is now £17,122.

Done. Right? Wrong. Because now we also need to remember to recalculate the total cost for our whole budget! Although formulas can feel like hard work, particularly when you're not used to using them, this is nothing compared to the effort of keeping track of a budget you are running manually. Formulas are ways of making the program do the work for you. One small change to one part of your budget might affect a huge number of other figures, and without formulas keeping track of this and avoiding mistakes will be very time consuming indeed.

Table 9.13 Spreadsheet costings for adding

	A	B	C
1	Set Build	1240	
2	Staff Costs	14,547	
3	Printing	389	
4	Transport	2891	
5	Accommodation	3433	

In the case in Table 9.13, we need a formula to calculate the totals for us. By now, you should be able to recognise that the cells we want to deal with are B1, B2, B3, B4, and B5. So, to our formula:

=SUM(B1+B2+B3+B4+B5)

Easy, right? Notice how I'm now using the symbol '+' for adding up. We can actually simplify this further, if we have a long string of numbers such as this, by using the ':' symbol.

=SUM(B1:B5)

This is telling our program: calculate the total of all these cells. Now, if a value changes, all we have to do is input the change and the program will automatically recalculate everything else for us.

Profit shares and open book

When you are in your earliest stages you are likely to be working with very limited resources, maybe even pitching in together to help get the project off the ground. As you grow and start to get your first small bits of fruit from the tree, you may still be a long way from being able to pay contributors their expected rates. In these circumstances, you could consider recruiting collaborators with the promise of sharing any future profits that your project goes on to make.

All of these stages are both real and necessary for any new theatre company without a huge amount of starting capital. You should always be aiming to pay people, and it is both a moral and legal responsibility to ensure that you do pay people when you are able to do so. But until that stage, both profit share and open book can help you on this tricky journey.

Profit share does exactly what it says on the tin. If the production makes a profit, those funds will be distributed between the people involved. Unless you have a very good reason not to, these profits should be shared equally amongst everyone, and this should extend beyond the actors to include all who are involved. Remember that you are sharing *profits*, not just any money made, and it can be helpful to remind your team of this so that you don't create a false impression of being dishonest. A production can have really healthy audiences, but it doesn't necessarily mean that it has been *profitable* if those ticket sales haven't helped to cover the costs of putting the show on the stage. Profit is the money left over once all expenses have been accounted for and is distinctly different to income. As producer, this can be tricky to navigate as not everyone will have this lingo, so it is really important to take time to bring everyone onto the same page.

A brilliant way of communicating the financial position of a production is through the open book model. This relatively new way of working is a fantastic tool, particularly for profit-share productions. The open book model makes the budget and running costs of a show available and transparent for all members of the company to see. Rather than leaving anything to guess work and rumour, sharing the budget and costs can be a really useful tool so that all of your team can see what profit there is, if any, and what the money has been spent on. The budget should take the exact same form as listed previously, with individual budget lines, actual costs, and forecasted expenses, so that everybody has access to the full financial picture, should they choose to view it. This raises your trustworthiness, as your spending can be seen and analysed by the company, and helps the company to feel more involved and part of the entire creative process. It is a sad fact that most theatre is economically tricky, to put it mildly, so the open book model can also be a good way of highlighting the profit situation to others in your cast and crew. Often those not involved in the producing side of staging theatre can be blissfully ignorant of the immense costs involved in pretty much every stage of the process, and can be left suspicious when a healthy audience doesn't appear to return any profit. The open book model details this fairly and transparently. If you are going to do this, it can also be useful to link in copies of receipts so that your team have confidence in the numbers you are inputting.

When using an open book model, it is best executed when it becomes part of the shared language of the production itself, so take time to share the process and logic behind it and to take your team through it, bearing in mind that they may not have the confidence with spreadsheets that you now feel! Remember to spell out the difference between income and profit, and that you will be recouping your costs before profit is counted. Don't set out to bamboozle people with numbers in the hope that they won't pay attention; people will respect your position much more if they feel you have made a genuine attempt to democratise the process to include them. They are also much more likely to support you when things are going wrong, as they will see clearly how much of an impact your poor ticket sales are having on the bottom line, for instance.

Chapter Resources

Financial management

'Accounting,' Bench, https://bench.co/blog/accounting/
'Bookkeeping – What is bookkeeping?' SumUp, https://sumup.co.uk/invoices/dictionary/bookkeeping/
'Budget Templates,' Open Book Theatre Management, http://openbooktheater.co.uk/freebudgets
'Gross profit vs net profit,' Starling Bank, www.starlingbank.com/resources/business-guides/gross-profit-vs-net-profit-explained/
'How to pay yourself as a Ltd company UK,' *Honest Money,* YouTube (8th June 2021) www.youtube.com/watch?v=SRt2sGH14xw&t=212s

Mahfouz, Sabrina, 'Applying for Arts Funding: A guide,' in *Smashing It: Working class artists on life, art & making it happen*. Ed. Sabrina Mahfouz (The Westbourne Press, London, 2019), www.docdroid.net/JDQXwhJ/smashing-it-a-guide-to-applying-for-funding-pdf#page=2

'Preparing annual accounts for a private limited company,' Gov.uk, www.gov.uk/annual-accounts

'Resources,' Freelancers Make Theatre Work, https://freelancersmaketheatrework.com/practical-resources/

Rice, Anthony, *Accounts Demystified: The astonishingly simple guide to accounting*, 7th edition (Pearson, Harlow, 2015)

'Theatre tax relief,' Gov.uk (26th April 2016), www.gov.uk/hmrc-internal-manuals/theatre-tax-relief

'Touring budget template,' House Theatre, 2015, https://housetheatre.org.uk/resources/touring-budget-template/

'What is depreciation?' Zero Accounting, www.xero.com/uk/guides/what-is-depreciation/

'What receipts should I keep as a sole trader?' Go Simple Tax (19th February 2020), https://sumup.co.uk/invoices/dictionary/bookkeeping/

'What's the difference between a receipt and an invoice?' SumUp, https://sumup.co.uk/invoices/dictionary/bookkeeping/

Zarzycki, Nick, 'Debits and credits: A simple visual guide,' Bench (29th June 2021) https://bench.co/blog/bookkeeping/debits-credits/

Zarzycki, Nick, 'What are assets, liabilities and equity?' Bench (25th November 2019) https://bench.co/blog/accounting/assets-liabilities-equity/

Budgeting

'Approaching budgets,' Arts Admin, www.artsadmin.co.uk/for-artists/resources-directory/approaching-budgets/

Bridges, Jennifer, '7 steps for a successful project budget,' Project Manager (3rd December 2019), www.projectmanager.com/training/create-and-manage-project-budget

Burton-Morgan, Poppy, 'The ethics of budgeting,' UK Theatre, (18th April 2017), https://uktheatre.org/who-we-are-what-we-do/uk-theatre-blog/the-ethics-of-budgeting/

Hishon, Kerry, 'How to create a budget when you've never done it before,' TheatreFolk, www.theatrefolk.com/blog/how-to-create-a-budget-when-youve-never-done-it-before/

'How to budget,' ArtQuest, https://artquest.org.uk/how-to-articles/project-budgets/

'Making a production / touring budget,' Bradford Producing Hub, https://bdproducinghub.co.uk/making-a-production-touring-budget/

'Sample Budgets,' Red Table Theatre, http://redtabletheatre.com/open-book-theatre/sample-budgets/

'UK Theatre Tax Relief', Gov.uk, www.gov.uk/hmrc-internal-manuals/theatre-tax-relief

10 Raising Funds

Finding funding

Finding funding is one of the biggest challenges facing any new business. Luckily, there are a range of options available if you do your homework. Searching and applying for funding is a time consuming process and is not for the faint hearted, and unfortunately it does sometimes feel as though these intimidating systems are designed to deter new artists from applying. However, as more and more people search for funding and as their resources become tighter, it is reasonable to appreciate that funds need to have strong systems in place to make best use of their limited money and manpower in order to reach the people they want to support.

Sources of funding

Any healthy business must aim to have a *sustainable and diverse income stream*. Put simply, there must be more than one method of generating income for your business and, preferably, no overreliance on any particular stream. This approach will allow you to be flexible and to avoid dependence on one particular form of income, which in turn can make you more flexible and prepared for change. There are many ways of raising and making money for your business, each with their own pros and cons, and each dependent on your specific skill set and experience.

Raising money for your business can take many forms. You can look at *loans, grants, trusts,* and *foundations, philanthropy, crowdfunding, sponsorship, donations*, or a mixture of several. Several of these methods may have terms attached – grant awarding bodies are notoriously specific about who and what they will fund – and depending on your business structure and the type of project you are looking to raise money for, these options may or may not be available to you.

Crowdfunding and donations

Crowdfunding can be a real bonus to your fundraising efforts, particularly where you already have a strong audience base and an effective strategy for reaching them through newsletters or social media.

DOI: 10.4324/9781003281726-10

Crowdfunding is an approach to raising money in which you launch a project on a website with a *funding goal* in mind, and members of the general public make donations of various sizes to help you reach that goal. In return for their generosity, donors are awarded with rewards to incentivise their investment.

In theory, crowdfunding is a wonderfully egalitarian method which carries none of the burden of grant reporting and which allows people to fund projects that are meaningful to them. It can be a great feeling to know that your project exists in part because of those people who believed in it enough to want to fund it.

Crowdfunding, however, should not be seen as a funding panacea and, while there are stories of incredible runaway successes, as with everything online, saturation has made such a result increasingly unlikely. In reality, it is probably unlikely that your project will attract the attention (even less, the money) from complete strangers, and so the success of any crowdfunding campaign will be in the efforts of your cast and crew to push the people in their immediate network to donate and spread the word. Running a successful crowdfunding campaign is arguably no more or less work than other fundraising methods, but it is at least as *much* work, and you should certainly get away from any notion that it is the easy option if you want to ensure success.

When launching a crowdfunding project your first decision is to pick a platform. There are a number of considerations to take into account here, despite the fact that they all appear to do much the same thing. First in your decision making should be the company policy about payment and unfinished projects. Broadly speaking, the platforms make their money by taking a percentage of your raised funds: so the total you raise is unlikely to be the total you actually receive. The percentage is only small, but this can add up across many donations, and the more you hope to raise the more you will be giving away. You will need to set a funding goal for your project, but the key difference comes into play for those projects who do not reach this target. Some platforms will give you the option of allowing you to keep the funds you do raise, but in exchange for this security they will usually charge you a higher rate for the privilege. On the other hand, some platforms will charge less on your donations, but projects will only be deemed successful if the funding goal is met. If you're even a pound out, the money will be returned to the investors. This is a great security for investors, as they know that their money will be safe if the project doesn't go ahead, which should give them more confidence to commit in the first place, but it does pose a challenge for the fundraiser. As always, you need to balance the pros and cons in your particular situation.

Key to getting your project right is to set a realistic funding goal to begin with. A crowdfunding campaign is an expulsion of energy from launch until the very end, as it is motivating for both you and your potential investors to see a project making consistent progress towards its goal. There is little more disheartening than a funding goal that has stalled.

Most projects will come with a set end date, although there are options for open-ended projects. Although this can be tempting, the momentum and sense of time commitment to a project with a clear deadline does put some wind in your sales to push to reach your goal, and again gives investors a clear message that the project is ready to move forward.

By any assessment, the most important part of any crowdfunding campaign is the *campaign page* itself. Here you will lay out the project, with options to include images and videos, and to detail the rewards available. This is your sales pitch and your shop window, and you should work closely with your team on getting this right. Remember that people are looking for authenticity and competency, so move away from hyperbolic language and instead be open and inspiring about the plan for the journey ahead.

You will normally be asked to share key milestones and to upload supplementary material. The world is your oyster here: it might be a good idea to show concept art, costume drawings, the set model, etc. You could record a trailer, but it will be quicker and more effective to record a short video of yourselves introducing the project. Having a personalised approach to your pitch will help people to build a connection to your project and to feel as though they are supporting you directly.

Rewards are given to investors in return for a set level of payment. An investor who donates £5 may get a shoutout on social media, whereas an investor who donates £500 will get that and more. You are able to define the number of reward levels and what those levels are. Your reward levels will influence your audience's behaviour, so if your first reward is for a donation of £50, consider whether that would be too high for your audience and whether it would therefore dissuade some potential investors. In the reverse situation, if there are a raft of rewards for £5, £10, £15, £20, are you downplaying the expectation and discouraging investors from sending you £100?

When setting your rewards, you need to ensure that you have the time and logistics to act upon them. This can be a much bigger job than you may realise at first, especially for those smaller rewards which are going to be the most popular. It can be really easy to come up with reward ideas and much more difficult to deliver on that promise, especially when you realise that sending everyone a personalised badge and tote bag is going to cost a huge amount more than you expected. In reality, most people are not donating to your project for a reward but the satisfaction of knowing they have supported your project into fruition, so don't spend more time worrying about rewards than is absolutely necessary. As a rule of thumb, if your reward is going to dent your budget more than to the tune of a pound or two, change the idea. The best rewards are meaningful and manageable: a shout-out, a mention in the program, a thank you letter from the cast. If you're going to the lengths of designing personalised gifts which will become somebody else's clutter, it's probably worth a rethink.

Crowdfunding can be lucrative and can generate a buzz around your project. It can double up as advertising to let people know that your project is happening. It's as easy to send the link to a celebrity on Twitter to donate (and this has worked for us) as it is to send to your grandparents for a few coins. At its best, it's an easy way to support because it doesn't require a huge outlay from an investor, and every donation visibly makes a difference. Projects that not only meet their funding goal, but exceed it, have generated an exciting level of anticipation before starting, which can be a huge boost to morale and eventual ticket sales. It can also be a way of tangibly evidencing support for a project. A worthwhile use of your time would be to establish a crowdfunder in which only very small donations are allowed; less than £1. If you can use this platform to evidence a significant number of people who have donated, it can be a great resource for evidencing your audience's involvement with your mission, which can really boost funding applications.

You should not underestimate the time and constant effort running a successful crowdfunding campaign will take. It is a *campaign*, and the work is only just beginning when you go live. It can be easy to share your page on social media endlessly and feel as though you've done a lot of work, but when was the last time you donated to something you'd seen randomly pop up on your timeline? For fundraising to be positive, you need both depth *and* reach. Often crowdfunding is less about sharing to millions of people and more about asking your aunt and uncle to donate £5 and getting them to ask their neighbour to do the same. It's hard graft, where numerous slow gains gradually build towards a greater result, in much the same way as selling tickets. It can be a significant amount of effort before you've even begun your project and potentially demoralising if it isn't successful. If a lot of donations helps to show support, it can feel as though a project which hasn't reached its goal has not only failed to raise the funds needed, but failed as a creative idea as well. This can be hard to pick yourself up from.

Finally, you need to be really attuned to crowdfunding fatigue to judge the likelihood of success. In my experience, crowdfunding is a good one-off to run every couple of years, and not something to rely on consistently. Asking your parents for £10 may not seem like much, but when you then ask them to buy tickets a few weeks later and to donate another £10 and another £10 to subsequent crowdfunders, the supposedly small contribution quickly becomes more of a drain. If your potential donor pool hasn't changed, expect it to become twice as hard to raise the same amount of money a second time round.

Philanthropy and high net-worth individuals

The arts have always gone hand in hand with both philanthropic giving and *patronage*. As long as there has been art there have been wealthy people willing to pay for it, and to a degree much of our theatre infrastructure still stands upon this central premise today, particularly in America. The relative rights and wrongs of this are not our concern, but exploring methods of patronage and philanthropy can be worth doing if you have a strong enough case. The key challenge with this method of income is access, and you will have a substantial head start in this area if you already have connections to this world through your own contacts or the contact of a relative/colleague. Although some high net-worth individuals establish foundations through which applications can be fielded, in the majority of cases these seemingly mysterious people are just people, usually working in all manner of different fields and professions, who want to give something back.

The challenge with starting from scratch in this area is that it can actually be illegal to straight up ask somebody for money. This pretty much rules out searching for the names of rich people and ringing them up, although this would be a crass strategy even if it was permitted! Instead, you should try and look for experience in this field when recruiting to your board and think carefully about who you might have connections to. People who run a business, who have retired or come into inheritance – there is no stereotype or one-shoe-fits-all when thinking about people who could potentially be donors, and while some may be professional philanthropists, many more may be wanting to make a contribution to the arts but not knowing where to begin.

If you can't think of anybody in your own circle, take time to look at other venues and companies in your region and see who they are funded by. This information will usually be contained in their company accounts and perhaps on their website as well. If there are local grant giving trusts in your area, draw up a list of them and get in touch. One sheet of A4 should do it: give them a really quick overview of who you are, what you're trying to achieve and what your next twelve months look like. Be explicit that you're not asking for money, but use the letter as a way of establishing a relationship. Many of the people running local trusts will be high profile individuals themselves or may have connections to those who are, and this can be a good way of building an initial relationship and getting the word out there. This is not to be confused with applying to those same trust funds for money through their own established channels, which we explore further below.

The same strategy can be employed for contacts you already know yourself. Don't pop up asking for money, but make a formal introduction and outline your mission and values. If the individual feels they align with it and can support you – and remember, there are many types of support above and beyond financial – the ball is in their court to take the next steps.

Philanthropy takes many forms from one-off donations to monthly membership schemes, and large theatres often have dedicated members of staff to manage and cultivate this essential part of their economic strategy. At your scale this is unlikely to be the case, although you may consider establishing a membership scheme when your size and profile grows. On a smaller scale again, passing around a bucket at the end of a performance is a sure-fire way of attracting a bit of an additional boost to your income. When collecting donations in this form though, make sure you are accounting for it properly, as cash payments require their own handling process.

Philanthropy and patronage is a long-term game with long-term energy required to make it a success. You are unlikely to achieve success if you see this process as simply hoping that rich people will give you money. Instead, see this as a relationship with individuals who believe in your mission and want to help make it work. It's much more than a cheque and a thank you.

Donations of this kind are as varied as the people themselves, and it is up to you to decide what sort of people and what sort of involvement you are comfortable with. How will it hurt your values as a carbon neutral company if one of your donors works in the oil and gas industry, for example? By the same token, are you comfortable receiving a large donation from an individual in exchange for them having a say into your output or a place on your board? There is, of course, no right or wrong here, and on the flip side, there can be much less paperwork and restrictions in accepting money from a donor than from being beholden to the demands of a grant.

Sponsorship

Sponsorship is a method often ignored by theatre companies. Sponsorship between brands perhaps conjures up images of huge global brand names joining together to launch products and can feel remote and impractical for a small, local theatre company. Nothing can be further from the truth.

Broadly speaking a sponsorship usually involves an exchange between two parties. One company may pay another money in exchange for their logo being posted on a website, for example. As a theatre company, you have plenty of opportunities to provide exposure to a brand, most notably through your theatre program. You will likely be familiar with theatre programs being crammed with adverts; this is sponsorship in action. Each of those adverts has been sold for a reasonable sum of money, which may have helped get the production you are watching off the ground.

When considering sponsorship, you usually need to start with audience and exposure. A brand is going to want to know that you can get their message in front of eyeballs, and you have a much better chance of doing this if you can evidence an audience.

When thinking of brands to establish a sponsorship with, think local and think about thematic crossovers in purpose and audience. An advert for another theatre performance is much more likely to be attractive to your audience when they're leafing through your program than an advert for equestrian winter wear. This is not to imply that horse riders wouldn't visit the theatre, but there is a more tangible link, a greater shared audience interest and a better chance of a return for the first idea.

If asking for money feels too intimidating or premature for the size of your business, consider what non-financial support you could benefit from instead. An easy place to start is to find a local print shop. In exchange for printing your flyers or programmes for free, you could agree to include their details on the print out. This is the sort of option that is easy to navigate, doesn't take too much of your time, and can save you small chunks of money without too much compromise on your part. Local print shops are in a lot of competition with online printers, so they may be keen to partner up. Why don't you start with them as a way of growing your confidence and see how you get on? As your potential audience grows, you'll be able to negotiate better deals in your favour in exchange for greater returns.

The steps above will get you started in the world of sponsorships, but as you move forward and the size and scale of your sponsorships grow, you will need to formalise this process to protect both parties. A sponsorship managing any significant volume of money or exchange of work is a formal business contract between both parties and therefore requires the correct legally formalised and biding documentation, which you are strongly advised to seek professional legal support to help implement.

Loans

Loans will be familiar to you from the parlance of daily life, and business loans are no different. Business loans need to be applied for in a different manner, and the information you need to produce will be different, but the fundamentals of what a loan is and how it works are exactly the same as the other loans you will have come across in your daily life.

A loan is different from a grant in that it needs to be repaid to the bank. Repayment takes place over an agreed number of years at a set cost, and comes with the added joy of *interest*. Low interest loans are better, as they cost you less over the long term, but they are increasingly hard to come by, and businesses with any sort of risk will find themselves hard pressed to convince the bank to offer more favourable loans.

Business loans are usually approved by a bank manager (or equivalent) and this decision will be based primarily upon your business plan and financial forecasts. It is unfair to say that the bank manager isn't interested in the artistic or social benefits of your business, but they are naturally tasked with ensuring they are lending responsibly to businesses who will be able to meet the repayment schedule. To this end, their key focus will be on financial strength and leadership competency: do they believe the idea has legs and that the person running it can make it successful?

Bank loans are difficult to secure, despite the promise of some online lenders who promise huge decisions in less than fifteen minutes. To some degree, applying for a bank loan *should* be difficult: it's probably one of the biggest decisions you can make, and if the process promises to be quick and easy and to ask no questions, you should probably do a bit of digging.

In some countries there may be government backed schemes to encourage banks to support start-up businesses, who are risky by their very nature, but whose success will grow the economy into the future. Search for terms such as 'start-up loan' or 'new business loan' to see what may be available. Due to their more targeted nature, however, they are more likely to come with specific eligibility criteria, and you should be able to find out pretty quickly if your project would be eligible or not.

You will often have to include evidence in your plan to show how you will continue to repay the loan even if things don't work out for your business. It can be almost impossible to untie yourself from the requirement to repay a loan, regardless of how well things have gone, so only consider this option if you are really confident in your success, as a last reward, or as a small part of a wider fundraising strategy. Loans involve your personal assets being tied up as guarantee of repayment, which may put your property and your financial security at risk, so only go ahead with these if you are confident and have received independent advice.

Grants: trusts and foundations

Grants are sums of money paid to organisations to deliver specific projects. Grants can range from a couple of hundred pounds to multi-million projects and almost always come with a set of conditions attached about how and when the money can be spent. At the end of the grant, there will usually be a process of evaluation and monitoring, to check that the money has been spent properly and to reflect on the project's impact. In exchange for all of this paperwork, grants are significantly preferable to loans in that they don't have to be paid back.

Your first port of call should be your national government and their associated arts department. These departments have a dedicated remit to fund and support artistic work, and will offer a range of grants for different projects based on scale and form. Because of their size and profile, national funders such as the Arts Council will tend to be hugely oversubscribed with very low success rates, and applying to them is a significant investment of time and effort. However, the profile and reputational advantage of securing funding from a body such as the Arts Council can be a significant tick towards increasing your validity, reputation, and profile, and no serious arts organisation would avoid applying to them altogether.

Local governments tend to have their own cultural departments and funding pots to support artistic work in their local area. This money will tend to come from central government but is a separate process than applying through a national funder such as the Arts Council. To find out what opportunities may be available in this space, you should simply search for the name of your local council followed by Arts or Culture. Even if they are not offering financial support at present, it is beneficial to strike up a relationship with the cultural arm of your local council so that you can be in their minds going forward for a whole range of things.

Lesser known grants are also available for organisations such as your own, which companies tend to ignore in favour of focussing on national funders. This is a huge mistake and you could potentially be missing out on a large income stream by avoiding these funds. There are funding search websites you can use to find these, but you can also use your search engine to type phrases such as 'community/arts/education grants' and see what you uncover.

Apart from government departments, there are a plethora of grant funders available worldwide. Often, these are charitable foundations set up in the name of some well-known philanthropist, and their sole job is to find worthy causes on whom to bestow their annual funding pot. When you begin to look into this world you will quickly realise that, rather than struggling to find anything, the challenge here is to manage the information overload, as you will quickly find numerous potential sources of funding to entice you. As with all grant, trust, and loan givers, however, there are always numerous requirements that will quickly bring your number of viable options into a more manageable shortlist.

Grant strategy

Grants are likely to be such a significant part of your fundraising journey that they need a dedicated strategy to manage effectively. Otherwise you will find yourself losing track, wasting time, and duplicating effort, only to be met with a series of rejected applications. Applying for grants is a big undertaking that requires immaculate focus and attention to detail, and while I don't say this to deter anyone from applying, you do need to demonstrate professionalism at every stage of the process if you are to stand a chance of success.

You should think of your initial grant journey in three stages. Firstly, you need to conduct a deep dive *search* to find out what funds are available. After this, you need to *refine* and finally you need to *prioritise*. I will walk you through these steps below.

Finding grants

The key with grant searching is to be specific but detailed. Grants come with conditions in order to apply (more on this below) so it is usually a waste of time to be broad with your searching in the hope that you can apply to funds that don't really fit your remit. Instead, you want to deep dive into your specific segment, and for this, Google is your friend. Search for terms such as Arts and Culture followed by terms such as Grants, Funder, or Philanthropy. You should search through several pages of Google here to ensure you get all of the good ones. If your work does legitimately cross into areas of education, community engagement, or other social causes, you may want to incorporate that into your search terms also.

Searching Google can be time consuming, and luckily there are tools to help. Grant search websites exist to allow you to enter your criteria in exchange for a pre-populated list of appropriate funds. At their best, these websites easily help you to find lesser known funds and make sure that results are accurate to your search criteria, to cut down on time wasted searching through funders who then turn out to be ineligible. However, such valuable resources tend to come at a cost – often in the region of several hundred pounds a year – and they are certainly not recommended for your first funding applications. If you are based in the UK, however, you should certainly check out Charity Excellence, which mercifully offers this service for free.

You will be finding a lot of potential results and it will quickly become confusing, so it is recommended that you create a table to track your information. The function and usefulness of this table is expanded upon below, but to begin with, make sure you record the names of appropriate funds with links to their website.

Refine

Once you have started to find grants you will quickly start to feel overwhelmed by the number of options. However, the sad fact is that many of these exciting options may not be suitable for you. The second stage of the process is to refine, and for this you will need to spend time on each funder's website researching their *priorities*, their *eligibility criteria* and their *deadlines*.

Each funder will outline a range of priorities in their work, and this will tend to be incredibly specific. Funders have their own systems for deciding what work they want to support and why, and this should be your first port of call. Do not waste your time applying for funds to which you are ineligible. It is difficult for strong projects to get grant funding, so bending your project to try and make it eligible for a particular fund is almost definitely going to fail and be a waste of your valuable time. Much better to focus on making strong applications to those funds for which you are a strong fit.

Eligibility criteria should be your next port of call and these will again be incredibly specific, highlighting who is and isn't suitable for their funding. Very often you will find that funders will be specific about the types of organisations they will fund (usually charities, usually not individuals or companies for profit) and this should have been part of your research and rationale when choosing an appropriate legal structure. Some funds, particularly those in the arts space, will require that you have specific *policies* in place: a safeguarding policy is a regular prerequisite. In a lot of cases, funders will ask you to complete a pre-funding questionnaire to determine eligibility before proceeding to a full application. This saves them time, and is once again a deterrent against applying for funds to which you are not completely eligible.

Finally, you should search for deadlines. Some funds will have very specific application windows whilst others may accept applications on a rolling basis.

Add all of this information into your table. You should make life easier for yourself at this stage and discard those funds which you now realise are not suitable for you, so that your table remains a list of viable options. However, it is worth seeing the benefit in retaining a record of funds for which you may become eligible in the future. Just because you have missed this deadline or because you haven't been open long enough doesn't rule out applying to this fund in the future, and you will thank yourself later for saving this research now.

Table 10.1 Grant application tracker

Fund Name and Link	Priorities		Eligibility Criteria		Deadline	Rating
Arts for All	1	bring people together and build strong relationships in and across communities	1	Must be a registered charity.	Ongoing	1
	2	improve the places and spaces that matter to communities	2	Will fund start-ups.		
	3	help more people to reach their potential, by supporting them at the earliest possible stage	3	Won't cover salary costs.		

Prioritise

You will now have a reasonably sized list of viable funding options and you will probably be eager to get started with applying. Before you rush ahead, however, you should organise your workflow to make best use of your time and funders' deadlines. Firstly, you will find it instructive to rate each funder based on its crossover with your aims, so that you can identify those funders you should apply to first, and those who may be a longer-term prospect. Each application may take several months, so prioritising your workload is very important to help you maintain momentum and a sense of progress.

At this stage, your ongoing table might look something like Table 10.1.

Grant calendar

You may find it helpful to visualise your grant application journey through the use of a grant calendar. This will help you to map out what you are applying for when, so that you can make sure that you have enough time to apply to each grant fully, and for you to monitor your progress. How long each grant will take to apply for is the million-dollar question, and with experience you will get quicker, but the reality is that different grants have different systems and some are more involved than others. As a general rule, the more money you are asking for, the more time you should expect the grant to take, but you will need to apply the same diligence and attention to detail if you are applying for £1,000 as if you were applying for £100,000.

You will be disappointed to hear me say that you should avoid copying and pasting the same application for multiple different grants. A bit like when applying for a job, the essential ingredients may stay the same and you may lift bits and pieces, but you need to convince the funder that your application is a perfect match for their fund, even if you are applying to many people! You will be working with a very strict word limit, and copying and pasting applications often leads to unnecessary padding and irrelevant content.

Increase your chances

How much should you apply for and when? There is no hard and fast rule for this, and unless eligibility criteria stops you, there is technically no reason why you cannot apply for a large sum of money right away. Be aware, however, that a lot of grants will typically ask to see three years of statutory accounts as a way of validating the health and general management of the organisation. Early on you are not likely to have this, which increases the risk to the funder. Similarly, many grants will request that you have at least two board members who are not related to each other, sometimes three as a minimum. In some cases, funders will also ask for you to have a business bank account with at least two signatories.

You should stereotype funders as being hyper risk-averse, and with good reason. Clearly it is their job to ensure that their funds are dispersed appropriately to worthy causes, with money being used properly to benefit targeted groups and projects. When you are starting out you are unlikely to have much of a track record or experience, you won't have much to prove that you can manage funds well and you are unlikely to have the backing of more experienced partners to vouch for you. All of this can be a challenge, and the solution to this is invariably to start small. Applying for a small amount of money for a project you can easily deliver is a relatively well-worn strategy for building a relationship with a funder and using this to demonstrate that your work has impact and that you know how to manage funds.

If your smaller grants have gone well and you have shown yourself trustworthy to manage public funds (ie. you didn't change identity and flee with the money to the Caribbean!) you are then in a much better position to apply for larger sums of money in the future.

Although it can be tempting, avoid submitting multiple applications to different funders at the same time. It might seem like a great situation to be in if they all agree to fund you, but you will suddenly have responsibility for duplicate funds to run one project, which is messy and potentially dishonest. If different applications are to fund different parts of the same project however, this helps to avoid this situation.

Match funding

Different funders have different approaches to match funding and they will often be transparent about their position on this. Some funders prefer to be the sole (or even only) funder on a project, as this fits their priorities and helps them to support you more. Other funders will see this as too expensive or risky, however, and will prefer to fund projects where they are not being asked for 100% of the project.

Unless explicitly stated, it is good practice to try not to ask a funder for 100% of a project cost, where at all possible. Use in-kind funding to help with this, particularly when you are struggling with resources. In some cases, funders like to see that you have a stake in the project yourself and would want to see you make a contribution through savings. Anecdotal evidence suggests that having over 50% match funding can increase your chances of success when applying to government schemes such as the Arts Council, although there is little hard evidence to back this up. Ultimately you should ask for what you need, but be aware that match funding can play a role in the decision a funder ultimately chooses to make.

Either way, a funder will usually be transparent about their relationship with match-funding, so have a look in the eligibility criteria for clarity on this.

How to write a successful application

Pretty much all public subsidy is under intense pressure and the majority of applications are rejected. In a lot of cases this is because of simple errors that could have been avoided. It is an unavoidable fact that many good projects are rejected purely because of numbers. With that in mind, let's consider ways in which you can ensure you stand the best chances of success when applying for a grant.

It is worth reiterating that nothing can replace proposing an interesting project with a clear idea of its intended reach and value. By this stage, you should have spent a significant amount of time researching your intended funder, to find out what work they support, what work they don't support, and whether you fit their eligibility criteria. As mentioned earlier, funding priorities are essential to any funder and they will usually be spelt out explicitly on their website. If you aren't a good fit at this stage, don't waste your time by hoping you will win them round. They are simply too oversubscribed to make exceptions to the guidelines they have laid out, and failure to read the guidance thoroughly won't do you any favours. You should also research to see whether the funds awarded are restricted or unrestricted funds. As the name implies, unrestricted funds mean that you can use the money in any way you see fit, whereas restricted funds are required to be used for a specific, stated purpose only. This can have implications for your accounting and for the delivery of your project, so knowing where the funds fit at this stage is important.

To do this, we are going to consider the social problem the funders want to solve and what your solution to this is.

In your group, think about answers to the following questions:

- What is the problem you are trying to address and why is it worth solving?
- What impact will your project have and what outcomes will you produce?
- When will you achieve these outcomes?
- How much will it cost?
- How does your project deliver value?

You should work through these questions in the order they are written. The first two questions are perhaps the most fundamental, and if you can't answer these or you feel as though you are shoehorning your project to make it fit these questions, you may need to revisit your overall plan. Not every project is deserving of a grant, and in order to be successful your solution needs to be an articulate and achievable response to the problem at hand.

- What is the problem you are trying to address and why is it worth solving?

To help with this question you should prepare a *problem statement*. A problem statement briefly sums up the problem you perceive and links directly to your mission and values.

To prepare your problem statement, first compile two lists. In the first list, write down as many adjectives you can think of that relate to the problem you are trying to solve. In the second, write down the adjectives you can think of to describe the solution. Your problem list is likely to feel fairly negative, whereas your solution list should hopefully sound positive.

Taking inspiration from these lists, try and write your problem statement in less than two hundred words.

- What impact will your project have and what outcomes will you produce?

To help with this we need to know our *milestones* and *outcomes*. Milestones help us to reach our outcomes and are a way of visualising our process towards its conclusion. An example of a milestone may be: appoint a youth theatre director, whereas an outcome may be: a three-day run of a performance. When we're thinking about what we will produce we should aim for our outcomes to be SMART.

A SMART outcome should be:

- S (pecific)
- M (easurable)
- A (chievable)
- R (ealistic)
- T (imely).

An outcome such as 'produce a good show' is not SMART. Firstly, it isn't specific: what show? This will be really difficult to measure because the concept of a 'good show' is entirely subjective and will mean different things to different people. It may be achievable and realistic, but without a better understanding of what 'good' means, this will be hard to prove or disprove either way. Finally, by not appointing any sort of timescale to this, when will we be able to judge whether this target was met or not?

To rework this into a SMART target we might say: 'produce *A Clockwork Orange* for an audience of more than one hundred people by August 20XX.' This is better because in August we will be able to go back and assess how well we did against this specific target.

Other examples of SMART targets might include:

- 'Out of one hundred participants on our drama school training workshop, at least seventy-five of them will have secured a place at a recognised drama school before 20XX.'
- 'Secure a minimum of three national reviews for our production of *The Crucible*.'
- 'Achieve a 50/50 gender split on all productions by the end of 20XX.'

Work your proposal into Table 10.2. This may be difficult at first but will really help you to articulate what can sometimes seem abstract or generic. Use this to help formulate your outcomes, and remember that these need to be SMART.

- When will you achieve these outcomes?

This clearly links to your schedule, and if you haven't already you should develop this to help visualise your individual milestones, rather than to simply show the end goal. Milestones are all linked and so a knock-on to one milestone will affect all others. Visualising those milestones helps you to know that you have enough time to reach your end goal and helps you to be adaptable in the face of challenges. Visualising your milestones can be done in a number of ways: the example in Table 10.3 is a particularly simple one.

- How does your project deliver value?

Delivering value to users is arguably what grant funding is all about, and this stage of the process is about linking back your solutions to this core. It can be easy to be so consumed in describing the benefits of our idea that we forget to go back to the people we are doing it for, and to avoid this we want to

Table 10.2 Grant aims and outcomes tracker

What is the overarching aim you want to achieve? This should be linked to the funder's priorities.	What will you do? What are your outcomes and activities?	What will change for the user?

Table 10.3 Milestone tracker

	Week 1	Week 2	Week 3	Week 4
Milestone 1		X		
Milestone 2				X

consider our *win themes*. Win themes are the *features, benefits,* and *evidence* of how our solution delivers value for the user, and they should be articulated and referenced repeatedly throughout your application.

- *Features*: what your project intends to do about the problem
- *Benefits*: what your project will achieve for the user, or help them to achieve
- *Evidence*: what evidence do you have that your idea will work?

Evidence can feel hard to settle on, but don't be intimidated by it. Evidence can include:

- Case studies,
- Testimonials,
- Track record – reviews, audience numbers, following,
- Secondary evidence – examples that have worked elsewhere that you intend to build upon.

Complete Table 10.4 to help write your win theme.

After doing all of this homework, you are now ready to begin to apply. Funding applications will have set questions and often very restrictive word counts, so the challenge now is to condense all your brilliant thinking to fit these requirements. Don't waffle and don't repeat points, and crucially, make sure you are answering the question you have been asked. It can be extremely tempting to copy and paste a generic application into a number of different funding applications, but you should avoid this. The questions are worded incredibly specifically with limited word counts, and you want to make sure you are spending all of that limited real estate in answering the question you have actually been asked. It can be easier than you might think to start answering the question you want to be asked, rather than the one in front of you.

It is useful at this stage to explore what requirements your funder puts in place for successful projects, to make sure that you are able to achieve them and have built this into your planning. Some funders will ask for a form of written report at the end of the funding period, but increasingly funders want to see more solid evidence at key project milestones. Information about the specifics of this will be found in the grant funders' application guidance. It might be easy to dismiss this as something to worry about when you are

Table 10.4 Win theme tracker

Funding Priority	Which features of your solution address this priority?	What are the benefits?	What is the evidence?

successful, but the vast majority of applications will provide a question relating to evaluation, which is your chance to demonstrate good practice in checking in with your project, making sure it's delivering, and assessing the impact of your activities.

Top tips for applying for funding

- Make sure your budget balances:
  - Online application forms won't let you submit a budget that isn't balanced, but regardless, you should always make sure that your project isn't costing more to run than what you plan to make back.
- Be realistic with costs:
  - Do as much research as you can and get feedback to make sure your costs are reasonable, educated guesses. Crazy figures will turn a funder away and highlight inexperience more than any other part of your application.
- Use support in-kind:
  - Support in-kind is great because it demonstrates that your project has support from others, but more crucially, it adds to your income, which can help massively when trying to get your budget to balance. Where it is appropriate, find volunteers for your project. You can write their hours into your application as in-kind support.
- Use clear written English and avoid jargon:
  - Make it clear what you are planning to do, and don't bullshit. Let your project speak for itself rather than falling back on hyperbole or exaggeration – claims you make now will need to be evidenced at the end of your grant, so don't create a rod for your back here. Don't be afraid to borrow the funder's own language in your applications to really evidence how you are meeting their priorities.
- Check timescales:
  - Do you have enough time to do your project and is the start date far enough in the future to account for when you may hear back?
- Pay people fairly:
  - Use the resources available to generate accurate costings for staff and freelancers. Where you are paying a day rate, check with others to ensure that the rate is reasonable and fair. Most funders will raise eyebrows if your project doesn't include wage costs as they will want to ensure people are being paid fairly for their work. If you are honourably not wanting to take a fee, first check whether the funder

would support this, and then make it explicit so that it doesn't appear as if you're avoiding or have forgotten this important budget line.

- Be specific and detailed:
  - Some preformatted online forms will dictate the level of detail you should go into when submitting your budgets, but too much is better than too little when it comes to estimating costs, as it shows you have a good understanding of the fine details.
- Remember contingency:
  - Aim for 8% unless otherwise specified, and remember this adds to your overall total to create your final cost which then needs to be balanced with income.
- Character limits:
  - You will often have strict character limits on grant applications. Save characters by using symbols ('&' instead of 'and') and writing digits for numbers ('7' instead of 'seven').
- Supplementary documentation:
  - Don't forget your supplementary documents. Depending on the size of funds required and the funder, you may need to provide additional documentation, such as cash flow forecasts or annual accounts. This is essentially to prove that your business is legitimate and for funders to judge your past performance to decide whether you will be able to handle the money reasonably. New organisations may not be able to provide this legacy information, and funders will specify alternative documentation required.
- Start small:
  - A new organisation with little track record is almost definitely unlikely to be successful asking for a six-figure sum from a funder. Funders have a duty and responsibility to ensure that their money is invested wisely and that it will be spent properly. As such, funders tend to be risk averse. Build up your relationship with funders gradually by applying for smaller amounts, in the first instance, to evidence how you have delivered impact and handled it securely. Then use that track record to apply for larger amounts, either with the same funder or with others.
- Break up your request:
  - It can often be advantageous not to apply to one funder for 100% of the project cost. Different funders will have different opinions on this, but many will want to see funding coming from another source, including from yourself. They would argue that this helps to

demonstrate your commitment to the project, although this can clearly be a hurdle early on when you may not have anything to contribute.

- Build a relationship with your funder beyond simply asking for money:
  - Find out the names of the relationship managers and invite them to see your work. This will help you punch above your weight with more established companies.
- Have a Plan A, B, and C:
  - This might not be something you share with funders, but having a backup plan (and a backup for the backup!) gives you some more security to be adaptable. This means that Plan A is the perfect scenario, but that you have a reduced alternative in case you don't get the funding you need. Obviously you want to get that maximum amount to be able to run the project in its perfect form, but identifying what are the 'nice-to-haves' is a good next step, just in case. Beyond that, what is the minimum amount you need to run the project, albeit in a compromised form, and what's the level of compromise you'd be happy with? Of course, you might well think that it seems counterintuitive to have a cheaper way of running the project: if you did, you'd be applying for that amount! As I started by saying, this might be something you keep up your sleeve rather than announcing to funders that you have a cheaper way of running the project.

Chapter Resources

Grants and fundraising

'3 things every proposal win theme needs,' RMR Consulting, www.rmrconsult.com/proposal-win-theme/

Charity Excellence, www.charityexcellence.co.uk/

Lane, David, 'Arts Council funding: Insider tips and advice,' (22nd July 2018), https://davidjohnlane.com/arts-council-funding-insider-tips-and-advice/

'Project grant templates: Arts Council England,' The Uncultured, www.the-uncultured.com/resources-arts-council-england.html

The School for Social Entrepreneurs, Online workshops, www.the-sse.org/our-courses/workshops/

'Theatre Funding: Complete Guide,' 20 Bedford Way, https://20bedfordway.com/news/theatre-funding-guide/

11 Festivals

Creating work is one thing, but how do you get it out to the world and in front of an audience? You will be familiar with going to the theatre to watch the work of theatre companies, but how do those people start out and get to that stage?

For a large number of theatre companies, the answer is festivals. Festivals range from the big to the small, from broad to specific, from city centre to the ridiculously remote. They are as fantastically varied and wacky as the work they showcase, and at their best, festivals can be an opportunity to meet other theatre makers, showcase your work, and learn about your craft in the most exhilarating way possible.

Theatre makers have traditionally flocked to festivals for a range of reasons. Festivals can be an accessible way of actually getting your work in front of an audience, and can be a platform for niche or abstract work. Particularly in the last twenty years, the number of fringe festivals has exploded and it is now rare to find a self-respecting town without an annual theatre festival taking over its spaces and bringing culture to the local residents.

Festivals have become the nearest thing to a default 'path' for theatre makers to follow that it is worth taking a moment to consider whether this is still accurate. In an industry where a determined path to progression and success is notably absent, the idea of making a piece of theatre and taking it to a festival to be 'discovered' has become a popular route many theatre makers take each year. There are more than a few success stories to back up this dream, with a very real promise that it could happen to you.

With this track record, festivals have become a breeding ground for discovering new talent, which in turn attracts the attention of the rest of the theatre industry on the hunt for the next big thing. Huge international festivals such as the Edinburgh or Melbourne Fringe have become hotbeds for the very best talent to get noticed.

As a direct result of this success and the reputation afforded to larger festivals by both audiences and artists alike, fringe festivals have arguably moved from the fringe space they originally intended to occupy firmly into the mainstream. Although the range of content on offer is as varied and multidisciplinary as ever, the hunger of artists has been gradually exploited to the

DOI: 10.4324/9781003281726-11

point that any serious festival run is likely to cost five figures as a minimum. Short of a runaway sell-out success, it's extremely unlikely that you will make that money back, which has in turn been seen to create an exclusionary financial bubble where attendance at a festival becomes about the strength of your bank balance rather than the strength of your talent. With such a dramatic number of artists vying for attention, hard cold numbers mean that the fight to be noticed is one that most companies are not going to win. Every year thousands of artists leave festivals poor, demoralised, and still undiscovered.

Festival types

Fringe festivals broadly fall into two categories. On the one hand, there are a respectable number of festivals where anybody can apply, pay a sign-up fee, and perform. These systems exist to allow anybody to perform, and in the best cases this is what they have remained. Where these festivals have become too popular for their own good, and competition for places has become fierce, many of these are open to all in name only, and you can normally get a sense of this based on the initial application procedure.

Festivals in which anybody can perform can be a really egalitarian way of getting your way in front of an audience. The lack of gatekeeping means that you simply need to apply to be given a space under the festival's banner.

On the other hand, an increasing majority of festivals require some level of application in order for you to be entered into the festival. This can be for a number of reasons: to balance the number of applications, to curate work around a theme, or to establish a level of artistic quality. Having to apply to a festival for any of these reasons can become quite a big job in itself, but this does establish a precedent that the festival has some level of consideration for the work being staged. You can see this as a positive or negative, and you are likely to get a sense from the festival's website whether your level of experience will be appropriate for the festival you are applying for. Some festivals exist as platforms for established artists, whereas others may be focussed less on your track record and more on the strength of your idea. These are likely to be your focus and most useful to your efforts.

Festivals come in all shapes and sizes and there are probably more fringe festivals today than at any point in history. Although this drastically improves the likelihood of getting your work into a festival, this should come with a caveat, because festivals are not all born equal. Smaller festivals may be less demanding in the initial application process and may be less involved throughout the process – smaller festivals are often operated by one or two people, helped by an army of volunteers. In the case of very small festivals, they may often run out of a small single venue where all performances take place.

Smaller festivals can be great for building your experience level and for attracting some attention to your social media pages, but it can be negligible what the benefits are beyond this. As we will see, festivals of any size are expensive and take a huge dispensation of energy. What you get out of it depends on having clear aims going in. If your aim is to perform and get your work in front of an audience, a small festival can help you do this and develop your practice.

On the other hand, there is a reason why a small number of festivals attract so much cost and attention, and this limits the usefulness of smaller festivals if your goal is to gain respectable reviews and get noticed. It can be difficult to get an audience for any fringe show, and while larger festivals have increased competition between a greater number of shows, they also attract an audience keen to see fringe theatre. In smaller festivals, you can often find yourself trying to convince the local community, who may not even have much of a knowledge that the festival is happening.

Getting into a festival

You should apply to your chosen festival as soon as you are able. Applying early shows that you are keen and ready, and gives you the maximum time to work through logistics and ensure that you are prepared. All festivals will have a range of deadlines for applying, and subsequent deadlines for sending across marketing materials for inclusion in the festival brochure. Excitement can sometimes inspire you to submit a last-minute application for a festival, but all logic would advise against this, particularly if you have missed the brochure deadline, as this will be the primary tool through which most audiences will make their viewing decisions.

All festivals will require you to submit an application form (even the free ones) before you are selected. This will include a wealth of practical information about your show – run time, whether you have an interval, tech plan, etc. You may feel that it is too early to know this information at this stage, particularly if you are applying early, but you will need to know this soon so that you can find an appropriate venue. In a lot of cases, tech at festivals is extremely limited anyway and running time limits are imposed, so you will find that there are a lot of parameters guiding you with this.

If you are applying to a curated festival or to an oversubscribed venue, you may also need to sell your show a bit to talk about the idea and its reason for being made. Use the same skills you have employed in your grant-writing applications, but remember that venue managers will often be most interested in staging good shows. Don't overload your application with review quotes and supplementary information unless it specifically asks for this: let the strength of your idea be the main element of your sales pitch.

In the vast majority of festivals, the festival is an entity in its own right, which is distinct from the venues in which you will perform. More often than not it will be down to you to find an appropriate venue for your show. Festivals will provide you with a list of venues, including technical info and contact details. In the simplest of cases, this is a case of finding a match, contacting them, and getting booked. In reality, particularly where a venue is oversubscribed, getting an agreement with a venue can be a challenge. In the most established festivals, you may need to have built a long-term relationship with that venue manager, so that they get to know you and your work.

If possible, your best strategy for selection at any festival is to attend the festival as an audience member the year before. This can be expensive but is an invaluable research trip, helping you to see what sort of shows are staged, what work is popular, what stands out, and what doesn't. It'll also give you an opportunity to scope out venues and to start conversations with the venue managers, so that they know about you and your show when your application lands on their desk in a few months' time.

You can find or build your own venue. Fringe festivals are a hive of creativity with performances taking place in literally every conceivable space possible. Finding or creating your own space can be an exciting way of doing something different and of generating a buzz, especially if that location is being used in a novel way, which may catch an audience's attention. Finding your own venue brings its own set of challenges, though. You will need to scope out the viability of the space itself and establish ways to make the site safe for performance. This may fall under your existing insurance but depending on the nature of the space and what you plan to do to it, you are likely to need a range of additional permissions from the council and the fringe office. The fringe organisation will need to approve your venue to be included under their banner, and they will naturally bring a range of practical and safety concerns for you to address. If this is not enough of a challenge, you need to work extra hard to make sure audiences know how to find your venue when it has been approved.

Programming at major festivals is a huge undertaking and venues will have their own micro-preferences. A venue might be known for staging stand-up comedy, or dance, for example. By doing your research into these venues you will be able to make sure that your show is a match for the kind of work they tend to prefer. This not only increases your chance of being selected, but also improves the viability of your offer to festival audiences.

Getting into a larger festival can be a challenge and you are best advised to do your homework before thinking about taking a show to any festival. For logistical reasons, venues will often impose strict run-time limits and tech support will be rudimentary. These restrictions are not guidelines and you will come unstuck if you try and take your two-hour show to a one-hour festival slot and hope nobody notices.

Choosing a show

Festivals are unlike any other performance environment, and to a degree the shows are unique too. The logistics of festivals will often dictate a set of restrictions, usually around run time and tech time, which may be your biggest obstacle to staging a full-scale three-hour performance epic. But should this be your goal in the first place?

Festivals are breeding grounds for new work and new talent, and audiences come with that expectation in mind. A typical audience member might attend a show in a fringe theatre in the morning, another performance in a churchyard after lunch, a third at the back corner of the pub, and a fourth in the middle of a shopping precinct. Audiences know the context and, to a degree, this is part of the charm. Shows that work with this context will excel.

Although curated festivals may select a specific program around a particular style or theme, the majority of festivals are a broad church with work of all shapes and sizes. In theory, this means that anything can be staged, but in reality, most festivals will have pockets of popularity and trends each year. Festivals known for discovering new work tend not to be the best place to perform a revival of a classic, for example, and at any rate these will often be difficult to fit into a sixty-minute run time. You can negotiate for a longer performance slot, but audiences are looking for variety. Your three-hour show is a serious commitment and might prevent an audience member from seeing two or three other shows in that time, so it is a confident producer who would go down this route.

Festivals are so unique that it can sometimes feel as though the work that excels is work that has really played the game of the festival environment. Although this can be a bit gimmicky, and tempting, you ultimately need to find a show you believe in and do this to the best of your ability. Choosing a show by trying to play a game will almost definitely not work, not least for the fact that the daily slog of selling tickets and trying to vie for attention requires nothing less than complete dedication to and belief in your show. You won't be able to convince anybody else to see your show if it has been developed cynically to be popular.

Festivals tend to have trends. In any given year there may be seven shows about a particular topic, and none about this topic the year after. It's a funny old business and impossible to predict. However, this is yet another reason not to try and play the game. Chances are, if you're trying to develop a show because of a trend from last year, the crowd will have moved on by the time it comes to your production opening.

Festivals can feel like competitive environments, especially if you are hoping to get your work seen, and to this end you should try as much as possible to make the work you are taking your very best. You can never predict this, of course, and so logic would dictate that it can be helpful to build up a record for your show in advance. This approach is favoured by many companies intent on getting their work programmed: develop a show through some scratch performances and audience feedback, secure some reviews, build an audience, and then take it to a major festival. This is great in practice but obviously brings its own disheartening questions about whether fringe festivals really are as fringe and open as they purport to be. But even if you can't secure a run at a regional venue to develop your show in advance, any performance testing and feedback is valuable to help make sure that your work is in a good shape by the time it gets to the festival. What you do want to avoid is your festival performance being your first performance, as learning and revising the show on the job will add to your stress, take away from the business of selling the show, and ultimately won't show you off to the best of your ability.

Your aims and outcomes

Although this may sound unnecessarily corporate, the success of your fringe journey will depend upon setting realistic goals for yourself before you apply. Even the notion of what success means will be different to every single one of the artists performing at a festival: some will want to get programmed for a tour whereas others will be enjoying a holiday with their friends. Every reason is valid, but establishing those goals early gives you something to measure yourself against and ensures all members of your team are on the same page.

You should be ambitious but realistic with your goal setting to ensure your best chance of success. Although being well known, having lots of money and a strong track record are not prerequisites for a successful fringe run, it is a fact that shows with momentum behind them can find the journey easier to navigate. They have their own challenges, of course, but they are certainly starting from a different position to a new company hiring the corner of a pub for a couple of days.

This is not to dampen your enthusiasm, however; instead, to prepare your expectations to match the volume of work (and luck) required if you are hoping for career progression. Short of producing the next big thing, the effort required to get reviewers and programmers to see your work almost certainly will be hard work. Both reviewers and programmers have a difficult job to balance seeing the shows they have a big recommendation for – and nobody wants to be the person who missed the memo on these things – and leaving enough spontaneity in their diary to discover something on a whim.

Setting goals will change your whole approach to the festival, from what you put on your poster to what you do after your final performance, and it is essential to provide some coherence to your festival experience. Every single festival run is exhausting and expensive, even if you do unleash a runaway hit, as this comes with its own challenges and learning curve. Being focussed in your efforts is a first step towards making your whole experience enjoyable and successful.

When to go

Smaller festivals can run for a day or two, whilst it is not unusual for larger festivals to run for a month or more. Booking a performance for a day or two can be a really nice introduction to the festival atmosphere, whilst keeping the whole project within budget. However, for those of you attending a festival with broader development aims, a run of a few days is likely to be sufficient to build the scale and momentum you will need to achieve results.

It is important to remember that festivals operate within their own distinct ecosystem, and the experience of being at a festival – as both an audience member and an artist – is not the same as doing that experience anywhere else. Festivals are a crazy, wonderful, hideous, exciting, terrifying explosion of creativity, and when they're over, the world returns to its normal self. Anybody who has visited Edinburgh outside of August will hardly believe that it is the same place.

As such, audiences don't typically book for shows in advance, outside of a few exceptions – normally, established comedians. Audiences are flexible. They want to be wooed and tempted, they may circle a few options and leave others down to flyers they get handed on the day. The same goes for reviewers, programmers, and pretty much everybody else in town. The magic of any good fringe festival is discovery, and all the marketing in the world cannot compare with the word-of-mouth buzz of a show you just have to see.

Given that a successful festival run relies so heavily on word of mouth, with companies relying on good reviews to further bolster interest, it is part and parcel that you need to be there for long enough for people to hear about you and to come and see you. It is also much easier for venues to schedule a show that will run for the duration of the festival than to program multiple smaller runs. Good fringe venues will want to support your work to get it seen, and they are clearly in a better position to do this when they can get to know you and the work you make.

Choosing a venue

We have already touched on the importance of finding the right venue earlier in the chapter. In many respects, choosing your venue will be the most important decision you can make. More established venues will be harder to get into, but can come with a whole host of support and reputational advantage. On the other hand, smaller venues may be less exacting and able to be more flexible with things such as performance times.

If you have an opportunity to visit your venue as an audience member you should take it. A conversation with the venue manager may also be able to give you a quick tour, which will be invaluable in shaping your show to the logistics of the space. Venues in fringe festivals are often ad hoc, and you should alter your expectations from what you might be used to in other performance contexts. It will often be impossible to achieve a perfect blackout and most spaces will include noise-bleed from surrounding bars. With audiences seated in a make-shift arrangement, there may be no version of a rake, meaning that anybody except the front row can struggle to get a good view. Small spaces with packed audiences can heat up quickly and become unbearable. Many of these logistical headaches can't be avoided, and to a degree your audience will know what they are signing up to and won't judge your show against this, but they are worth being aware of so that you can work with them. A delicate show requiring a number of intricate slow blackouts may not be best served in this context.

Your venue's tech pack is going to be an essential document to refer to before, during and after applying. If anything in the pack doesn't make sense, or isn't clear, feel free to contact the venue for clarification, so that you are certain about what you are signing up to.

At festivals such as the Edinburgh Fringe, shows can have as little as fifteen minutes' turnaround time between performances, and you risk your show being walked off the stage altogether if you try and run over! It's also very unlikely that you will be able to stage your show with a Broadway musical level of tech requirements, even if you wanted to. Apart from the limited amount of time available for companies, venues in fringe festivals are often pubs or other spaces not typically used for performance. Tech – in so far as it exists – becomes a case of what is available rather than what you want. You may be able to add extra tech, but this will be at your cost, and decisions of this nature should be balanced against the incredibly tight turnaround you will already be working with. Similarly, with set pieces, venues will be working around the size of any access doors into the space, and any limited storage space. You need to make sure that your set can get into the venue and be clear with what happens to it when you are not performing. In this context, set and logistics need to be as simple as possible. Although this can feel limiting, this does put the spotlight back onto the words and the story, which is ultimately a good thing. If these are strong, your audience will come with you. Remember that your audience understands the context of a fringe festival and will likely have seen several other performances in similar contexts on that day. They are not expecting West End levels of technical finesse, what they do want is a buzz, and a chance to see something engaging and exciting.

Performance times

Performances at fringe festivals take place all day, every day. Forget your usual routine of performing at 7.30: festival performances can be at ten in the morning, one in the evening and pretty much every time in between. To the uninitiated, this can feel second rate, but don't be fooled. Festival audiences operate in different ways to the usual performance crowd and there is a hunger and appetite for work all day.

Your times will be agreed with your venue at the contract stage, and you should talk with them to lean on their expertise, as they should have a good understanding of what kind of work plays well throughout the day. Although each festival is different, theatre tends to be scheduled before the early evening, when audiences tend to move towards grabbing some drinks. In the majority of multidisciplinary festivals, stand-up comedy tends to hold the power in the evening, for obvious reasons. Performing at 7.30 can deplete your potential audience significantly, and could mean that the audience you do have are already a few drinks down, and are not in the headspace you may need. On the other hand, if your show leans in to elements of comedy and needs an audience who are, for want of a better word, responsive, this may be a perfect fit. It is not unknown for some shows to perform at midnight, so there really are no hard and fast rules. Again, do your research. Some festivals won't involve you in this process, as they will handle the scheduling themselves, for their own logistical reasons.

Venue contracts

When you have made contact with a potential venue and they have agreed to host you, the venue will move to draw up a contract. Your contract is a serious piece of business and there will be ramifications for failing to meet your end of the bargain, so make sure you get advice and clarity around anything that doesn't make sense, so that you are fully clued up on what you are agreeing to.

Your contract will stipulate a range of limitations and restrictions, which can feel quite punitive at first glance. It is important to remember the difficult position any fringe venue is in; purely balancing the number of shows moving through its space in such a short amount of time is a huge effort, and they really need artists to work with them to make that a smooth process. Again, there is a tangible benefit to getting in early with venues: not only will you get better performance slots, but the earlier you know your performance limitations, the sooner you can ensure your work fits around them.

There is no set length or format for your contract. Some venues will do little more than copy and paste a contract from the internet, whereas venues with more experience may have huge contracts that make sure every 'i' is dotted and every 't' is crossed. Their contract may have needed to grow to this length due to hard learnt lessons in previous years, so have pity on them!

The most important part of your contract is the venue offer. Discussing payment can feel awkward for a new company, particularly when you're dealing with an established venue in a large fringe festival. But if you have got to this stage, you deserve to be here, and your venue needs and wants you as much as you need them. So do try and be an active participant in this process and don't feel as though you don't have a say. The deal you agree now will go a long way towards hopefully making your show break even, so you want to push for it in your favour.

Your venue should not be seen as some remote corporate presence who you have no relationship with. The best venues are partners in your journey, and many of the more established venues at festivals such as the Edinburgh Fringe will have their own marketing and their own champions making sure the right people come and see your work. They are your co-creators and co-conspirators, and they wouldn't be where they are if they weren't interested in supporting and celebrating theatre makers. There are always shady venue managers, but especially in established festivals, they tend to be found out pretty quickly. Whereas this might be your first festival with a huge amount resting on your head, your venue is a bit like a wise old guardian who has seen it all before. Their experience and advice can be invaluable.

There are a range of deals available when booking a venue, and this process typically tends to mirror the process of getting booked at any venue. There is a full breakdown of financial deals, with what to expect, what to look out for, and what to avoid in Chapter 12.

Relationship with the fringe and your venue

Your relationship with the festival itself and the venue you are performing at goes far further than being simply transactional. Depending on the size of the festival you are performing at, they are likely to have a range of support and guidance available to make your fringe journey smoother. Your fringe office is like Festival HQ, usually offering everything from artist support to help with show promotion. The very largest festivals will run events throughout the year where you can meet the teams and get answers to your questions, so that you can attend the festival itself as ready as possible.

Your journey through the festival itself will be unpredictable with many highs and lows, and your fringe office and venue will be the people to talk to for help with all of this. If they can't help you with a particular issue, they will at least be able to point you in the direction of someone who can.

Accommodation and transport

One of your biggest costs when applying to any fringe festival is likely to be the most mundane. Transport and accommodation costs quickly add up as festival cities seek to capitalise on the influx of artists and audiences, meaning prices for even the most basic rooms can be two or three times higher than at other times of the year. This is yet another advantage of being the early bird, and your festival website will likely have a list of recommendations for good accommodation options. If you know the area you may well be better served, but when heading to a new city or a new country, organising accommodation can be a daunting task.

Consider the different forms of accommodation available to you before booking – group dorms will tend to offer the best value for money but could become intense after multiple weeks of a cast spending every waking moment together. Consider the dynamics of this, and assume that tempers will run high as energy dips. Your accommodation should be your way of escaping the madness of the fringe, if only briefly.

Commuting to your festival or staying out of town can offer better value for money. Staying with friends or family who live in the area is the holy grail and could potentially shave thousands off your budget. These are not without their drawbacks though. The cost of travelling – even if it's a bus ticket – can quickly add up when multiple people are travelling into town and back every day for a month. Added to this, the inconvenience and time for commuting, not to mention the sense of feeling out of it, can really add to the isolation and pressure of a busy fringe environment, where it can easily feel as though you need to continue giving more and more. Speak with colleagues and reach out to companies whose work you saw as an audience member and garner their feedback and thoughts.

Press and marketing

It is perhaps the most well-known adage in festival parlance that you will end up losing a tonne of money and performing to one man and his dog, at best. Every performer, without exception, has tales such as this, which they seem to wear as a badge of honour.

Performing at a fringe festival is a strange mix of jubilation and constantly feeling as though the party is happening on the next street along, and with so many demands on their attention it is little wonder that finding an audience can be one of the hardest challenges of the whole affair.

No show is guaranteed an audience at a festival and from your starting position, nobody will have heard of you and everybody will need convincing that their time will not be wasted. As a result of this culture, audiences won't often book in advance as there is very rarely a need to: on the special occasion when something is likely to sell out, a buzz is created beyond any marketing efforts.

For the majority of companies then, your marketing will be the main reason people choose to come to your shows, or not. Typically, you will need to provide content for the festival brochure and website and for on the ground flyer-ing at the festival itself. There may also be opportunities to stick up posters and your venue may produce its own show program.

Your most important deadline for marketing is the printing deadline for the festival booklet, which contains the information of everything at the festival that year. This is the most important simply because of its reach: this will be the one thing audiences cling on to when making their decisions, and many will pre-plan their festival experience based on these listings.

Listings in the festival brochure will typically be organised by category (dance, comedy, etc.) and will tend to be listed in order of performance dates, although they may also be alphabetical. There is another advantage then to getting your show on early! Your brochure entry will consist of a small image and a copy of probably fifty to one hundred words. In so many ways these will be the most important fifty words you will write, and the success of your show could depend upon them capturing enough attention to hook a reader's interest. To give yourself the best chance of success here, cut straight to the point in telling us what your show is about and avoid hyperbole, review quotes, or other descriptive language. Life is too short to read about another 'timely,' 'important,' or 'innovative' show – let the description of the show leave us in no doubt about its value!

To help with your brochure entry, get hold of brochures from previous years and look for good examples that catch your eye, and those that don't. Depending on the size of the image, text can be a negative if it is difficult to read, and colours become hard to see next to one another when viewed in a tiny format. Your best option is a simple, eye-catching image that grabs our attention and makes us ask questions and want to know more.

Flyer-ing at festivals is something akin to a life experience, in both good and bad ways! Flyer-ing is not for everybody and takes buckets of courage, enthusiasm, and energy to be successful. Given that you will need all hands on deck from your cast and crew to help spread the word about your show, you need to make sure that everybody is prepared for this work. And believe me, I call it work deliberately. You can sometimes hire promoters to hand out flyers for you, but this will add to your budget and is not a guarantee of success: often it is the personal sell and connection between artist and audience member that convinces many to come. A faceless fringe entity handing out flyers for a show they don't know much about may not carry the same weight.

Speaking personally, a gentleman once hit me with his umbrella so that I wouldn't break his stride as he walked past me, so I can vouch for the fact that flyer-ing can be brutal. In smaller fringe festivals, the general public may not be attuned to what is going on and they will therefore see you as yet another inconvenience on their way to work. By contrast, flyer-ing at larger festivals is a bit like trying to sell sand in the desert. Your potential audience will be wooed in all directions from other companies who seem better resourced, more confident, and more imaginative than you are feeling when you're on your third week and running out of energy and money.

Your flyers themselves need to be clear with an easy to read title and simple instructions about where and when your show will run. Festival audiences will seldom prepare more than a few days in advance, so it should become part of your daily routine to be flyer-ing right until the last minute. If you can afford to, print your flyers on reasonably thick paper so that they can withstand the weather and being squashed in a bag for a week. If you are lucky enough to get some glowing reviews, you could print them ad hoc and stick them onto your existing flyers, to save having to pay for a reprint.

Posters are another option for your marketing efforts but you will need to triple check your local postering laws to ensure you are in your rights to put them up. Lots of cities have local by-laws restricting where posters can be placed in order to keep the city clean, and if you contravene these rules your poster will be removed and you are also likely to be hit with a fine. Your festival itself may have designated poster spots, or you could ask around local businesses to see if you can place your posters in their shop windows. Posters are a great way of embedding your show in the audience's subconscious, but their benefit can be negligible, particularly at the scale of a small company working with only A3 posters. In a competitive fringe environment, it is also likely that your poster will be covered over by somebody else before you've got round to double checking it!

Consistency is key when it comes to your marketing efforts. Once you have hit on a distinctive and eye-catching design, stick with it. Exposure is a great way of creating a hook in an audience's mind, and if they have seen an image pop up repeatedly it helps when being handed a flyer if that show triggers a memory.

If your show has a newsworthy element, you should consider contacting press to run a preview. You are obviously going to think your show is newsworthy, but this requires you to think about this from the perspective of a journalist, who will be trying to come up with engaging content for their readers. Stories with a local interest, a topical theme, or a well-known name are all likely to be of interest to journalists, and running a preview can be a useful way of building some pre-festival buzz. To contact journalists, you will need to put together a *press release*. Your press release should be limited to A4 and should be sent as a Word document (or copied into the body of the email) so that the journalist can edit it easily. Your press release is not a sales document and shouldn't be a de facto show blurb in disguise. Instead, it should focus on the newsworthy element of your production. Some journalists will essentially use your press release as it is written, so make their life easy and conceive of it in this manner, using appropriate journalistic language. Always make sure you finish your press release with contact info and a summary of ticket information.

Reviews are the cornerstone of many a festival experience and a good review can help attract the attention you need from those with the power to make decisions about your next steps. Every journalist wants to find those shows with potential and they are particularly keen to be the person who 'discovers' a hidden gem. This does put a huge pressure on their schedules, however, and even with the best will in the world, journalists can only review a certain number of shows in any given period of time.

You should reach out to reviewers via their email address, which will usually be on their publication website. Unless they have specifically indicated otherwise, avoid contacting them through social media tags and the like, as this can be incredibly intrusive. When contacting them, avoid attaching large files and don't waste time in getting to the point. Consider your request from their perspective and make it easy for them to find out what you want, what the show is about, and where/when it is on.

Reviewers will expect *comps* – complimentary tickets – to your show, and you should offer this as a courtesy. This is pretty standard practice and your venue will have a system for managing this: it might be written into your contract to have a small number of comps allocated per performance. In order to arrange this, your venue will need to know the name of the person collecting them so that they can be handed out to the right person in the midst of the pre-show box-office rush.

In most other circumstances you will have a designated *press night* for your show in which the great and the good all descend en masse to review your work. If you're lucky, this will come after a number of *preview* performances. Such a luxury is impossible in a fringe environment, where reviews may happen at any stage during your run. You can push for reviews to happen as early as possible, but you will find yourself grateful for any review at all once you get to grips with how much of a challenge it can be to secure one!

Reviewers are only human and although you will want your glowing review to be published as quickly as possible, it may be a couple of days before it goes live depending on their deadlines and schedule. Absolutely don't pester them for this as your reviewer will not appreciate this, and they won't have forgotten about you.

Reviews can, of course, not go the way you would have hoped. A negative review can be a blow at the best of times and never more so than when you feel as though everything is on the line at a festival. They are hard to deal with, and in a festival environment you don't have the luxury of choosing not to read them, because a good review can be such a good boost to tickets. You can take heart from the fact that there is usually such a rush of noise and activity at a festival, your bad review will hopefully go relatively unnoticed and will quickly disappear into the annals of time. If you can bring yourself to appreciate its perspective, there may well be a useful learning curve to further develop your performance.

Depending on the size of your festival, you may have options to employ *press agents* to do a lot of this leg work for you. A good press agent will have the contacts to get your show on the desks of editors and reviewers, and their recommendation can be the difference between being picked up or not. However, these services don't come cheap and you will need some substantial budgeting efforts if you are going to incorporate this into your offering.

The run

A month-long run at a fringe festival is an emotional and draining undertaking even from the most optimistic perspective. The sheer energy required to sell and perform your show night after night, not to mention schmoozing, networking, organising reviews and press, and hopefully having a good time is an undertaking that it's impossible to fully prepare for. If you have opportunities throughout your run to visit friends or even to escape the bubble for a few days, you will thank yourself in the long run. It may feel as though everything is riding on the success of this show, but life does go on and your mental well-being is not worth jeopardising, whatever the outcome.

The run itself will tend to fall into distinct chunks – the optimism of week one blends into the tiredness of week two, week three may see a pickup if your reviews are good, and week four equals exhaustion. It's a long slog and a long time to spend with anybody, never mind someone you are working with. It's also a good idea to know yourself in this environment, and look out for those triggers that make you difficult to be around so that you can better protect and support those around you. Visiting a festival is made more bearable by working with people you trust on an equal basis: the experience is draining enough without being landed with the title of 'person in charge' when your actors decide that they are only performing in your show and aren't equally responsible for its success.

Living and working in such close quarters will inevitably become suffocating and you should establish some company ground rules in advance of starting, so that people feel able to take a break or spend some time alone. Although you won't plan to argue, having a robust set of principles for how to get today's show on if you had a blistering drunken row the night before can make all the difference.

Fewer cast and crew can make a big difference to your overall project budget but the payback can be in the lack of manpower. One person selling a show is patently not as effective as twenty. However, twenty people sounds great in practice if everybody is equally motivated to sell the show and works equally to do it. Your collaborators may not have the entrepreneurial spirit that you have – they may have signed up to be an actor, after all – and the idea of practically begging strangers in the middle of a rain-soaked afternoon may not float their boat or be in their comfort zone. There is nothing wrong with this in principle, but festivals require everyone to pull their weight beyond the show itself and you should only take people who respect that. Nothing creates resentment quicker than half a cast doing all the work while the other half, through awkwardness or laziness, put their allocation of flyers in the bin and then go and get a takeaway. Trust me: it happens.

With a run of a few weeks, it is inevitable that your audience will fluctuate. Typically, you would hope that your audience will grow as word of mouth spreads that your show is the best in town, but in reality it may well be a haphazard affair in which getting an audience of double figures becomes a successful evening. Whether you have a sell-out audience or an audience of one, they have all chosen to spend their time with your show against competition of literally thousands of other options, so give them the same focus, love, and respect as you would a sell-out crowd. The magic of the fringe is that you truly have no idea who that one person might be; they may be somebody you really want to impress.

Speak with your venue if you don't feel the run is going particularly well. They will be able to offer advice and they may even put in a good word or two to help get your show some attention. They are not obligated to do this though, so don't expect much if you suddenly start wanting their attention after not showing them much respect previously. Remember: your venue should be your partner. Equally, speak to your venue and the fringe office if your show is going really well. Some of the attention and conversations coming your way may well be overwhelming if you don't feel experienced enough to deal with them. You won't be the first company in that situation, so seek out that advice as they will be keen to help.

Finally, remember to engage with other artists! There will be hundreds if not thousands of people similar to you, with all of the same hopes and fears, hang-ups and celebrations, and this is one of the best ways to meet likeminded people and connect with your peers. Yes, this can be a great way of making connections and finding future collaborators, but equally it's a wonderful way of connecting with other human beings going through this same crazy process. They may know things you don't, or they will be likely to have had similar experiences to you – including playing to one man and his dog!

One day you will have a wonderful moment when you realise that you're speaking to a company with less experience than you and suddenly you'll be the knowledgeable one!

Building on success

With hard work and a sprinkling of luck, your show will attract a reasonable crowd, garner some positive reviews, and gain attention from theatre programmers. This may be the pathway to your show having a future life beyond your festival, and this can be an incredibly exciting moment in your development.

Theatre programmers may attend your show and be interested in booking it for a performance. It is always a good idea to be available to network in the bar after your show, as this is most likely where conversations like this will be struck, or they may come as part of an email after things have died down. If you're really lucky, multiple programmers may be interested in booking your work as part of a tour. As with almost everything else, your festival head office and venue will be on hand to provide support and guidance, if you feel that you need it. This is obviously an incredibly exciting scenario to be in, and although conversations will often be struck up after a show, it is most likely that any deals and agreements will take place in a more structured meeting, perhaps over coffee at a mutually agreeable time.

Although the excitement can take hold, try not to rush into any agreement for further work, especially until you have considered the cost and time implications of doing so. In the next chapter we will explore, in detail, the logistics of working with venues and the various agreement options available to you, which will be exactly the same if you have been approached at a festival to any other context. Any programmer who appears to be rushing you into a deal or not respecting your need to ask questions and seek advice may well be someone to think carefully about before going ahead. Good programmers understand and respect artists and if there are any warning signs, make sure to seek assurance before going ahead, otherwise a positive moment now can become a headache later on.

Next steps ... next year?

Depending on which way you look at it, one of the great joys or great cons of the big fringe festivals is that it is often rare for a first time act to hit it big there. Whether it's building the experience of actually surviving the fringe, or whether it's simply the fact that more festivals increase your chances of the magic dust falling on you, what is apparent is that seasoned artists make plans to visit their major festivals as a regular occurrence. For some companies, this becomes the focus of their whole year – they may not perform much throughout the rest of the year, but come festival time they always take a show to their chosen big festival. In some ways this is a good tactic, as they can grow and foster a festival-specific audience who return to the festival, again and again, to see their next show.

Stand-up comedians will attest to the power of repeat fringe performances, as many have to slog it out for multiple years before they get a promoter interested in booking them for TV. Some comedians go further and claim that without an annual fringe slot they can be seen to have fallen off the radar.

Performing in festivals is by no means the only method for presenting work and getting it seen by an audience. Although it is often presented as being the obvious step, this is by no means a given, and doing so too early or with too little prep can be a misstep. In the next chapter, we will explore the many other ways in which you can create work and get it staged.

Chapter Resources

Festivals

Boot, Claire, 'Fringe with benefits: Top 5 fringe festival benefits,' TicketSource (27th March 2022), www.ticketsource.co.uk/blog/fringe-with-benefits-top-5-fringe-festivals-benefits

Care, Christina, 'How to put on your first fringe show,' Spotlight, www.spotlight.com/news-and-advice/tips-and-advice/how-to-put-on-your-first-fringe-show-part-1/

Delikonstantinidou, Katerina, 'International Theatre and Performing Arts Festivals,' Critical Stages, www.critical-stages.org/7/international-theatre-and-performing-arts-festival-guide/

'Edinburgh Fringe survival guide,' Bush Theatre, www.bushtheatre.co.uk/bushgreen/edinburgh-fringe-survival-guide/

Fisher, Mark, *The Edinburgh Fringe Festival Survival Guide: How to make your show a success* (Methuen Drama, London, 2012)

'How to take a show to the Edinburgh Fringe,' *Spotlight*, YouTube (23rd January 2019) www.youtube.com/watch?v=mEXU6WgwXH0

'Planning your fringe,' Edinburgh Fringe Festival, www.edfringe.com/experience/how-to-plan

'Pleasance futures,' Pleasance, www.pleasance.co.uk/futures

Taylor, William, 'How the seemingly chaotic but wildly successful fringe festival makes it work,' Fast Company (18th August 2011), www.fastcompany.com/1773957/how-seemingly-chaotic-wildly-successful-fringe-festival-makes-it-work

'The Fringe guide to doing a show,' Edinburgh Fringe Festival, www.edfringe.com/uploads/docs/participants/Fringe%20Guide%20to%20Doing%20a%20Show.pdf

The VAULT Festival, https://vaultfestival.com/

Underbelly Festival, www.underbellyfestival.com/

'Video resources for artists,' VAULT Festival, https://vaultfestival.com/video-resources-artists/

12 Putting on Work

There are as many ways to present work as there are stories to tell. The key when selecting a platform for your work is to find the best outlet for your artistic ambitions, whilst hopefully balancing this with financial security. Across the life of your company you will perform in a range of contexts, for different audiences and for different reasons, and having a general sense of the broader landscape can be a helpful step towards plotting your longer-term ambitions early on.

Art vs money

There are few places where the dichotomy between the need to tell stories and the need to make money come into more focus than when it comes to finding a home for your performance. Some doors will only open if you part with your hard-earned cash whilst other opportunities may seem hidden behind gatekeepers. It can be easy to rush ahead for the excitement of a perceived opportunity without considering the potential cost, whilst the very fact that this system exists seems to make barriers unavoidable.

Added to this is the endless search for exposure. Here's how it tends to work. You approach a theatre with a view to staging some work with them. After much wasted time and chased emails, the beleaguered programming manager or artistic director tells you that they'd love to work with you but they need to build up a relationship with you, to gain a sense of your work. They ask you to invite them to your next show. You slave away endlessly at great expense to develop a fantastic show, secure a great fringe venue, and send your dates along. The artistic director replies to tell you how sorry they are that they're not available on those dates. Repeat ad infinitum until you lose the will to live.

Partnerships

Collaboration is the name of the game and apart from being a great way of making interesting work, it can be a really useful way of getting work staged, programmed, and funded. Working with co-partners demonstrates a collaborative and interdisciplinary approach to your work, which is increasingly viewed promisingly in funding circles, as a way of reducing risk and increasing reach. Successful partnerships obviously bring a lot to both parties and could take a whole range of forms, from a co-production with another theatre company to a sponsorship in your theatre programme. Considering artistic co-production can be a beneficial avenue for getting work staged, particularly where your partner brings something additional to your offer (increased resources, contacts, or artistic experience). Obviously, you should not see partnerships as a one-way street, and there should be a communicable benefit for both sides. This is especially important to articulate when you are the smaller partner.

Partnerships are particularly useful when it comes to funding applications. The fact that both parties have agreed to work together is appealing in itself, as this should add value and reach to the work you could achieve individually. Partnering with a more established organisation can give your application some gravitas, and you should consider who will be the main applicant on funding applications, to best support you in this.

Remember that partnerships could and should be varied and supportive, so really take time to think beyond the obvious. If you were producing a piece of work about homelessness, for example, it could lend credibility to your show and help in the development of the show itself to partner with a major homelessness charity. Looking for meaningful connections with other stakeholders can open up a range of opportunities for community engagement, funding, and artist development, and when making such enquiries be clear about what you want from an initial conversation and be articulate about what you can offer them in return. This might take the form of organisational development, through workshops, skills sharing, and knowledge exchanges. When such things are agreed, make sure they are accounted for in your production budget and consider your time and costs before agreeing to any additional activities.

Finding venues

If you are looking for one or multiple venues and you don't know where to begin, do research on companies similar in size and/or artistic output to yours. Get hold of their flyers or visit their website and see where they have booked and how long for. This will give you an indication of what is possible (although you won't know if it's been successful or not) and should help you to find venues you may not previously have been aware of.

Dealing with venues

Getting your work programmed at a major theatre can seem to be the icing on the cake for your new organisation. There are numerous ways in which to get your work onto a stage and venues will normally be transparent about this on their website. The first thing you will want to find out is whether the venue produces its own work, whether it is a receiving house and whether it is purely available to hire. Each of these different brushstrokes have different implications for the kind of work the venue will stage and the artistic and financial opportunity available to your company as a result. When dealing with venues there are a number of things you should take into account:

- Artistic programme:
    - Look at the other kinds of work that venue produces (or receives). Does your show and company fit into the style of work they already host? Does the venue stage work by emerging companies such as yours, and if they do, are there specific routes-to-stage for work companies such as yours? Do they have a new writers programme or associate companies, for example?
- Venue capacity:
    - Does the size of stage and audience capacity fit with the type of work you want to make? Bigger is not always better – you should think about set and lighting requirements or limitations, sightlines, and artistic impact. Will your intimate one-person show work well on a huge stage? At this point, you may need to approach this process in reverse. The type and scale of venue you can work with (or afford!) may be out of your hands, which in turn dictates the type of work you should make. A fifty-seat pub theatre might force some creative rethinking for your twenty strong Chekhov cast with a revolve stage! On the other hand, you should use this limitation to your advantage. Big stages are intimidating, as well as harder to find an audience for, and working in a smaller space can be an exciting way of shaping your craft without an overreliance on sets and gimmicks. This is how most new work is developed, at least to begin with, so embrace it.
- Programming options:
    - How do you get your work on a venue's stage? Do you need to be programmed as part of a wider artistic season? Can you simply pay a fee and hire the space? Each route-to-stage has its own positives and drawbacks, outlined below, so make sure you do your research.
- Touring requirements:
    - If you're lucky enough to be thinking about booking multiple locations for a tour, an added challenge can be finding venues that are broadly similar in terms of the layout of the space and the practical requirements of your show. If one venue is a traditional proscenium arch theatre, another is a black-box studio, and a third is an outdoor performance space, these may all be really fun to perform at, but

what headaches will this cause to your production if it plays on a different size and type of stage each week? In reality, no two performance spaces are exactly the same, and you should do your research into the quirks and peculiarities of each before going into rehearsal, so that you can avoid staging anything that will be impossible for a venue to facilitate.

- Audience:
    - Who are the audience for the venue and would they want to come and see your work? Look at the type of shows the venue currently programmes and, if possible, visit the venue and see some work here so that you can get a feel for who it is for. This is probably the most important issue to be honest with yourself about. Does your audience live in this theatre? If not, does your work have the potential to bring them in? Look also at the marketing efforts of the venue – from the posters and in-house marketing to social media followers – and get a feel for how well shows are promoted. Where venues offer a mix of programming or hire arrangements there can often be a hidden hierarchy where programmed shows are given focus over hires, which the venue takes little responsibility to promote.

- Values:
    - This may seem a low priority when you are simply desperate to have your work staged, but finding venues whose values and work aligns with yours is an important way of establishing a strong working relationship that is more likely to last beyond the specific piece of work you are currently developing. You shouldn't see venues as little more than a platform for your work at the end of the process, as the best theatres have a range of schemes and opportunities to work with artists throughout their creative journeys, in ways that benefit both sides. Equally, programmers tend to prefer companies who have done their research and who are able to articulate why a particular venue is a good fit for their work. The temptation to do a scattergun approach just to get your work staged should be replaced in favour of cultivating strong relationships with venues where you can actually see an overlap in artistic and wider values. Your work is more likely to be something they are interested in, and even if a particular show isn't right for them at that moment, this is a much stronger way of building a relationship for the future.

Contacting programmers

Where your venue is available to hire, this is usually quite a simple process to initiate. A hire email will typically be available on the theatre website for you to contact. If the website has been scant on details, be sure to ask these questions in your initial correspondence, particularly around cost and dates, so that you can quickly assess whether the venue is a viable option for you. If it is, the programming manager will confirm arrangements with you before sending over a contract for you to sign. There may be additional policies for you to agree to – such as health and safety – and the programming manager will detail when the hire fee is to be paid. Draw up a list of any questions thrown up by the contract and ensure you receive satisfactory and clear answers before you sign and pay, so that you are clear on what you are agreeing to.

In the majority of cases, however, you will be looking to strike up a relationship with venues where an artistic programme is commissioned, either to find a home for a show you are planning to develop, or to access opportunities to create a new piece of work with them.

Approaching venues can feel intimidating and it can sometimes feel as though this process is opaque, which is why it's important to do your research and certainly to make sure you aren't contacting them in any sort of hurried rush. Venues operate on their own very different timescales, so it is borderline impossible that they will want to programme your show at short notice when they have never heard of you before. Find those venues whose values and opportunities strike a chord with you and set about establishing a relationship.

Those responsible for programming at venues have a duty to find work that will be of interest to their audience, and as such they are naturally going to be cautious about staging work whose artistic merit they are unfamiliar with. It can take a long time, sometimes several years to build meaningful relationships with venues, and although this can feel frustrating, when viewed from their perspective the approach is understandable.

Programmers might want an opportunity to engage with you and your work, so this should be your first approach. Drop them an email or a phone call to ask for a coffee. This can be a nice way of putting a face to a name, introducing yourself, and finding out a bit more about how the venue works with artists. They may even show you around the theatre. Obviously, this may be more practical for venues in your local area, and you may not establish the same sorts of relationships when working with venues further afield. However, broadly speaking, you are more likely to start your career (when building these relationships is so very important) working with venues in your geographical region. The reasons for this may well be logistical, but also because venues will often have a preference or stipulation (dictated by their own funding guidelines) to primarily support artists in their local region.

Programmers are some of the hardest working and busiest people in the whole theatre ecosystem, so do politely nudge them but be aware that they are not obligated to meet you for coffee on your every whim! It is also very unlikely that an introductory coffee will result in a three-week run at their venue next spring, so treat the process as it is and be respectful of this.

Programmers will want to get a sense of your artistic output and the best way to do this is to invite them to see your work. If you are looking for a home for a pre-existing piece of theatre, it would be ideal to invite them to see the show so that they can judge whether it is of the right quality for them and whether it would fit within their broader artistic output. If they aren't available or the show isn't currently being staged, a good quality recording must be your next priority. If you are planning to develop a brand new piece of work, programmers will only be able to judge the possible outcome of this through getting a sense of your existing artistic quality and aesthetic, so the above still applies. However, the risk factor increases dramatically for an unknown quantity, which a programmer can't see or get a sense of. You should be happy to send over a script, but if you are looking for a home for new work, it would be prudent to explore what opportunities the venue has for nurturing new performances. Lots of venues will have some form of a new works department – in many mid-sized theatres these tend to be run by the same people – and they will have a plethora of script submission windows, scratch nights, and R+D opportunities for seeking and helping to develop new work. The clue is in that word *develop*, however, and work can take many months and years to create – through scratch nights, feedback, drafts, and re-drafts – before it is ready to be staged in a main space for a paying audience.

How to build a relationship

The process of meeting programmers and building a relationship tends to be slightly different if you are looking to develop work outside of a festival context. Remember, programmers are much more likely to give you the time of day if you are genuinely interested in forming a relationship between the venue and your work, rather than if you are simply trying to sell them something. You might think about inviting programmers to see your work (or a recording of it), or you might invite them to see you perform at a scratch night. If the venue has space and you have the budget for it, you can often hire space within a venue for R+D. This can also be a good way of fostering a relationship with a venue, which provides programmers with a much easier way to get to know about the work you are creating. Remember, good venues and good programmers are interested in artist development as much as they are in good shows, and you should see your entire creative *process* as a way of engaging with venues, not just the end result. With this in mind, feel free to invite them to rehearsals, and don't feel the need to explain away all of the roughness; they will understand and appreciate this. What they'll be looking for is a group that has vision, integrity, and focus, with a way of bringing stories to life that is unique and interesting to their audience.

Likewise, your relationship with a programmer may result in more than just a booking. Subsidised venues, in particular, are often obligated to support the development of artists, and to this end, programmers may be able to help you with things such as funding applications, advice, and feedback. However, they are not automatically obligated to help you and you should not see this as a right you can demand, but instead part of a healthy, respectful, and mutual connection. Where you have asked for feedback and support, do be mindful of the programmers' workload before pestering for a response right away.

Feedback on work

When a programmer has come to see your work (or has viewed an extract) they will either decide that it is right for their venue or not. There may be many reasons why a piece of work is not right: it may not match their audience, it may be too similar to something else they're already programming, or it may not be up to the artistic or technical standard they are looking for. Although this can naturally be a disappointing outcome, you should always seek opportunities for developmental feedback, and feedback from programmers can be some of the most useful for shaping your creative practice. It is useful to try and agree that feedback will be part of the arrangement when first asking the programmers to attend, but again, do be mindful of timescales when a programmer has come to your show before pestering for a response. It takes time to fully consider a response to a piece of work, particularly if the programmer has to tactfully and helpfully explain why that piece isn't right – so do be mindful.

The production pack

What should you include when you are contacting venues with an eye to them programming a piece of work? A production pack (also known as a touring pack) is a document containing information about your work. Be sure to include:

- The title of the show
- A short synopsis
- When the show is available
- Run time and interval requirements
- Artwork and trailers
- Additional info about your offer
- A possible post-show Q+A (what wraparound activities could you offer?)
- Access requirements
- Technical and staging requirements
- Target audience
- The sort of deal you are looking for
- How you work
- Contact details.

Remember that you will have very little opportunity to capture the interest of a programmer, so make life easy for them and pay attention to your formatting and structure. Put the important information early on in the venue pack so that they can find it quickly.

If you aren't a graphic designer – and you don't need to be – check your show pack with other members of your team to look for spelling and grammar mistakes and to get a second opinion on formatting. Don't feel the need to make your document sing and dance, it will only increase the file size, be slower to load, and be less likely to impress a programmer, who is relying on your information doing the work, but definitely avoid funky fonts and crazy colours.

Some other considerations to bear in mind:

- Unless it specifies an alternative, send your pack as a PDF. This means it's harder to edit, you know the formatting will hold up, and they're easier for venues to save and print.
- Make your pack accessible and avoid small fonts (don't go below 10pt) and things that make your text difficult to read.
- Add links to suitable video footage (if you have any) on YouTube or Vimeo.
- Add brief captions or ALT text to any images to increase accessibility and to aid with context.
- Follow up your pack with an email a week later. If you prefer a phone call, try and email to agree on a suitable time to be more respectful of their workload.

Booking venues

It can be exciting to get an offer to perform at a venue, whether through building a relationship or as a result of being approached after a festival performance. Whichever way the process comes about, do make sure you keep a clear head before agreeing to anything: booking a tour around Denmark might sound incredibly exciting, but it also sounds expensive. Add to this the fact that you may have customs fees to pay, huge costs to transport your set and different rules around copyright, performance licences, or censorship and you may end up having to make a lot of compromises just to get your show to the stage.

As you would with any major life decision involving a contract, don't rush into anything, make sure you are crystal clear about what you are agreeing to, and ask for help if you need it. There is very rarely a disadvantage to taking time to double-check and think about any agreement, and if a programmer seems to be rushing you on this it might be worth asking why, and making sure that the proposed deal is in your best interests.

If you are lucky enough to be in the position of booking something with enough weight to warrant this process, it may be prudent to seek out a producer who has previous touring experience who can come on board or at least offer guidance.

Venue locations

When looking to book multiple venues, make sure you have an awareness of their geographical location. Venues will often have conditions in place to limit crossover of content and stretch on audiences, so if you are looking at two venues quite close together they may not want to program you on this basis. If you need help with this, speak to your programmer about *catchment areas* or *exclusion clauses*, the details of which may also appear in your contract.

International locations

Before booking international locations, make sure you take time to check your funding stipulations for any clauses to inhibit this. In the UK, the Arts Council will only fund tours in which a maximum of 15% takes place outside of England, for example. The UK, Europe, and the US have fairly different systems for producing and developing work, including how that work is funded and created, and what audiences are used to seeing, so do your research to make sure you are prepared for this. The International Network for Contemporary Performing Artists is a really useful resource to explore for help with working and collaborating internationally. For artists in the UK, there are now additional challenges to consider since the decision to leave the European Union, many of which result in further costs. UK Theatre has an excellent questionnaire to test whether you are 'Brexit ready,' with all of the latest advice and guidance on a range of issues, which is linked at the end of the chapter.

Programming deals

There are a whole range of ways in which you can secure a venue to perform in, each with their own advantages and drawbacks. There will be many variations within these, but it is super helpful to be familiar with the key terms around deals that pop up again and again. Don't panic if this process feels intimidating – it's actually relatively simple when you break it down.

Box-office split

A box-office split is an agreed percentage split of the money made on ticket sales. A 70/30 split on a £10 ticket, for example, will see £7 come to you and £3 go to the venue. When negotiating a box-office split, make sure you are clear who gets the bigger percentage, and ask if this is not explicit. This larger percentage should almost always be in your favour, and you should seriously reconsider if this is not the case.

A box-office split shares the risk between venue and company and is a reasonable alternative to a hire when it can be negotiated. However, as the venue hasn't put down any money for you at this stage, the risk does still fall most strongly with the company if you fail to sell many tickets. To avoid this, look at the capacity of the venue and work your split on the capacity you think you could realistically achieve. If this covers your costs, great, but if not, think carefully about signing up.

With any financial deal, make sure you are clear whether VAT is being deducted or not, so that you are clear what price your split is being negotiated from. A box-office take of £1,500 will only leave £1,200 once the venue deducts their 20% VAT, meaning that your 60/40 split will be decided from this figure, rather than the original £1,500.

Ensure you are clear whether there are any other additional charges to be deducted (typical ones to look out for are credit card commission, restoration levy, and music licensing payments) so that you know what price you're getting the split on. Depending on the specifics of your contract, you may see deductions for something called a 'contra,' which is an accounting term but can be simply understood as the base cost the venue incurs to actually run the theatre. Usually this is presented as being non-negotiable, but you should still question the 'first rate' quote you are given to see how it breaks down and whether there is any room for negotiation. In an ideal world, any rental fee should be less than the contra, although this gap can shrink as the size of the theatre increases.

You should also interrogate your contract for any mention of the 'take-off figure,' which reflects the minimum weekly box office income you will need to achieve in order to cover your weekly running costs and salary payments. If your weekly take doesn't reach this figure, you'll be in a difficult situation financially. In this scenario, you will need to explore options for 'shortfall and notice weeks,' which represent the number of week's notice you (or the venue) will give after consecutively making a shortfall, before deciding to close the show early. You legally need to give a minimum of two weeks' notice to your cast and crew, but in this situation you will likely want to get out as quickly as possible, and although this isn't a scenario you will aim to be in, it's worth ensuring you are clear about the possible outcomes if this arises.

Fee/straight guarantee

A guarantee means that the venue agrees to pay a set amount to stage your show. The guarantee is just that: regardless of how many tickets you sell, the venue has agreed to pay you this guaranteed amount for each performance.

Apart from the obvious benefit of receiving payment, this also places a responsibility on the venue to help sell your show, because that is the only way they will make their money back. If you sell out or sell nothing, you will always take home your guarantee, so it is in the interest of the venue marketing department to support your show to reach an audience.

Although a guarantee is an attractive idea, it's only worth it if the guarantee will actually cover your costs, and of course, there is a chance that you could make more money by opting for a box-office split, if you are confident that you will sell a lot of tickets.

Split against guarantee

A bit of a 'best of both worlds' – a split against a guarantee follows the same process as the guarantee, but ensures that if you make more through a box-office split, you would take home that instead. This ensures that you benefit from both systems, giving yourself a guarantee but ensuring that a particularly successful show can benefit you also. Arguably this supports both artists and venues, and encourages both parties to be invested in making sure the show reaches the biggest audience it can.

Hire

The most 'basic' venue arrangement and arguably one to avoid whenever possible. Venue fees can be expensive and usually need to be paid up front, which can be an obstacle to getting started. With a venue hire, you have already covered the costs of the space so it makes no difference (in theory) to the venue if you sell any tickets or not. The motivation to promote the show therefore lies primarily with the company. The advantage of a hire is that anything you sell at the box office is yours, so if you know you will get a large audience this can potentially be more advantageous to you. Hire venues are also easy to get booked in to, if you can afford the entry fee, so can be a great way of actually getting some work on the stage in your early days.

Make sure you get clear advice from the venue on what is included in a hire fee, as box office, venue staff, and technical support is not always included as standard. This varies on a venue-to-venue basis, and if any of these aren't specifically mentioned, it is advisable to clarify with the programming manager before making payment. Some theatres hire-in shows and create their own work, and in order to prioritise and showcase the work made in-house, there can sometimes be a hierarchy of how that work is marketed on the website and social channels. When looking at any hire venue, research is your friend, as it can sometimes be a minefield of unexpected surprises and low audience numbers.

If your theatre does offer an in-house box office system, it is always advisable to utilise it (even if it does incur an additional fee) as this can streamline the process for audiences and imply greater professionalism in the eyes of audiences. Websites such as Ticketsource do offer do-it-yourself box office systems, but you still pay a commission on tickets sold, and audiences usually have to pay a booking fee which further increases the cost of the ticket.

When booking a for-hire venue which is not close to your base, you need to think carefully about your strategy for attracting audiences. Look at the venue's social channels to see how well (if at all) they promote their hired-in work, and see whether there are opportunities to send flyers and posters. Venues can have a hierarchy of poster displays, in terms of both size and prominence (a personal favourite being the A4 posters sometimes displayed over toilets …), so try and get information about this before you spend a lot of money on posters that will be barely visible. If you can afford targeted advertising on platforms such as Facebook, this can be a helpful way of bridging the geography gap, but depending on the target audience for your work this may or may not be a viable option to consider.

First and second call

A first call ensures that box office income is split in one or more calls, either in favour of the artist or the venue. It may be agreed, for example, that the first £500 of box office receipts would be guaranteed to the producer. This is the first call. After this threshold is reached, it might be subsequently agreed that box office receipts from £500 to £1000 will be paid to the venue. This is known as the second call. This method of agreement is most common with larger touring venues, however, and is unlikely to feature at your current scale.

It is worth pointing out that this is a negotiation and you do not need to be a silent party in this process. Obviously, you want to get your work programmed, so it can be tempting to sit silent and accept whatever comes your way, but you can politely start the conversation if a proposed deal isn't quite working for you. At the end of the day, venues will understand if the numbers don't make an option viable for you, and they need you to feel confident to create the fantastic work they have booked you for, so don't be afraid to go back and forth a few times to find an arrangement that suits both sides.

Royalty payments

There may be members of your creative team who are entitled to royalty payments from your production. Most commonly this may be the writer, but perhaps also the composer and designer, and occasionally actors. Whether this applies to you will depend on the specifics of your contracts with the creative team, and when working professionally with venues this can get notoriously difficult due to the way such standards have been agreed on in the past. At its simplest, royalty payments off the top are payments made to the creative based on net box office receipts. As with all contracts, if you are unsure of anything you must query it with the most appropriate person, but you should also ensure you are aware of standards and legal requirements in your territory.

Contra charges

Contras relate to the expenses incurred by the venue in the staging of your production. Generally contras can be split into Marketing contras, Facilities (cleaning costs etc.), and Technical. It's important that you check what is included in your contract, because these are costs you will usually be expected to pay back from your box office earnings. For hire venues may operate in a more limited way, stipulating set fees to be applied if, for example, you fail to take your rubbish with you at the end of a run. Always check and always ask if you are unsure.

What are programmers looking for?

Programmers are all unique and each person will be looking for different practical and artistic qualities, depending on the nature of their venue and their artistic offering. However, there will be a set range of practical considerations that will be common to most programmers, which you would do well to lay out in your initial contact. This shows that you know your work, that you are making life as easy as possible for the programmer, and helps to avoid time wasting if a programmer finds out after much effort that the show won't work for them.

Generally, programmers will want to know:

- Why you are making this piece of work and why you are making it now?
- Why their venue is a good fit?
- Who your target audience are and how you can work with the venue to reach them?
- What kind of financial deal are you hoping for?
- Whether the show is reliant on additional funding and whether it is already secured, or likely to be secured at all?
- What other venues you have had conversations with and who else can endorse your work?
- What your technical expectations are and what resources will you require?

If you are proposing to tour an existing piece of work you should, realistically, have a good response to these questions already. Where you aren't sure of things, certainly don't lie or exaggerate – programmers don't want to read marketing speak all day – but be as clear and open about your offering as possible. With anything relating to programming, it is actually much better to be honest, even when it means admitting that you're not sure, than to try and bluff your way and hope things will sort themselves out. Often, admitting where you have gaps can be the first important step towards improving your offering overall.

Programmers will make decisions about what to program in any given season based on a number of factors, including, but not limited to:

- Other shows in the season
    - Finding opportunities for artistic connection whilst avoiding artistic clashes
- Audience potential
- Personal taste/venue preference
- Reputation of the people involved
    - For some venues, big names may be the way of ensuring the audience come in, in other venues, not so much so
- Quality of the work
- Technical requirements
- Geographical factors for touring shows

- Staffing implications,
- Box office implications (if your show proposes halving the number of seats available in the auditorium, for example)
- Sales pitch.

You can immediately improve your chances of building a relationship with a venue by being mindful of the questions posed above and doing what you can to make a programmer's life easier to work with you and to accommodate your request. There is no ideal time to contact a programmer, as each venue will be working to its own printing and programming deadlines, but you should make sure you are ready within your own artistic journey before reaching out, so that you are attuned enough to make contact in the appropriate way and to ensure that you can respond appropriately to whatever developments come your way.

Although venue relations is about much more than selling your work, you should remember that everything will speak for you at this stage: the quality of the photos you send along, the choice of font used in your sales pitch: everything forms an impression that will guide a programmer's decision to engage with your work or not.

Finding audiences with venues

It can be tempting to think that having venues book your work means that the responsibility for getting bums on seats now transfers nicely to a marketing department somewhere inside the theatre building. Unfortunately, no show is guaranteed an audience, and venues will often want to work *with* you to maximise the opportunity to get your work seen by as varied a range of people as possible. This has a tangible benefit for you also, as audiences who enjoy your work now are going to be more inclined to follow your journey and therefore build your following for future work. You should always be keen to engage in a conversation with the venue about audience development as they will have a lot of knowledge and expertise about the kinds of groups they reach and those who they don't reach so well.

Audiences have been traditionally measured through numbers, and this is important to ensure that you get a sizeable crowd and that costs are covered. But you should also consider the wider move towards depth of engagement as a measure of success, as this is a much more promising way to build deeper, longer-lasting relationships with audience members. The first stage in this process is to identify the potential target audience for your work, a task that we explored in detail in Chapter 5.

Being specific about who your work is likely to be enjoyed by is going to strengthen the focus of the work itself and will really help programmers and marketing departments to know how your work fits into their broader remit. It will also be a big step in their initial decision making: it is going to be a waste of time on everybody's part if you propose a sketch show in a venue predominantly known for staging contemporary dance. Working with the venue throughout the process is always best for audience development, as the venue will have a stronger grasp of their audience than you will, and until you reach the enviable stage of having a loyal audience following you across the country(!) you will do well to listen to the venue's reflections on who their audience is, and who consumes the work presented there. When thinking about your target audience, it can be beneficial to liken your shows to that of other work. This can feel a bit awkward when you're trying to sell the unique benefits of your artistic vision, but it can be a big help to programmers to see links between audiences who booked for such-and-such a show last year, who will likely be interested in your work also. This can be useful in a broad sense 'audiences who like *Game of Thrones* are likely to enjoy this show,' but extra brownie points if you can talk about work previously staged at the venue to really drive home why your show would be a good fit for their space.

Developing audiences with venues

Audience engagement then is about numbers, but it is equally about depth of engagement. Depth of engagement works well for both sides and is something you should give some thought to early on, if possible. Remember, this is about quality and you should therefore avoid tacking things on or opening yourself up to any old idea: it'll feel like a wasted opportunity and it'll also stretch your resources thinly. Research the work of your chosen venue and see what they currently offer and also where possible gaps exist.

Engagement with audiences can take a whole range of forms. You could open up your rehearsal room or lead a workshop with local artists, particularly where there is overlap with your play. If your work is a devised piece, you could run a workshop on devising techniques, for example. Consider ways in which audiences can engage with your show beyond the performance itself, both before and after the performance. This can be particularly interesting if your show has a wider contextual background, which audiences may want to deep dive further into. Think about opportunities for audiences to produce their own creative response. Several well established theatres in London operate rapid-response programmes, where new writers will go away and create a ten-minute response to a play they have seen the week before.

There are an endless variety of ways to engage in meaningful, sustained audience development, and ideally you should consider this as part of the broader development of your show itself. Meaningful audience development should not be an add on, and the effort it can require to establish these plans will pay off in the long run. Do make sure that your content is generally engaging, and that there is a focus on active rather than passive response from your potential audience.

While it can feel intimidating and overwhelming to consider ways to engage an entire audience for your show, remember that this is in addition to the marketing campaign of your venue and your own established audience. These activities will work better when they are targeted at small, defined cohorts, and you are not being expected to run some sort of activity for every single audience member on top of the show itself.

Performance dates

There are a few considerations to bear in mind when booking performance dates, and if you are in a position to give thought to them, they will potentially make your performances stronger. Traditionally, theatres tend to book external work between Autumn and Spring, but a bit of research into your preferred venues will give you an idea of how this is applied in practice.

Things to look out for when selecting dates:

- Bank holidays
- Key dates such as Valentine's day, Eid, Halloween, Bonfire Night, etc.
- Half terms and university semester dates
    - Lots of students go home during these times
- August
    - In the UK, most theatres scale down as much of the industry flocks to Edinburgh
- Summer holidays
    - Lots of people go on holiday
- Sports matches
    - Especially important finals.

Site-specific and non-traditional work

You may be considering building a new space for performance or staging a performance in a non-traditional space such as a park or a shop. Lots of incredibly exciting site-specific work is made in this way, and if it helps to enhance the story you are telling it can be a very beneficial storytelling tool.

As you might expect, there are a range of unique challenges to consider when dealing with site-specific work, and where possible this should be done before you begin any creative work on the piece itself.

Your first step should be to contact the land owner and summarise your thoughts about how you would like to use their space and when. In some instances, this can be a very easy step to achieve, but often it can be notoriously difficult to reach the correct person. When you do make contact with somebody you should ensure that they have the authority to conduct such a discussion, as they may be acting on behalf of the landlord and may not have ultimate say. Pay close attention to spaces you believe to be public property, as parks and pathways are often owned by local councils or national bodies such as the National Trust.

Given that you want to use the space in an unusual way, it is probable that a hire fee will be the most likely outcome, as the space may need to compensate for lost earnings during the time you would like to use the space. To mitigate against this, think about how you can work around the usual requirements of a space if it is still functional, so that the business can continue to operate without disruption. You may be able to use this leverage to negotiate a better fee.

Buildings that are regularly hired will probably have a set hire fee for events such as filming and performance, but where your request is truly unique, it is likely that a landlord will be plucking a number out of thin air. This can be tricky. Be prepared for a savvy landlord to throw the question back at you by asking what your budget is, and be sure to lay out clearly that you're a small company. It's amazing how quickly non-theatre people can think any sort of performance is of Hollywood scale and, therefore, has a Hollywood price tag. As always, if you have no way of covering the costs being offered, do not accept the agreement.

When you have secured a venue (or built your own) you will need to look at applying for a theatre licence. Regular theatre venues are licensed to perform plays all year round, but you will need to secure a temporary licence for your pop-up venue as a requirement of the Licensing Act 2003. Any public performance of a play needs to be granted a licence, and for the avoidance of doubt, a play in this context is defined as 'any dramatic piece involving speech, singing, or action and the playing of a role, ballets, and musicals.' You must apply for a theatre licence through your local council, and you should check time frames before making plans to progress further, particularly in case your application is rejected.

You will have to pay particular attention to everything outside of the performance times themselves: specifically thinking about your get-in, tech run, and storage of set. You may need to educate the landlord on these issues, and it is better to do this early rather than to drop it in as a surprise at a later date.

There are an endless number of logistics to think about when producing site-specific work:

- Is there parking available?
- What about toilets?
- Is the site safe and accessible?
- Is there enough power: note, theatre lighting very rarely plugs into your standard plug socket!
- Is it warm, especially in the evening?
- Does the space have sound bleed, making it difficult to hear or to obtain silence?
- What about blackouts? There are often regulations regarding emergency exit signs, which need to be visible (and therefore on) at all times, which could spoil that essential blackout at the end of act two.

- Is there wing space and a place for your actors to get changed safely and in private?
- Is there lighting outside the venue when people leave after the show?

This is not to say that site-specific work is impossible, far from it, but you should know from the outset that you are at least doubling your workload if you go down this route, and the wilder the location, the greater the level of planning you will need to embark upon before you even begin. Added to this list of headaches is the fact that audiences may have a difficult time finding you: both in terms of hearing about the show and booking tickets, to actually locating you on performance day.

An important addition to this list is the obligation to consider health and safety in a far more hands-on way than you may be used to when dealing with pre-existing venues. Although you have obligations to your cast, crew, and the general public when presenting any work, when creating site-specific performance, the buck really does stop with you in making sure you are covered for any eventuality. You have legal duties to ensure that you have systems in place to assess and control potential risks, to reduce the amount and severity of any manual handling, and to avoid working from height where possible. Additionally, the person in charge of a premises has duties to ensure that the means of getting into and out of the venue are safe, and that all equipment brought onto the premises is safe and does not present a health risk. The majority of injuries incurred in theatre of all kinds results from manual handling and working at height, so this is not to be taken lightly, and producing theatre in non-traditional spaces opens up additional risks in both of these areas. You will also need employer's liability insurance in the majority of cases. You should seek out training or, even better, work with trained technicians. There are resources listed at the end of this chapter that detail your obligations and provide links to further training and support.

There are a number of really good ticketing websites, where you can set up your own box office. Payment options vary, with most websites taking a small commission from each ticket sold. If your performance location is likely to be difficult for audiences to find, it can be prudent to put this information onto their e-tickets. A useful tip when producing any show is to check whether Google Maps is accurate! Huge numbers of audience members will rely on such navigation tools, so make sure to let them know if the search result is off by a street or two, for whatever reason. When selling e-tickets, do take time to consider those who may be disenfranchised by this method of purchasing tickets: not everybody has access to a smartphone and is internet savvy.

As is the nature of site-specific work being something completely original, you should generally give yourself a substantially larger planning time for a piece of this nature. Given that the piece is likely to be in direct conversation with the space itself, it is much better to know the challenges and opportunities of a space early on, as surprises down the line can be of significant detriment to the piece itself.

A note on fringe theatres

How to put this tactfully ... not all venues are made equal. You may have an understanding of this already from your time as a student or an audience member, but trust me, it's a whole new adventure when you start to produce your own work. Particularly in the early days, when you'll be excited to get your hands on any space you can, you will likely come across a whole plethora of weird and wonderful quirks which can range from minor irritation to existential threat. I wish I was exaggerating.

A brief summary of personal experience may give you a flavour. In our time, I have arrived at venues (which will remain nameless!) where the backstage area smelled strongly of urine and another where the dressing room floor was littered with needles (yes, really). In another venue, a stage technician decided to lock a door to a balcony where our actress playing Juliet was supposed to go through for quite an important scene in that play! Not knowing what was going on, and trapped in pitch black backstage, the actress panicked and forced the entire door off its hinges, which made for (a) quite a unique interpretation of Shakespeare's balcony scene and (b) a very angry tech crew.

Common surprises to look out for:

- What is the general condition of the dressing rooms and are there separate spaces for men and women?
- How big is the backstage area and where is it located? In many fringe venues, backstage is separated by little more than a curtain, making it effectively the same room. This means backstage needs to be completely silent at all times.
- Doors and squeaky floors. Adding to the last bullet point, keep an eye out for backstage doors – they *always* squeak or slam, or, if you're really lucky, both. Squeaky floorboards can also make backstage movement a cacophony of noise if you're not careful.
- Where are speakers located on the stage? In fringe venues, they are often at the front of the stage, which can have the effect of drowning out your actors when they are trying to talk at the same time. It also limits your ability to 'locate' sounds in a 3D space.
- How silent are your speakers when they're not in use? Many cheaper sound systems will let out a distinct hiss when 'silent' which cannot be removed without turning off the power altogether.
- Is there sound-bleed from other spaces? Ones to watch out for are the bar or the street outside. These spaces may seem quaint when you arrive at 10am but by 10pm the noise can be quite different. If your venue has multiple performance spaces, be ready for a flurry of noise if another performance starts or finishes during your run. In one memorable moment, we had a wedding party walk in on Act four of *Hamlet*. Weird for us, probably much weirder for them.
- What inputs do you need? If you want to play music from your phone or laptop, you will need a *mini-jack* connector. Check if this is supplied or if

you need to bring your own. If you're planning to use a projector, check the inputs. Depending on the laptop you have available, you may need to find an adaptor. Again, check with the venue in advance and see what is provided.
- Can you stick things to the walls or floor? We once performed at a fringe theatre where the floor was painted black (as opposed to a 'proper' theatre floor). When our designer got trigger happy with the gaffer tape the venue weren't happy at the end of the run when removing the tape took half of the floor with it!
- Is there a fixed *lighting rig*? A fixed rig means that the position and choice of lights cannot be changed. In some fringe venues this limits lighting cues to little more than a general wash.
- Does the theatre magically transform into a pizza oven when full? There should be laws against this, but at the time of writing there regrettably aren't. Venues of all sizes struggle with this dilemma, but small fringe venues with a full house ascend to a whole new level of torture, usually about forty-five minutes before the end of the performance. If you don't have audience members passing out (it's happened) or being violently sick (yep, this happened too) then you're likely to see your audience transform into a mass of fluttering programs as they desperately try to fan themselves to cool down. Not exactly conducive to focussed performance. And this is to say nothing of your heavily costumed actors ...
- Is there a seating rake? In the vast majority of fringe venues, the answer to this question is likely to be an overwhelming no. Beware of how this affects your audience, though, where basically everyone except the front row are sat in restricted view seats. This can make staging very difficult. Any action that involves an actor kneeling or lying down is basically out of the question: no one will be able to see it!
- How dark are your blackouts? Some venues are a long way from dark at the best of times, especially if they let in natural light. Others will have inconveniently placed fire exit signs which will need to remain on throughout your show, and therefore illuminated. When you do find a venue where you can achieve a satisfying blackout, you then have the next problem of a backstage area that is so dark your actors risk falling into the depths of hell. If there isn't a dedicated backstage light, bring a small desk lamp from home and cover the bulb with a dimming blue gel. This will provide enough light to see by, whilst preventing bleed into the stage space.

Commercial venues and transfers: West End and Broadway

For many readers, the idea of performing on the West End or Broadway may seem like a far-flung pipe dream. However, it may surprise you to know that you pretty much simply strike a deal and book a commercial venue in a not dissimilar way to how you may work with other venues, but obviously on a much larger scale. It is good to be aware of this part of the market, not because you're likely to be performing on Broadway in your first year of existence, but so that you are clued up about how this fits into the wider ecosystem and so that you have knowledge to fall back on if you are lucky enough to be considering this.

Unless you happen to be incredibly wealthy, it is probably most likely that you will come to this stage in your career after a successful tour or regional production. The show may well have been a hit critically or commercially (or hopefully, both!) and it may have been judged that there is an opportunity for a much longer run in the commercial sector.

The first and most important thing to say here is that if you are seriously considering this prospect, you should at least be at the stage of employing an experienced producer who has both the knowledge and the experience in the commercial sector to steer the ship. The commercial sector is not to be underestimated, and with some nine shows out of ten failing to break even, it's a risky venture even for seasoned commercial producers.

Commercial producers bring an unfair reputation with them, and they carry the added injustice that most people in the creative industry can't really explain what they do. This is unfair ignorance at the best of times but particularly so when thinking about shows on this financial scale.

In brief, a commercial producer will:

- Get a project off the ground by supporting a project they believe in.
- Hire key creatives to initiate the project.
- Raise the finance through a long-developed list of contacts.
- Budget the production and work with the creatives to help realise their artistic ambitions whilst being realistic to the resources available.
- Book a venue.
- Head up the marketing campaign.
- Head up press relations.
- Monitor ticket sales and regularly assess how well the show is performing.
- Close the show when the time comes.

This is the shortest list I could put together, which doesn't even begin to scratch the surface, so finding a good producer who believes in your project and who has the experience to make it work is invaluable. However, Broadway and the West End are notoriously fierce places to do business, and if there was a guaranteed pathway to financial or artistic success we'd all be doing it. Just because your show has the possibility to perform in the commercial sector, and just because you have a producer who is paying your wages, it is not guaranteed that the show will (a) attract an audience and (b) be a critical or commercial success. For every vacancy that pops up in a commercial theatre another show must have closed, and unless you develop the next *Lion King*, that is likely to be the outcome of most ventures into these seas, so consider your producer as a key collaborator, and not as a panacea or a distant overlord.

Furthermore, although you can, in theory, take anything to a commercial venue, there are obviously high stakes involved and high costs for venues, regardless of whether your show is a hit or a flop. Therefore, there are often restrictions in place to safeguard who can book venues and under what conditions, to protect both sides. In the UK, only full members of The Society of London Theatres (SOLT) can register a show in the West End without registering a *bond* with the London Theatre Council. A bit like when you're buying a house or a car, there are a lot of clauses tied up to protect the money needed to protect the venue and the producer. There are conditions for producers to meet to establish their reputation and reliability (usually regarding whether they ever have to call on an emergency bailout deposit) which helps to ensure that those dealing on the West End have some sort of track record on which you can rely.

Finding a commercial producer

If a commercial producer doesn't come and find you, many will have their own production company websites or you could ask venues you already know for their recommendations. Many of the more established regional venues will have had transfers and co-productions in the past and they will be able to offer advice, at the very least. If you're going all-out to find a producer off your own back, look at flyers for other productions as the production company will usually be listed. Although the mechanics of producing in the commercial sector are broadly the same regardless of form, you will probably find it easier to work with a producer who has a history of producing musicals, for example, if that's the sort of work you're looking to transfer.

Commercial work is high stakes and not something you will likely be seriously in a position to explore at this stage. Information is included here to develop your understanding of the sector at large, and it is particularly important not to be ignorant about the ways of working if opportunities for commercial theatre ever come your way. Don't push all business matters towards your producer and go in ignorant, as the potential pitfalls to yourself cannot be understated. At the same time, it is virtually impossible to self-teach yourself in the absence of experience in this area, so do not attempt to bring work into the commercial sector without the backing and support of an experienced commercial producer. The cost of obtaining this experience will more than pay for itself in these dangerous seas.

Understanding commercial avenues

Very generally speaking, the commercial route will choose you rather than the other way around. This is a crude way of saying that events will normally overtake you; if you have a show with commercial prospects, it is very unlikely to be a viable prospect if you're dreaming up a plan for Broadway in your bedroom. The reason for this is simple: the commercial theatre needs bums on seats, and not just any bums, but paying bums. Without a serious commercial prospect, it will be virtually impossible for a producer to raise the substantial finance needed to get your show off the ground, and harder still to attract people to come and see it. A well-known show or a lot of audience and press buzz from a previous run will probably be needed as a minimum, as well as the draw of well-known stars. This can seem unfair and this is not to make judgements on the artistic merit of your work, but you need to approach commercial theatre with a commercial mindset to judge the potential and to be realistic about the outcomes. As such, this summary is included here to support your broader contextual understanding of the theatre landscape only. Venturing into commercial work should only be done with, at a minimum, the support of an experienced commercial theatre producer.

There can be a tendency to apply a hierarchy to performance opportunities and to fixate on things such as venue size and reputation. In my opinion, this is a mindset to move away from. For the vast majority of companies I have worked with and observed, the journey of creating work is circular and winding; success looks very different to how it may do in other industries. Look at the work of the companies you admire and look at them from a company perspective: how often are they creating work, where were their last five shows staged and how were they funded? What other work does the company, or the directors, carry out in order to subsidise this and fill in the gaps?

One of the joys of this industry is that there is as much opportunity, joy, and money to be found in running some local workshops or performing at a festival as there is being an associate company or performing at a big venue. How you map progress in this climate matters, but it is not as linear or as clear-cut as if you were running a business selling products. With each year that passes you would hope to sell more of your product, and to increase the amount of money that you made by doing so. For theatre and for theatre companies, success may look very different, and it should not necessarily be measured by venue size or the number of five star reviews you have achieved. In this difficult industry, being able to continue may be enough of a bar of success for most: it is a bar many fail to meet eventually. So, define success for you and your company, don't worry about where you 'should' be on that path, and remember to keep your focus on the work and its purpose for being.

Chapter Resources

Touring and venues

Independent Theatre Council, 'Resources' www.itc-arts.org/about-us/resources/
Live & Local, www.liveandlocal.org.uk/
NRTF, www.ruraltouring.org/
Small Venues Network, www.smallvenuesnetwork.org.uk/
Spot on Lancashire, https://spotonlancashire.co.uk/

'The day in the life of a theatre programmer,' House Theatre (8th August 2013) https://housetheatre.org.uk/the-day-in-the-life-of-a-theatre-programmer/

Tour finder, http://tour-finder.org/

UK Theatre, 'Are you Brexit ready?' https://uktheatre.org/theatre-industry/guidance-reports-and-resources/are-you-brexit-ready/

UK Theatre, 'Example Deal Memo' (2011)

UK Theatre, 'Venue Agreements Guidance' (2017)

UK Theatre / SOLT, 'Producing, Presenting and Touring Handbook,' (2019), https://uktheatre.org/theatre-industry/guidance-reports-and-resources/producing-presenting-and-touring-handbook/

Venues North, http://arconline.co.uk/venues-north

Royalties

The Writer's Guild of Great Britain, *The Working Playwright: Agreements and Contracts*, https://writersguild.org.uk/wp-content/uploads/2015/02/WGGB_booklet_jun12_contracts_i.pdf

Site specific

Get Licensed, 'Theatre Licence,' www.get-licensed.co.uk/licence/theatre-licence

Health and Safety Executive, 'Theatre,' www.hse.gov.uk/entertainment/theatre-tv/theatre.htm

Smith, Phil, *Making Site-Specific Theatre and Performance: A Handbook* (Red Globe Press, London, 2018)

TheatreRites, 'Masterclasses with Sue Buckmaster: Making site-specific productions,' YouTube (22nd September 2020) www.youtube.com/watch?v=Gax4Mo9-C9Y

Warren, Jason, *Creating Worlds: How to make immersive theatre* (Nick Hern Books, London, 2017)

Connections

International Network for Contemporary Performing Artists, www.ietm.org/en

Practical

Ticketsource, www.ticketsource.co.uk/

13 Business Sustainability

It should be a key priority for your organisation to want to still be here in many years to come. This is the end goal of any business, and considering the implications of growth, sustainability, and development can require a specific mindset to embrace it fully.

Part of the contradiction about thinking of the future is that it can be the easiest thing to move to the bottom of the priority list. The demands of the here and now and the ever-pressing to-do list can dominate our thinking and get in the way of meaningful strategy, succession planning, and reflection. Indeed, the placement of this chapter within the book may seem to reaffirm that this is an area of less focus and responsibility. This couldn't be further from the truth. It is important to recognise, however, that during your first show your priority and focus is just getting the project to happen. Now that you've bagged your first production, however, it is time to start thinking strategically.

Why strategy is important

Strategy can be easy to overlook because there appear to be no immediate consequences for its omission. Indeed, your business could operate for many years without a single thought for strategy. You will be extremely busy, you will still be creating work, and you may fail to see why it should drain your already stretched time. Growth and doing are not the same thing.

In this situation, however, there is likely to be something wrong that you are not quite able to diagnose. In focussing on the day-to-day details, we can mistake work for progress and effort for vision. It is, in fact, very easy to be busy, but this doesn't automatically lead to growth.

Without strategy and growth, your organisation can stall. If you are still in the same place (whatever that means to you) in five years' time, you may find yourself frustrated. In business, to stay still is effectively to go backwards. A tech firm making the same model of smartphone or laptop may have incredible success, but the long list of obsolete tech giants should also warn us of the dangers of complacency. Without strategy, organisations of all shapes and sizes are unable to respond and adapt. Any organisation that fails to adapt has a very short shelf-life.

Thinking strategically can be a helpful way of ensuring our organisation meets its goals and mission. The mission statement of our Theatre in Education company might be to deliver engaging Shakespeare productions to young people growing up in poverty. But if we are forever bogged down in the specifics of rehearsal, selling tickets, and organising the next show, we aren't thinking about how the business could be reaching more young people and how successfully it is meeting those goals.

As a result, our latest show may have reached fifty children in two schools, for example, which may be an improvement from our first show which only reached thirty children in one school. But this is small progress, and as business leaders in this scenario, we may struggle to understand how we can scale our organisation to reach one hundred or ten thousand young people.

So strategic thinking, sustainability, and growth go hand-in-hand, and encapsulate a swathe of areas that can help our organisation to continue to develop in the changing world of the 21st century. Let's look at how this can work in practice.

Moving beyond performance

As part of your general growth strategy for your business you may be thinking about expanding into areas beyond performance itself. This may be something simple, such as running a post-show talk or workshop, or it might signal a wider organisational change. It is important when considering growth and change, that any developments to your business don't stray from the principles set out in your constitution. Youth theatres, theatre in education, and workshops are some key examples of possible ways in which your organisation may branch out, although the sky really is the limit with this. From a growth perspective, your theatre company will always be at something of a disadvantage if it remains afloat from a wider structure of development and support, such as being an Associate Company or resident artists with a venue, for example. It is a simple fact of the business model that running a theatre company alone costs more to run than you can make back through show deals and ticket sales, so finding methods of sustainability early can be a solid strategy going forward.

Of course, sustainability may apply to yourself and your fellow company directors as much as to the organisation at large. Hoping for your theatre company to pay your bills may be a stretch for many, in reality, but that doesn't mean that yours is an ineffective company or that you shouldn't continue with it. Sustainability may be as much about finding a way for you to continue to supplement your income so that you can continue with your company, as much as it may be to find ways of making your company financially viable. Many of those who run theatre companies also work as teachers, box office staff, or with any number of valid and varied methods of paying the bills. Once again, it is worth repeating that this is nothing to be ashamed of. This is the reality for many in the arts, and although an Instagram feed may not give off this impression, the vast, vast majority of people working in the arts are forced to work in other ways to help pay their way. Perhaps it shouldn't be this way, but often it is, and it is something to be proud of and not embarrassed by.

> **Task:** Return to the work you did back in Chapter 4 exploring your skill-set as a company. Build upon, or repeat this exercise now, thinking about your organisation as a whole and considering its future life. What are the areas with opportunities for you to expand into? Repeat this task for yourself and your own skills. How are those skills transferable?

It is a fact that running a theatre company is something of a risky enterprise, especially when you have livelihoods to support through regular wages. As a result, theatre companies are naturally quite precarious and the people who run them are often forced to hold down second jobs. If you have got this far and have had a success with your first show, it is incredibly important that you give some time and energy to the longer-term strategic plan for your organisation so that you can try and avoid the pitfalls. Without a direction and a plan for stability, you will experience the fate of most emerging theatre companies. After a small number of successful shows, your company will run out of steam and the members will leave. If you're lucky, it'll be amicable.

How can you practically plan in any tangible sense? The future is uncertain, and plans will inevitably change, but having a flag to aim for gives a very different focus than a company dealing only with the day-to-day, hoping that the future sorts itself out.

The problem with launching into your next show is that you avoid the harder problem of making your business secure. It is incredibly likely that your first show cost you a lot of money. In the unlikely event that it did make a profit, that figure is likely to be small and will likely not account for your own time, which you probably didn't pay yourself for. If we were to imagine that everyone involved, including you, were paid for all the hours of work that you did, that deficit may become quite substantial.

This is not a negative. As I said earlier, the arts are a precarious industry that relies heavily on subsidy and goodwill as much as on financial gain. What you are experiencing is not necessarily a failure of your own entrepreneurialism, but instead an honest reflection of how difficult this industry can be and therefore a warning signal as to why you need a plan to deal with it. Even if, after all your group reflection, you decide that you don't want to branch out into education or outreach, you still need a viable plan to figure out how you can make the *business* of staging plays more sustainable for your company into the future.

Measuring and charting progress

Even if you are really clear that your aim as a company is to gain National Portfolio Organisation (NPO) status, for example, it is recommended that you chart your mid- and long-term goals so that everyone can see them, and progress can be measured against them. The future for your organisation may be obvious and logical, but when you reach those goals, which hopefully you will do, you will want further goals to ensure that you continue to grow and develop, in theory, exponentially.

> **Task:** Work together to create a goal tracker. This can be a simple document with four columns. You can see an example in Table 13.1. In the first column, a goal has been identified. It is better if this is something specific, but for longer-term goals this will naturally be a bit more speculative. The second column lists the things that need to be achieved for you to meet your goal. Think about all the things that need to be in place to ensure your goal happens successfully. Then identify a date – again, you can be as specific as you like here. The fourth and final column is about prioritising. What tasks need to be done first? Which are non-negotiable, and which are nice-to-have?
>
> *Table 13.1* Identifying goals
>
> | Goal | Aims | Date | Importance |
> | --- | --- | --- | --- |
> | • Secure a booking for our first school workshop. | • Ensure all members have a DBS check.
• Contact school to find out Head of Drama. | • November 20XX
• December 20XX | Essential |
>
> It can be helpful to do this in reverse, to think backwards from your end point. For me, this was about thinking when I wanted to leave the company. This gave me a target to ensure that the company was in good enough health so it could be continued in my absence. Working backwards has the added benefit of allowing you to see if you have time to meet all your subsequent steps on time. This document should be a living piece of work, constantly updated and developed and always heading somewhere.

What growth means

There are many ways to grow your business. Although the aim of this growth may be to make more money, anything that helps to improve your efficiency and productivity, or to make you better at what you do, is an essential part of the growth ecosystem. Before we consider planning for growth on the broader scale, let us explore ways in which your operations can be streamlined and improved to help you get into the growth mindset.

Below are some suggestions for how to think about growth:

- *Think about systems.* Growth involves finding ways to move your time from the day-to-day responsibilities to think about the bigger picture. If there are options to automate or outsource certain tasks, this can free you up to focus on your longer-term goals.
- *Have plans and backup plans.* Consider what aspects of your business are being approached ad hoc, or without a distinct focus and strategy. Are you creating your marketing strategy as you go along? Do you have a plan for capturing and growing your audience? Go back through this book and spend time to implement any of the key areas you might have previously overlooked.
- *Measure what works.* Growth only becomes relevant when you can see it tangibly. Goals are a way of provoking growth, but you can only measure your success in setting and meeting these goals if you can measure their impact through hard, cold numbers. Being able to see that your changes resulted in two thousand more people following you on YouTube means that you can make a judgement around the success of that intervention. This requires ambitious Key Performance Indicators (KPIs) for you to track your goals against.
- *Improve your communications.* If you have a website, does it load properly on mobiles or on different web browsers? Does it rank highly on search engines? Does it load quickly? Are your images out of date?
- *Consider your online measurement.* Utilise search engine optimisation (SEO) and analytics software to measure the impact of your online activities. Almost everything online can be tracked and measured, and the benefit of this is that you can draw out narratives from the data to figure out where best to spend your time. You might be spending a huge amount of time and money filming a video trailer for your show, for instance, yet your videos are being viewed fewer than ten times.
- *Network and collaborate.* Forging connections with others is a key way of exploring new ways of working into the future. This can have clear artistic and social benefits and can also be a great way of punching above your weight in terms of your company profile. Working with a larger organisation – a local charity, for instance – can be great if you can explore submitting a joint funding application together. If the larger, more experienced company are happy to lead on this, this can help you to access funds and resources that you wouldn't otherwise have access to.

Growth in practice

Failing to plan for growth was one of the biggest mistakes I made in running my own company, PurpleCoat. My eagerness to put on another show was masking my fear and inexperience in knowing how to grow the company to become more sustainable. As a result, I often felt frustrated that we weren't reaching more audiences or working on bigger stages. In effect, despite what we were achieving artistically, we had stalled as a business.

We began to explore the possibility of launching a Youth Theatre, which would explore the works of Shakespeare and his contemporaries with working-class young people. Our initial experiment in this area had gone well, but the young people involved had had to pay a participation fee to help us cover our costs. We galvanised our team and applied to Arts Council England, which would, amongst other things, help us to ensure that access was free for the young people involved. We were successful in gaining grant-for-all funding from ACE, which was a huge boost.

Exploring work in a youth theatre context was a great moment for us. As we moved further and further in this direction, we started to realise that we were more and more excited by these elements of performance and the very DNA of our organisation began to change. This was really exciting. The Youth Theatre was a tangible way for us to define and meet our aims and we were able to scale because of securing our first set of public funds.

As a small-scale theatre company without attachment to a venue, we were spending a significant amount of our overheads on rehearsal studios and venue hire. We were creating strong work artistically, but our business model was weak, even with funding. An overreliance on a particular funder meant that we were entirely at the whim of that funding being renewed for the long-term success of our company. When this funding was not renewed, we were back at square one with a company we did not know how to grow.

The summary above makes our challenges and their solutions sound clear and obvious. However, in creating work we were proud of, a lack of future-proofing and strategic thinking became easy to overlook. Our plan to expand into youth theatre work was a good one, and the initial success should have galvanised us to be even more strategic. But suddenly we had public funds to account for, young people to recruit and rehearse, and shows to stage. All too easily, the need to spend time thinking about the future became less and less important.

We lacked a text such as this to provide a pathway through what can be a treacherously uncertain road. As the saying goes, you don't know what you don't know. We certainly had ups and downs at PurpleCoat, and we got some things right and other things wrong. But I am pleased to say that by finally making the decision to pause and to step away from the desperate urge to constantly stage another show, we were able to truly reflect and grow, not just as an organisation but as individuals and artists, also.

Remaining unattached to a venue, the size of our impact was limited by the scale of venue and marketing we could afford. This was financially prohibitive and left us vulnerable when those spaces began to close. This was not sustainable.

We always knew that having our own physical space was the first step towards being able to reach more people. Our work focuses around improving access to culture amongst disenfranchised social groups. We knew there was a need locally and that we had the artistic skills to create engaging work, but we needed a platform to support that development. This was a very good first step: finally, we were thinking about strategy and considering tangible steps to improve our business model. For us, the goal wasn't about attaching ourselves to another theatre, but about having our own space to create, and where we could encourage and support others to do the same.

These were the early seeds that led to PurpleDoor; our performance venue focussed on providing free-to-access culture created by and for working-class local people. We sought funding to help us develop the idea, and we were able to spend the following two years enhancing our proposition and developing our own skills. Being supported through this process was life-changing, and our business proposal grew as a result. As our skillset grew, so did our confidence, and we are in a much stronger position now with a future we feel in control of. Being supported to identify our strengths and weaknesses and being funded to address these was a great way of developing our capabilities as leaders.

The development of PurpleDoor has taught me several important lessons. Although the overview above can seem to be a somewhat negative reflection of our journey to this point, the idea and ethos of PurpleDoor would never have happened if it wasn't for the work we did with our youth theatre. The seeds of something positive were around for a long time; we just needed to give ourselves the time to let them grow. For us, the intense workload of staging show after show after show was part of a deeper sense of insecurity, imposter syndrome, and having something to prove. While this wasn't entirely helpful, it has given us the drive and resilience to still be here now, despite the challenges we have faced.

Another benefit of taking time was the renewed focus this brought to the quality and direction of the art we produce. We always had a defined political outlook and a distinct sense of what made our work different, but spending time away from creating made us reconnect with what we love about the process and rediscover what we had to say.

Future planning is part of the very DNA of our process now. The huge amount of energy and passion required by any fledgling project can easily blur the lines between one's personal and professional life and ambitions. In effect, you become the project. While this is perhaps inevitable in the early stages, it is not helpful to your well-being long-term, nor is it constructive for the organisation. If a company is to flourish, it must grow beyond the founder and it must be able to stand on its own two legs. If the success or failure of your company depends entirely upon the continued and unhealthy commitment of your entire time and energy, you will find it harder and harder to retain the passion that got you into the game in the first place. With PurpleDoor, I have set clear goals for when I want to depart the company. Partly, this reflects my own view that arts organisations should avoid management sticking around forever, but also this is about a healthier realisation in my own mind and body that I and my life are separate entities to that of any work I complete, and that it isn't a failure to admit this. In fact, it is quite the opposite.

There are many ways of applying future planning to your organisation, and to a degree it will depend on the specifics of your business how you choose to go about this. However, there are a range of principles any business can follow, which will help your strategic planning and hopefully ensure that your business always knows where it is heading next.

The first thing to consider is about making time. In our rush to keep putting out more content, we never had the time to stop, pause, and reflect, and this led to tunnel vision. Carve out a slot – perhaps three or four times a year initially, where you will specifically discuss and plan for the next steps. This should coincide with your trustee meetings, where you will be expected to lay out a plan for the future of your business and hopefully secure their approval.

The most comprehensive way to plan for future development is through a business plan. Contrary to what you might believe, a business plan is not just for securing funding for your business at the start of its life. A good business plan continues to do what it says on the tin: to lay out the plan for your business for the next twelve months. Your plan could be for more or less time than this, but this is a useful timeframe to work within when thinking long term. Shorter than this will require rewriting the plan every five minutes, and much longer than a year is difficult to predict, particularly for a new business. Your business plan, just as it did originally, should lay out what you are about, what you have achieved, and what you plan to achieve in the next year. This forces you to keep a strategic overview of your direction, to embed growth and ambition into your plans (rather than repeating the same thing forever, which is rarely a recipe for success), and to outline how you will measure success. You should ensure that your new plan contains SMART Key Performance Indicators, as tangible ways to measure your progress against your goals. You should also reflect backwards upon how much progress you have made on previous goals and address any goals you have had to change or alter because they did not align with your previous planning.

Doing this regularly, perhaps at the same time every year, brings your company together, sets a vision and checks that you are achieving what you set out to achieve in the first place. It forces you to assess your overall performance and to be ambitious with your future planning, and to continually reassess what is important to you as an organisation. An ongoing business plan can be relatively lean; however, producing it *should* take time and focus to give it the importance it deserves.

Environmental impact and evaluation

As we move further into the 21st century, the impact and development of the climate crisis will rapidly begin to be more and more of a concern for those in the arts and entertainment business. For better or worse, the climate crisis is something we cannot and should not avoid, and there are numerous ways to approach this from the perspective of an emerging theatre company.

Surviving in the climate crisis

Moments such as the Covid-19 pandemic remind us that the knock-on effects of climate change are wide ranging and unpredictable. Theatres and those who work for them were particularly affected during the Coronavirus outbreak with many companies, both small and large, falling prey to its significant impact. Even the most robust business with Plans B and C in storage for dealing with crises were extremely unlikely to have a backup plan for a global pandemic and worldwide economic shutdown. This is arguably not an excuse we can rely on for the future.

A traditional theatre company is entirely reliant on open venues and public attendance for its very existence. Without a place to perform and an audience to perform to, the function and purpose of a theatre company comes into question. How would your new business perform under a similar challenge? Many smaller companies adapted in creative and honourable ways during the Covid-19 pandemic, with a renewed focus on community and digital access. It may seem premature to consider how your new company will respond in the event of a further global crisis but considering a simple list of skills and approaches can be a good place to start, especially as your company grows and you start to rely on its success more and more.

> **Task:** As a group, conduct a brainstorm session exploring ways you could continue to create work if your usual methods of operation are prohibited. Think about the skills of individual members, possible methods of income generation and how quickly you could switch to Plan B. When you have done this, create a shared live document, which you can continue to add to and develop as your company moves forward.

The importance of Plan B

It may seem like an unnecessary use of energy but having a Plan B for your major activities helps to offset some of the natural uncertainty within the arts sector. If you could employ understudies, you probably would, and having a strong Plan B in place is a bit like having an excellent team of understudies ready to go. We are in an uncertain world and organisations able to adapt and develop to changing times will be the ones that are best placed to respond to it.

As we mentioned in the chapter on budgeting and finance, having a Plan B and C also increases your chance of actually getting projects off the ground. My business mentor tells me that she doesn't do anything without a Plan B and a Plan C considered, and I'm very inclined to follow her advice.

Measuring your carbon footprint

It is becoming more important for organisations and individuals to be mindful of their carbon footprint and to be proactive in trying to reduce it. As we move further through this century it will become increasingly likely that consumers come to expect environmental responsibility from corporations and transparency around the sourcing of materials. The theatre industry can be incredibly polluting when we consider the issues of touring, transportation, and the disposable attitude towards props, costumes, and set.

The first step towards enacting any change is to be aware of the current impact of our activities so that we have something to measure our progress against. Your first aim should be in moving towards net zero, although this is contested in some circles, and you should remember that all emissions are ultimately harmful. Some things to consider when exploring your carbon footprint are:

- Avoid an overreliance on disposable single-use plastics (such as water bottles) within your rehearsal room.
- Think about travel distance to rehearsal venues and suggest greener alternatives (public transport/carpooling etc.).
- Explore ways to save, restore, and reuse the raw materials of your performance, including props, set, and costumes. You might consider hiring sets (although there are transport problems to consider with this) or think about how to eliminate unnecessary elements altogether.
- Consider how you can highlight environmental issues in your work and use this to inform and educate your participants and audiences.
- Be transparent about your carbon impact and consider ways to share this with your audiences, including information about their own behaviour in attending your show.
- Avoid overreliance on certain transport types (particularly when transporting set and cast) and be mindful of how objects are delivered to you.
- Consider the impact of printing scripts, flyers, and other materials and think about recyclability where this is deemed necessary.

Luckily, there are initiatives available to support and help in your mission to be climate conscious. In the UK, Theatre Green Book is an organisation worth exploring; it is a theatre-industry wide initiative to lay out practical pledges and guides to make your work sustainable. Over three volumes,

Theatre Green Book aims to explore ways in which you can make shows, buildings, and operations sustainable, and is an excellent, comprehensive free resource well worth reading. Similarly, UK-based Julie's Bicycle is a not-for-profit offering a range of programs including courses in Creative Climate Leadership, to empower and connect theatre makers to make a tangible difference, and to be aware of their responsibility in facing this immense challenge.

The climate and audiences

Several of the key developments within climate practice seem to be at odds with the transient, touring nature that makes up much of the DNA of live performance. At a small scale, it can feel prohibitive and reductive to implement some of the measures listed above, especially when resources and finances are tight.

Some people prefer to consider the climate crisis through the social responsibility of running a theatre company. Thinking about how you can bring your audience into the conversation can be an effective first step to delivering a wider impact beyond your own practice. You may want to imbed themes of climate change directly into your work or facilitate wraparound education and outreach workshops to further educate audiences about the issues that matter to you. You may want to collect data about your audience's behaviour to help raise their awareness about their environmental impact (45% of our audience travel to us by car, which is twice as polluting as using the bus, for example). There are numerous creative ways in which to embrace this issue as part of your organisation's mission and to utilise everything that makes theatre so unique to help play your part in this growing issue. Audiences are rightly becoming increasingly aware of the issues for themselves, and are choosing to align themselves with those brands and organisations who reflect these values – not just in the climate emergency but across a whole range of broad social developments.

Archive and legacy

As your work begins to grow and you become more prolific, you will amass an ever-increasing body of evidence that collectively comes to define your company. Although some of this is out of your control, it is prudent to plan for your own archive, not least in case you do grow into the next Royal Shakespeare Company!

A simple hard drive with your production photos, videos, and related materials can be a reliable way to keep track of your legacy items. You never know when you may need any of this information; in a future funding application or if you decide to remount a show, for example, and having an organised structure for archival material is an easy win to support this. I save everything, including raw copies of large image files and video editing projects. This takes up a huge amount of space but means that I'm always able to access the highest quality material when needed. Anyone who works in IT would – correctly – advise you to back up your back-up, so that you will always be protected!

Saving raw original copies means, in its most practical form, saving original uncompressed photos and videos before upload. As soon as an image or video is uploaded to the internet, via a cloud server, it is compressed. This will reduce file size but may also reduce image quality. Often the compression isn't noticeable, but as technology advances and audiences get more and more used to higher resolution video and photography, you can extend the shelf-life of your digital materials by ensuring they are saved to the highest quality possible, by keeping the original files backed up.

A final point to consider with the archive is an overreliance on digital trends. As we move more of our lives onto social media and cloud platforms, this can be a risky future for our archive materials if the service closes or changes, or if we need to pay to continue access. Having a dedicated backup on a computer hard drive avoids these problems and is generally more secure. When considering archive, it is useful to think long term: it may seem as though a social media site will be around forever, but archive is about long-term practice and being prepared for the changes that will inevitably come.

Embedding reflective practice

In Chapter 7 we thought about the need to implement a post-show debrief to reflect on a performance and to draw a line beneath it. You can apply the learning from this task to help improve the quality of your work in several ways, both artistically and logistically.

Before starting work on a new show, return to your debrief notes and identify a list of targets. This may feel too prescriptive, so feel free to adapt this as you see fit. The important thing is to reflect and to translate this reflection into action. Reflection for reflection's sake can quickly become a waste of time, so getting into the practice of pulling some tangible goals from this can be a worthwhile activity.

Embedding reflective practice is about being in constant conversation with yourself about what you can do better and finding tangible ways to apply this across your whole organisation. This is a productive mindset to train yourself into so that your work avoids complacency and remains humble. There are always things we can do better, and proactively identifying and working towards goals helps this to become a more tangible and achievable process. Embedding this change can be harder than identifying it, and you are encouraged to think broadly across your company at large when thinking about how to make change. An actor in a rehearsal process may have raised concerns about the number of hours being worked, as an example, but the correct response to this may equally lie in considering your entire organisational work culture and what you expect from those you work with. Embedding change is difficult, and can sometimes resemble using a sticking plaster to resolve one particular drip, without realising that the pipes themselves need replacing.

To support this, write the problem down in the centre of a piece of paper, and thinking laterally; consider all the possible causes and implications of that problem. After this, write two or three solid SMART steps to address it. Doing this will quickly help you to recognise the areas where you need to focus your time most. By thinking backwards from the problem itself to the possible root cause, you will be able to identify how your wider vision trickles down to specific actions. To take another example, you might have had a lot of people turning up late to your show. It would be easy to blame the audience for being unreliable, but when you extrapolate this further, you realise that your Google Maps location is inaccurate, and that the instructions on your website are written in an inaccessible font. This may further imply a lack of customer focus on your business generally, which may require going all the way back to your Mission Statement. Changes aren't always so drastic but considering practical plans to address each area of concern helps to make sure that change actually happens, and keeps your eyes focussed on the big picture whilst tweaking the details.

You might work from your own thoughts, or you may use the feedback of your company members and audiences. When collecting feedback, it is helpful to be clear about expectations – you don't *have* to take on people's thoughts and you *do* have the right to ignore suggestions. Similarly, to avoid people becoming disenfranchised, think about ways you can share your changes so that people can see your desire to continue to improve your practice and your organisation at large. It is never a good idea to ask for feedback and then to run away when the results aren't to your liking, so transparency and openness in your process is always welcomed.

Chapter Resources

Climate resources

'Climate Emergency,' Howlround, https://howlround.com/tags/climate-emergency

Johnston, Sholeh, 'Tips for green, more sustainable shows,' *Guardian* (29th January 2014) www.theguardian.com/culture-professionals-network/culture-professionals-blog/2014/jan/29/tips-green-sustainable-shows-production

Julie's Bicycle, https://juliesbicycle.com/

National Theatre, 'Making theatre in the Climate Crisis – Designing Paradise and the Theatre Green Book,' YouTube, (16th August 2021), www.youtube.com/watch?v=Zwy021aMfGY

Reynolds, Will, 'Not costing the earth: Theatre & environmental sustainability,' UK Theatre (9th February 2020), https://uktheatre.org/who-we-are-what-we-do/uk-theatre-blog/not-costing-the-earth-theatre-environmental-sustainability/

'Sustainability,' Theatres Trust, www.theatrestrust.org.uk/how-we-help/sustainability

Sweigart-Gallagher, Angela, 'Sustainable theatre practices,' Sustainable Theatre, www.sustainabletheatre.org/narrative/sustainable-theatre-practices

Theatre Green Book, https://theatregreenbook.com

Growth

Dweck, Carol, *Mindset: The new psychology of success*, 2nd edition (Ballantine Books, New York, 2016)

'Growth mindset vs. design thinking,' Growth Thinking, https://mygrowththinking.com/growth-thinking-vs-design-thinking/

Wooll, Maggie, 'A growth mindset is a must-have – these 13 tips will grow yours,' BetterUp (26th July 2021), www.betterup.com/blog/growth-mindset

14 Failure, Endings, and Exit

You may have registered some surprise upon discovering this chapter and glancing through its content. I can count on one hand the number of times I have seen an acknowledgement that things can often go wrong in this industry and how to deal with it. Maybe this is inevitable. With an industry built upon so much inequality, graft, and luck, it is perhaps unsurprising that we don't talk about our mistakes and errors as often as we should. As a result, it can feel as though everyone else is achieving constant success and getting it right, a fact exacerbated by social media.

It is for these reasons that I am most passionate about this chapter out of everything contained within this book. It is my firm belief that a greater transparency around the struggles and inequalities of our sector can drive meaningful change to improve it. Furthermore, acknowledging that there is more to the adage that, 'the show must go on,' can be the first major step towards reducing the huge levels of stress and poor well-being within a sector, which can all too often feel as though success is only achievable through unsustainable sacrifice.

Conversations with failure

Due to the nature of our businesses and the environment in which they operate, anything less than a roaring success can often feel to be a crushing disappointment. Every single show requires such a commitment of time and effort, not to mention money, that it can sometimes feel as if putting on shows are only worth it if they will sell out and gain a raft of five-star reviews. Indeed, this may be a reality for some of you, where a half empty box office could spell disaster for any future shows. Such is the unsustainable precarity that much of the theatre industry is built upon, and which I hope this book has helped you to navigate that little bit more smoothly.

We need to renegotiate our relationship with failure for the sake of our companies and for our own mental well-being. Failure is a strong word with plenty of baggage; however, an empty auditorium or a poor review can often make us feel deflated and that we have failed tremendously.

We can have a healthier relationship with failure if we alter the way we think about the process. Not every show can be a success. If there was a golden formula, we'd all be following it. Indeed, many professional shows can fail to excite an audience and can be subsequently mauled by critics. Shows are beset by creative problems all the time, and we can reserve our harshest judgement for a show we feel has failed to meet its promise.

However, a poor show (whatever that means) is very rarely a reflection of poor talent. Many of the actors, directors, and theatre makers you admire will have had productions that have been stronger or weaker against a set of criteria: whether that be in relation to their artistic quality, their box office take, or their reviews. Indeed, artists can sometimes experience a slog of poorly received work before finally hitting the jackpot. It is important for us to recognise that our industry is built on unrealistic expectations and use that to come to peace with the ebbs and flows that are an inevitable part of a career in the arts.

Occasionally we can find ourselves in the midst of a bad show. Whichever way you square it, however positively you spin it, it's a stinker. You know, you're pretty sure the cast know, and the audience will know soon enough. Guess what: it happens! Sometimes this might have been completely out of your control: a lead actor needed replacing at the last minute. On other occasions, this lands firmly at your door. Your concept for the show wasn't right and it's too late to change it. What do you do when you find yourself in this situation?

The most important thing to remember at times like this is to recognise that your own assessment of quality might not necessarily condemn the entire production. As much as you may want to throw in the towel, there will be numerous other people involved who can see much to love in the production, not least in their own contributions. Indeed, a show that you look on negatively could have many positives when seen by an audience. It might not be the best show ever created, it might not be the best show you will ever create, but does that mean it's worthless? I have yet to see a show that didn't have something to offer.

Failure can be reframed if we remove the pressure from ourselves to be perfect. If we instead think of failure as the **F**irst **A**ttempt **I**n **L**earning, we move towards a recognition that getting things wrong is a vital and instructive part of any learning process. When we were at school, we were given numerous opportunities to practice new skills and ideas. When we got them wrong, our teachers would instruct us and eventually we would improve.

The important part of reconsidering failure is what to do with it once we have acknowledged it. This might be during a rehearsal process, or it might be long after a show has finished. Revisiting our discussion in Chapter 13, we return to the idea of reflective practice and implementing the changes from our reflection. If a rehearsal has gone disastrously wrong, there is no reason for you to repeat the process in the next rehearsal. There is also no reason for you to believe that you are an awful director who can't run a rehearsal process smoothly. With reflection and implementation, you can ensure that the next rehearsal runs much smoother.

Getting it wrong

I'm going to let you into a secret. It's so secret, you might never hear another person say it in your lifetime. Are you ready?

Sometimes, people get things wrong.

Period. Without a shadow of a doubt. In fact, it's so certain you could put money on it. So why do we judge ourselves so harshly when we do?

The previous section was about rethinking our attitude to failure. Yes, we can be our own harshest critic and yes, there are sometimes good things to be found where we can't see it. On the other hand, there are almost definitely going to be times when you get it wrong, full stop. Then what?

Things can go wrong a surprising number of times when you're running a business. In fact, things go wrong for me daily. The difference when you're in charge is that you will suddenly find yourself in a different position than you may have been used to when you were just another member of the team.

Let's think about some of the things that could go wrong, as a starting point:

- Your concept doesn't work once you start rehearsals.
- You got angry in a rehearsal and spoke unprofessionally to a colleague.
- You scheduled a rehearsal poorly and some actors weren't needed.
- You misread the tech plan for the venue.
- You forgot to order a prop in time ....

Etc, etc, etc. In fact, as you begin to think of all the things that can go wrong, it becomes harder and harder to be so judgemental on yourself. There is a lot on your plate, a lot resting on your shoulders. It's probably fair enough to admit that you will occasionally slip up.

But when things do go wrong, you must make a decision. As the leader and the person in charge, it is surprising how quickly other people will defer to you when there is an issue that needs resolving. For better or worse, you are the face of your business and the face of the show, and you must be prepared to deal with that.

In the worst-case scenario, you might decide to cancel a show. This is an extreme event, and you should consider the fallout from this action and whether that eclipses the issue you are facing in the first place. Don't underestimate the disappointment people can feel when something they are working towards falls through. This is not to dissuade you, but if you consider cancelling a show, ensure it is the best solution and not simply a reflection of your frustration. Obviously, the earlier you can cancel a show the better for everyone involved, not least the audience. You may be required to pay a cancellation fee with your venue if you decide not to perform, and you should consult this information in your contract before you begin this process. Ensure that you are fully transparent with everyone involved and make sure your cast and crew hear it from you directly. Never let a colleague find out through word of mouth or, worse, through a social media post. Whatever has happened and however bad things have got, you owe it to your cast and crew to tell them this directly.

Cancelling a show can feel like the worst thing in the world. I still feel the scars from the few occasions it happened to me. But it doesn't need to mean the end. There are many more shows to make, and one failure doesn't define you. When you are ready to move on, its vital that you address whatever led to the issues last time and respect the other people you were working with. Never see cancellation as a way to cut and run: that will create a significant amount of bad blood and is a poor reflection on your organisation as a whole. If you cancel a show and start rehearsing a new one the following week, this will be very harmful to the people still left disappointed by your first cancellation. People will, quite rightly, wonder what, if anything, has changed.

Dormant companies

There may come a time when your company isn't doing much – in fact, it's not doing anything at all. However, if you expect to resume business in the future, you may not want to close the company for good. In this case, your company is *dormant*. A company can be dormant for a long time and can be restarted at will. However, there is a process for being transparent about this, and a company being dormant does not absolve you of all responsibility for managing it.

Dormant for corporation tax

Your organisation is dormant for corporation tax if:

- It isn't trading and isn't making income.
- It's a new company that hasn't yet started to trade.

Dormant for Companies House

If your company qualifies as a micro-entity in the eyes of Companies House (turnover of £632,000 or less/ten employees or fewer) you will only need to file *dormant accounts*. You will need to do this annually, just the same as if you were in business, but if you have been dormant for a full accounting period, each subsequent set of accounts should be virtually unchanged.

Informing HMRC

HMRC may write to you themselves to let you know that they are treating your organisation as dormant. If this doesn't happen though, filing your accounts and tax return will demonstrate that you haven't traded or received any income during the last accounting period.

Restarting a dormant company

Luckily, the process of restarting a dormant company is relatively straightforward. After commencing trade again, you will need to file your accounts and register for corporation tax, which will again demonstrate that you are back in business.

Winding up a company

If and when the time comes to call it a day, you will need to familiarise yourself with your responsibilities in closing down a company. The process can be complex if you have a lot of assets or if there are conflicts of opinion amongst the company directors, but assuming smooth running, closing a company officially is a straightforward process.

The process of shutting down a company is more properly called *dissolution*. When a company has been *dissolved*, it no longer exists and your responsibility to it ceases. There are criteria that need to be met for a company to be applicable to be dissolved. Your company:

- Must not have traded (done business/sold things/made money) in the last three months.
- Must not be threatened with *liquidation*.
- Must not owe credit to anyone.

If you do not fall into any of the categories above, don't worry. You must follow a slightly different process called *Voluntary Liquidation*.

You can apply to close your company online through Companies House. If your company has a board of directors with multiple trustees, you will require the signatures of more than half for your application to be approved. Signatures can be secured electronically. Trustees will be emailed, and they will be asked to add their name for approval.

After your application has been submitted, it'll be published in something called a *Gazette*. The *Gazette* is the official journal of public record, which essentially means it is a place where important information is published. By law, a company's intention to close must be published here. This idea exists to allow people to be informed and to object, although, in practice, this will most likely be a formality.

Once you complete your dissolution application online, an article will automatically be published in the *Gazette*. After two months, if there are no objections, the company will be struck off the register. At this point, a further notice will be published, meaning that your company has now ceased to exist.

Providing your company has traded, you must send your final statutory accounts and a Company Tax Return to HMRC. On these, you should indicate that they will be the final set of accounts for the company. You don't have to file final accounts with Companies House. If you owe late filing fees, Companies House say, 'we will usually accept the dissolution and allow the company to close without paying the fine.'

Failure, Endings, and Exit 251

When you make the decision to wind up the company, you have a moral and legal responsibility to inform all interested parties and to ensure any staff are treated according to your company rules. When your company is dissolved, your organisation's bank account will be frozen from that date, so you also need to ensure you have sorted any money and assets. Accounts need to be emptied, as appropriate, and assets need to be sold off or disposed of. If you don't do this, any outstanding assets will be passed to the Crown.

Be aware that some company types and some external funding may place additional expectations on you when closing a company. For example, a CIC requires, as part of its constitution, that you specify an asset lock. This is a nominated organisation to whom your assets will be passed in the event of the company closing, so that they may still be put to appropriate social use. Check the fine print depending on your specific situation so that you don't fall foul of any rules.

After your company has closed, the name can be taken by somebody else with a different company number. Although the company no longer exists, information will be stored and available for twenty years after dissolution, either by Companies House or the National Archives.

Moving on: transferable skills

There are many reasons why you may have chosen to step away from your organisation, but regardless of the motivation, the skills, experience, and contacts you have gained through your time as an entrepreneur will not be wasted. In fact, we can regularly fail to appreciate the transferable skills we have developed, and detailed analysis and application of these can help you to plan your next steps. Viewed in this way, a company should never become a millstone around your neck, and it is perfectly possible – indeed, it should be desirable – that your experience has helped to develop and improve *your* skills so that you can move to better opportunities in the future.

> **TASK:** Think about all the things you feel you are naturally good at. Start with your obvious skills and talents but don't overlook the things you may take for granted. Start specific, if it helps, and then broaden out. If you run an efficient tech rehearsal, for example, could this be unpacked to suggest you're a good organiser?
>
> Visualise this in whatever way works best for you. You might want to list these in columns, or you might choose to draw up a spider diagram. Don't worry if you can't think of a way to summarise these in a fashion that sounds right, the important thing at this stage is to begin to interrogate where your strengths may lie.
>
> After you have completed this, start to look for themes or links between what you have written. Are a lot of the notes you have written technical? Or organisational? Do they relate to group or solo work?

A brief point here about confidence. Sometimes it can be hardwired in our DNA to downplay our skills and to lack the confidence to say that you are good at something. Try and think about those areas where you may be avoiding acknowledging a skillset or interest. Recognise the barriers in your own way to success and remember that this document is entirely private to you. It took me a long time to accept what was staring me in the face: I was so rigid in my self-categorisation as a creative person that I didn't want to accept that the huge amount of organisational work I did – 'producing stuff' – was my strongest skillset. Embracing that has not only made me a better creative but has opened new avenues in my career as well. In large part this was about confidence and overcoming the barrier I imposed on myself to what I could or couldn't do. Mostly though, it was a fear of failure, and a paralysing worry that doing anything other than creating work for my company in some way meant that I had let myself down.

It is perhaps only with experience that we begin to realise the varied and fascinating routes our lives take above and beyond what we have planned. When working with my students now I always tell them to have a goal. Putting your flag in the sand gives you direction and something to aim towards. It's a motivation, a driver, and a reason to get out of bed each morning. Without it, we're not sure where we're heading next or how our current actions are helping us to get there.

But plans change and we will often not reach the flag as we originally planned. Sometimes we'll go further, sometimes we'll end up reaching a completely different flag altogether. We are living in a time of huge societal, technological, and environmental change. We are living for longer, on average, and the days of the job for life are almost over. Many of us are working multiple jobs, or doing work for people remotely, with clients and bosses we may never actually meet. In this environment, we do ourselves a disservice to expect all our plans to succeed and our goals to never change. The truth is, most of us will end up doing lots of different things throughout our working lives, each as varied as the next.

Whatever your circumstances, own them for you. They are what make you unique and what help to mould the creative impulse that feeds your work and its right to exist. Take up space and question rules. Make your voice heard – you never know who will be listening.

Chapter Resources

Failure

Bailes, Sarah Jane, *Performance Theatre and the Poetics of Failure* (Routledge, London, 2010)
Edmondson, Amy, 'Strategies for learning from failure,' *Harvard Business Review* (2011)
   https://hbr.org/2011/04/strategies-for-learning-from-failure
Gardner, Lynn, 'Fail safe: how good can come of bad theatre,' *Guardian* (6th November 2012)
   https://www.theguardian.com/stage/theatreblog/2012/nov/06/theatre-good-bad

Marquit, Miranda, 'How to handle mistakes as a business owner,' Broadway Educators (22nd January 2016), https://due.com/blog/how-to-handle-mistakes-as-a-business-owner/

Mroczka, Paul, 'Theatre students have to be open to new ideas and failure,' Broadway Educators (27th June 2014), http://broadwayeducators.com/theatre-students-have-to-be-open-to-new-ideas-and-failure/

Patel, Deep, '10 ways leaders fix mistakes without making it worse,' *Entrepreneur* (29th October 2018), www.entrepreneur.com/article/322072

Powell, Henry, 'Theatre and failure,' https://theatreandfailure.co.uk

Closing down

Hellicar, Lauren, 'What is a dormant company? A guide for small businesses,' Simply Business (25th September 2020), www.simplybusiness.co.uk/knowledge/articles/2020/09/what-is-a-dormant-company/

'How to close a limited company,' Future Strategy, www.futurestrategy.co.uk/advice/how-to-close-a-limited-company/

Townley, Gary, 'Closing your company and applying for voluntary strike off,' Companies House (10th August 2021), https://companieshouse.blog.gov.uk/2021/08/10/closing-your-company-and-applying-for-voluntary-strike-off/

15 Final Words

At the time of writing this final section, I am knee deep in rehearsals for two Shakespeare productions, preparing to tour around the UK and Ireland. They're going pretty well, I think. At the same time, we've had six people drop out because of various commitments. I've not yet had the whole cast in the same room together because Covid, and work, and life keep getting in the way. We have one cast member who has just joined us, who has five rehearsals to learn both shows. God laughs at plans, and all that. By the time you're reading this book you'll be able to search up the photos, the reviews – good and bad – and likely you'll form a judgement about how successful you think the shows were. I hope this book might give you pause on that.

The year I have been writing this book has provided the perfect anecdote for me to end on. At the end of the pandemic, I quit my job, moved out of London and came back to my hometown to start our own theatre venue. I also decided to embark upon a PhD, and I'm super glad that I did. Then we started producing these Shakespeare productions with a possible programming opportunity next year. And finally, I was given permission to write this book. It has been, to say the least, quite a year. And a perfect proof that you very rarely know all the answers or what is round the corner.

I have no idea how I have juggled all of my commitments this year, but writing this book has given me the perspective to reflect on my own habits and to know how to build on them. In the arts we can often work ourselves to exhaustion – because of force of habit, desperation, or bad timing. Probably all three. I wanted to end this book by letting you know, whoever you are, that your struggle is noticed, and it is shared. I know the stress and the worry you'll be going through every day trying to prove to yourself and others that this silly, crazy idea will pay off. You are not alone unless you choose to be.

I am embarrassed to admit to you how much I have had to research, learn, double-check, and question in creating this book. Proof, if proof were needed, that we never stop learning and that we can never know it all, but also that it is ok to ask for help. To stop. To be. If I'd have known all this before starting, I probably still would have made the same mistakes. I'll probably still make the same mistakes in the future! That's ok too. Trying is everything, despite what Yoda tells Luke during his Jedi training, trying is the greatest

DOI: 10.4324/9781003281726-15

achievement of all. Who cares if you succeed? You tried. That is worth celebrating. Sorry Yoda.

Running a company is not the same as being a director or an actor. You need to be brilliant at everything, from creating posts on Instagram to knowing how to run a sensitive rehearsal. From understanding a lighting desk to knowing how to get the best deal on flyers. It is relentless, and with no manager and no structures in place, it only stops when you tell it to. It can be easy to sugar-coat and to minimise the sheer mental and physical effort that this work takes. And believe me, you *do* have to be good. If numbers, or social media, or networking, or directing, or budgeting, or managing, or scheduling, or video editing are not your strong suit, you'll quickly trip and fall. It is hard graft and a thankless task. Worst of all, you can be brilliant at almost everything else but if the work itself is uninspiring, or poorly executed, you'll struggle to hold attention. You'll look around at other, larger, better-funded companies and dream of the day when there are other people with dedicated skillsets to take care of those things. To relieve the burden.

But right now, it's just you, with the weight of the world on your shoulders.

I have come to realise, this year in particular, that money is not, in fact, the solution. We spent our early days bemoaning our lack of resources: if only we had a better rehearsal studio, or a better camera, or better props etc., etc., etc., we would be fantastic. Writing this book has helped me to re-evaluate. The greatest privilege isn't money. You could achieve a lot of what is in this book with extremely limited resources, and many of the great artists who have come before us have done just that. The greatest privilege I now believe, is time.

Time to create, time to stop, time to ask questions, to interrogate, and reflect. Time to solve problems, time to think of problems before they arise. Time to be creative, time to fail. Time to heal, time to live your life, time to discover who you are and what you want to be. In the course of my own journey, this hard work has created many sacrifices of money, relationships, and energy. But really what this all boils down to, is time.

You won't get everything right, you certainly won't get everything wrong. Have fun doing, but know when to stop. Most of all, respect yourself, respect the work, and make your time count.

Index

A/B Testing 91
Abridged accounts 43
Accessibility 3, 13, 24, 69, 81, 90, 93, 97, 101–102, 107, 109, 214–215, 224, 238, 240, 244
Accounting Reference Date 43
Acting Agent 56–58
Algorithm 98
American Society for Composers, Authors and Publishers 143, 145
Analytics 78, 88–91, 96, 236
Annual accounts 6, 42–43, 46, 48, **134**, 149, 154, 156, 159, 171, 176, 183, 189, 249–250
Annual return 42
Archive 74, 105, 242–243
Articles of Association 40–41, 45
Artistic Director 208
Arts Council 5–7, 33, 60, 71, 85, 110, 149, 179, 184, 190, 216, 237
Assets 135, 152, 156, 171, 179, 250–251
Associate company 210, 230, 233
Audience development 12–13, 65, 71, 81, 82, 85, 87, 110, 221–222; audience development plan 85–87, 110
Audience feedback 113, 128, 195, 201, 213–214, 244
Audience funnel 73
Audience journey 72, 73, 75, 96–97, 110
Audience persona 75–76
Auditor 43

Back stage 226–227
Balance Sheet 43, **134**, 153–156
Bank account 12, 46–48, 59, 149, 153, 159, 183, 251

Blocking 115
Board 36, 37, 44–46, 48, 121, 136, 147, 156, 161–162, 176–177, 183, 250; trustees 36–37, 42, 44, 45–46, 239, 250; governors 36, 44
Board observer 46, 48
Bond 229
Bookkeeping 47, 147, 149–153, 156, 159, 170; double-entry bookkeeping 150–152
Box-office split 216–217
Branding 13, 16–17, 29, 40, 57, 70, 73, 85, 87–89, 91–92, 101, 177, 242
Broadway 64, 198, 227–229
Budgeting 13, 120, 159–161, 163–166, 168, 171
Business profile 90, 101, 109
Business strategy 74, 232–233, 236, 238

Call time 117, 129
Call to action 93, 94, 101
Campaign plan 94
Cancellation clause 124, 248–249
Captioning 107, 215
Carbon footprint 19, 28, 122, 177, 241
Cashflow 159
Casting 21, 23–24, 57, 63, 112–117
Catchment area 216
CEO 44, 51
Chaperone 120
Charitable aim 37–38
Charity 37–38, 40, 45, 121–122, 181–182, 190, 209, 236
Climate crisis 14, 18, 27, 240–242, 244, 252
Cloud server 49, 149–150, 153, 243
Commercial venues 227–230

Index 257

Community Interest Company 38, 40, 41, 45, 251
Companies House 37, 40–43, 249–251
Company director 16, 36–37, 41–45, 47, 52, **134**, 156, 230, 233, 250
Company secretary 44
Complaints 83, 121
Comps 203
Computer aided design 115
Confirmation Statement 42, **134**
Contingency 161, 189
Contra 217, 219
Contract 52, 55, 60, 103, 114, 115, 124–125, 127, 130, 143, 144, 146, 178, 198–199, 203, 212, 215–217, 219, 231, 248
Copy 91–92, 93, 97–99, 108, 144, 201
Copyright 23, 40, 140–141, 143, 145, 215
Cost of sales 158
Covid-19 2, 3, 7, 28, 105, 240; pandemic 2, 3, 7–8, 13, 18, 27–28, 84, 105, 107, 113, 124, 240, 254
Cross-selling 103
Crowdfunding 14, 172–175
Curtain call 24, 128–129, 131

Data types 76; quantitative data 76–77; qualitative data 76–77
Debit and credit 151, 153
Debrief 131, 243
Debt 37, 152
Demographic 22, 70–72, 75–77, 112
Depreciation 152, 171
Digital theatre 64, 105
Director's notes 129, 130, 243
Directors' Report 43
Disclosure and Barring Service 119–120, **134**, 145, 235; DBS Update Service, 120
Disclosures 121
Discount codes 78, 103
Dissolution 250, 251
Document Control Sheet 136–137
Donations 75, 128, 172–175–176, 177
Dormant company 249–250, 253
Drama school 3, 7, 9, 33, 56–57, 61, 66, 186
Dressing room 125, 226
Dropping out 62–63, 254

Email signature 44, 97
Employee 43, 47, 55, 59, 61, 138, 249
Ensemble 5–6, 12, 50–51, 62–63, 118

Equity 58, 60, 64
Ethics 12, 24, 26, 144–146, 171
Evaluation 14, 76, 179, 188, 240
Exclusion clause 216
Expenditure 79, 160, 163, 165–166, 168

Failure 246–249, 252–253
Feedback loop 106
Festivals 14, 102, 126, 130, 191–207, 213, 215, 230; Edinburgh Fringe Festival 198, 199, 207; Fringe festival 126, 130, 191–192, 195, 197–202, 204, 206–207; Underbelly Festival 207; VAULT Festival 207
Financial year 42, 43
First and second call 219
Flame proofing 114,127
Flyers 6, 14, 24, 65, 71, 74, 78, 89, 91, 92, 95, 101–103, 108, 123, 177, 197, 201–203, 205, 209, 218, 229, 241, 255
Force majeure 124
Forecasting 159, 170, 178, 189
Foundations 172, 176, 179–180
Founder 4, 6, 14, 32, 34, 38, 47, 51–54, 97, 238
Freebie 73–74, 96, 103
Freelancer 38–39, 58–59, 61, 63, 64, 119, 120, 171, 188
Front of house 128
Funding goal 173, 175
Fundraising 36, 172–173, 175, 179–180, 190

Gazette 250
GDPR 79, 80, 133–**134**, 145,
Get-in 114, 116, 125, 130, 132, 224
Get-out 130, 132
Goal tracker 235
Governance 12, 36–37, 42, 44, 162
Government Gateway 41–42, 154
Grants 14, 149, 156, 158–159, 164, 172–173, 176–190
Growth 14, 43, 65, 85, 232–233, 235–237, 239, 245
Guarantor 37, 41

Hard to reach 67, 81–82
Health and safety 13, 114–115, 125, 138, 146, 212, 225, 231; first aid 139, 146; risk assessment 138, 139
High-net-worth individuals 175, 176
Hire 4, 103, 112, 122, 125–126, 131, 142, 210–213, 216, 218–219, 224, 237

Index

HMRC 35–36, 39, 41–42, 58, 149, 154, 171, 249–250
Human resources 45, 59

IN01 40
Incident report 121
Inclusivity 22, 82, 107, 110, 117, 144
Income 14, 39, 75, 79, 155–158, 162–166, 169–170, 175–176, 188–189, 217, 219, 233, 240, 249; income stream 172, 179
Incorporation 12, 32–33, 36, 39, 40–44, 89, 161, 180, 204
Independent Theatre Council 41, 48, 61, 64, 136, 230
Insurance 13, 137–138, 194; Public Liability Insurance **134**, 137; Employers' Liability Insurance 138, **134**, 145, 225
Intellectual property 140
Interval 27, 69, 128, 193, 214
Invoice 59, 149, 150, 171
Irish Music Rights Organisation 143, 145

Julie's Bicycle 242, 244

Key Performance Indicators 236, 239
Key words 98–100

Legacy 189, 242
Liability 36, 38, **134**, 137–138, 145, 225, 229; liabilities 152, 156, 171
Licensing 224, 231
Lighting rig 115, 227; fixed rig 126, 227; lighting desk 126, 255; plotting 126
Limited Liability Partnership 38
Limited-by-guarantee 37–38, 40, 44–45
Liquidation 250
Loans 14, 152, 172, 178–180
Logo 40, 87–89, 92, 98, 101, 104, 177
London Theatre Council 229

Market research 34, 38, 76, 80–81
Market segment 71
Marketing calendar 94
Marketing plan 85, 94, 108
Marketing strategy 13, 72, 74, 94, 103, 236
Match funding 183–184
Matrices 95, 110
Meeting Minutes 46
Memorandum of Association 40–41

Mentor 7, 10, 11, 15, 27, 45, 53, 59, 131, 241
Metrics 78
Milestones 174, 185–187
Mini-jack 106, 226
Minimum wage 58, 60–61, 168
Mission statement 29, 109, 233, 244
Music Theatre International 142

National Insurance 59
National Portfolio Organisation 235
Newsletter 74, 77, 79, 84, 95, 96, 103, 172
Non-traditional spaces 223, 225

Offline marketing 95
Open Book Model 60, 169–170
Outcomes 184–186, 196

Paper tech 124, 131
Partnerships 208–209
Patronage 175–176
Paul Hamlyn Foundation 10
Pay per click advertising 100–101
PAYE 39, 59, 64, 158
Performance licence 4, 23, 120, 142–143, 160, 215; performance rights 23, 135, 141–143, 146
Permissions 92, 114, 122, 135, 140–143, 194
Person with significant control 36
Philanthropy 14, 172, 175–176, 180
Point of sales system 159
Policies 133, 136, 138, 146, 181, 212
Portable Appliance Testing 127, 132
Post-show Q+A 214, 233
Posters 14, 24, 92, 94–95, 101–102, 104, 140, 196, 201, 202, 211, 218
PPL-PRS 142, 143, 145
Pre-show announcement 128
Press 79, 92, 103–105, 201, 203, 228, 230; press release 93–94, 103, 104, 203; press night 123, 203; press agents 204
Preview 104, 123, 203
Pricing strategy 74–75, 103
Problem statement 185
Producer 1, 39, 50, 52, 55–56, 58, 60, 68, 85, 103–104, 116–117, 125, 137, 166, 169, 195, 215, 219, 228–230
Production pack 214
Profit [X]; Gross Profit [X]; Net Profit
Profit and Loss 43, **134**, 148, 153–154, 156, 157, 158

Index

Profit share 59, 169–170
Programming 194, 208, 210–212, 214, 216, 218, 220–221; programmers 63, 196–197, 206, 211–214, 219–222
PurpleDoor 8, 92, 238–239; PurpleCoat 4–8, 33, 237

QLab 126
Question types 80–81; leading questions 80; impartial 81; bias 81

Recall 113
Receipts 44, 149–150, 170–171, 219
Registered Office Address 41, 44
Rehearsal 13, 24, 28, 31, 111–120, 124, 125, 135, 142–144, 211, 213, 222, 233, 243, 247–248, 254–255; rehearsal space 111–115, 166, 237, 241; rehearsal photo 104; technical rehearsal 54, 93, 125–126, 251; cue-to-cue rehearsal 127; dress rehearsal 127
Release forms 140
Research and development 213
Restricted view 227
Return on investment 78–79, 86
Reviews 5–6, 26, 58, 65, 92, 103–104, 122–123, 130–131, 187, 193, 195–197, 201–204, 206, 230, 246–247, 254
Risk management 161–162
Royalties 219; royalty free 140, 146

Safeguarding 119, 120, 133–**134**, 145, 181; safeguarding lead 119
Scheduling 52, 116–117, 124–125, 136, 186, 197–199, 203–204, 248
The School for Social Entrepreneurs 10–11, 190
Scratch night 195, 213
Search ranking 99, 236
Self-employed 38
SEO 90, 93, 97–100, 109, 236
Share 37
Sightlines 210
Signatory 47, 183
Site specific work 14, 223–225, 231
Skills audit 53, 64
Small and micro company 43, 154, 156, 249
SMART targets 185–186, 239, 244
Smoking on stage 114
Social enterprise 31, 37–38

Social media 9, 38, 53, 60, 79, 83–84, 88, 89–92, 94–97, 100, 103, 108, 109, 122, 174–175, 243, 255
Society of London Theatres 229, 231
Sole-trader 38–40, 149, 171
Sound desk 126
Split against guarantee 217
Sponsorship 172, 177–178, 209
Spotlight 57, 64, 207
Straight guarantee 217
Streaming 13, 105, 107–109
Striking sets 130
Style guide 91–92
Subject Access Request 79
Subsidised theatre 213
Support in-kind 166, 188
Sustainability 14–15, 27, 32, 232–233, 241–242, 244
SWOT 34, 53

Take-off figure 217
Target audience 66, 70–71, 93, 101, 214, 218, 220–222
Tax 36, 39, 42–43, 59, **134**, 147, 150, 153, 154, 158, 171, 249; tax return 42, 250; corporation tax 154, 249–250
Tax return 42, **134**, 154, 249–250
Technical plan 115
Theatre Green Book 241, 242, 244
Theatre-in-education 233
Theatre maker 1–2, 7, 14, 51, 65, 81, 191, 199, 242, 247
Tone of voice 84, 91, 93
Touring 115, 125, 131, 171, 210, 219–220, 230–231, 241, 242
Trademark 40, 135, 152
Trailer 71, 78, 89, 94, 107–108, 140, 174, 214, 236
Transferable skills 14, 251
Trigger warning 117, 144–145
Trusts 38, 172, 176, 179
Turnover 42, 43, 46–47, 154, 158

Unique selling point 74, 88
Unique Tax Number 42

VAT 150, 154, 216–217
Venue tech pack 198
Vision, Mission, Values 29–31, 87
Volunteer 44, 55, 120, **134**, 138, 188, 192

Wants and needs 67
Website development 13, 38, 44, 76–77, 90–91, 94–100, 102, 107, 109, 136, 140, 236, 244
West End 227–229
Win themes 187, 190

Worker 55
Working with children 119–120

Young Vic Director's Program 61, 64
Youth theatre 5–6, 56, 233, 237–238

For Product Safety Concerns and Information please contact our EU representative GPSR@taylorandfrancis.com
Taylor & Francis Verlag GmbH, Kaufingerstraße 24, 80331 München, Germany

www.ingramcontent.com/pod-product-compliance
Lightning Source LLC
Chambersburg PA
CBHW050531300426
44113CB00012B/2040